VOL

OLD TESTAMENT

THE NEW COLLEGEVILLE BIBLE COMMENTARY

FIRST AND SECOND CHRONICLES

John C. Endres, S.J.

SERIES EDITOR

Daniel Durken, O.S.B.

LITURGICAL PRESS

Collegeville, Minnesota

www.litpress.org

Nihil Obstat: Reverend Robert C. Harren, J.C.L.
Imprimatur: ✠ Most Reverend John F. Kinney, J.C.D., D.D., Bishop of Saint Cloud, Minnesota, December 12, 2011.

Design by Ann Blattner.

Cover illustration: *Solomon's Temple* by Donald Jackson. Copyright 2010 *The Saint John's Bible*, Order of Saint Benedict, Collegeville, Minnesota USA. Used by permission. All rights reserved.

Photos: pages 12, 38, 74, 119, 130, Wikimedia Commons; page 53, Thinkstock.com.

Maps created by Robert Cronan of Lucidity Design, LLC.

1	2	3	4	5	6	7	8	9

Library of Congress Cataloging-in-Publication Data

Endres, John C., 1946–
    First and Second Chronicles / John C. Endres.
        p.   cm. — (New Collegeville Bible commentary. Old Testament ; v. 10)
    ISBN 978-0-8146-2844-7
    1. Bible. O.T. Chronicles—Commentaries.   I. Bible. O.T. Chronicles. English. New American. 2011.   II. Title.

BS1345.53.E53   2011
222'.6077—dc23   2011046899

CONTENTS

ABBREVIATIONS

Books of the Bible

Acts—Acts of the Apostles
Amos—Amos
Bar—Baruch
1 Chr—1 Chronicles
2 Chr—2 Chronicles
Col—Colossians
1 Cor—1 Corinthians
2 Cor—2 Corinthians
Dan—Daniel
Deut—Deuteronomy
Eccl (or Qoh)—Ecclesiastes
Eph—Ephesians
Esth—Esther
Exod—Exodus
Ezek—Ezekiel
Ezra—Ezra
Gal—Galatians
Gen—Genesis
Hab—Habakkuk
Hag—Haggai
Heb—Hebrews
Hos—Hosea
Isa—Isaiah
Jas—James
Jdt—Judith
Jer—Jeremiah
Job—Job
Joel—Joel
John—John
1 John—1 John
2 John—2 John
3 John—3 John
Jonah—Jonah
Josh—Joshua
Jude—Jude
Judg—Judges
1 Kgs—1 Kings

2 Kgs—2 Kings
Lam—Lamentations
Lev—Leviticus
Luke—Luke
1 Macc—1 Maccabees
2 Macc—2 Maccabees
Mal—Malachi
Mark—Mark
Matt—Matthew
Mic—Micah
Nah—Nahum
Neh—Nehemiah
Num—Numbers
Obad—Obadiah
1 Pet—1 Peter
2 Pet—2 Peter
Phil—Philippians
Phlm—Philemon
Prov—Proverbs
Ps(s)—Psalms
Rev—Revelation
Rom—Romans
Ruth—Ruth
1 Sam—1 Samuel
2 Sam—2 Samuel
Sir—Sirach
Song—Song of Songs
1 Thess—1 Thessalonians
2 Thess—2 Thessalonians
1 Tim—1 Timothy
2 Tim—2 Timothy
Titus—Titus
Tob—Tobit
Wis—Wisdom
Zech—Zechariah
Zeph—Zephaniah

The Books of
First and Second Chronicles

During the era of Persian rule (539–332 B.C.), when the land of Israel was known as the province of Yehud, a Jewish writer with close connections to the Jerusalem temple authored a new version of Israel's sacred story. Crafted for the Jewish people of his time, Chronicles spans the time from the creation of the world through the end of the Babylonian exile and Cyrus' permission for Jews to return home in 538 B.C. These books tell the story from a special perspective. They emphasize the relationship with God centered at the temple and focus on Israel's monarchs as leaders in political and religious matters, cooperating with Levites, priests, and prophets. For example, in Chronicles there is little concern for the split between the northern and southern kingdoms after Solomon. Jerusalem is God's chosen city, the temple is God's special place of presence, and public worship and song are critical aspects of Israel's public life. God appears as mighty power, transcendent divinity, creator and sustainer of the world. There are no other gods as rivals.

These views come from the same storyline as that in the books of Deuteronomy through 2 Kings, often referred to as the Deuteronomistic History. The Chronicler, however, paints this picture with different shades and accents. Often, such differences can be easily traced when the Chronicler follows the story in the Deuteronomistic History rather closely. In fact, one can read 1–2 Chronicles synoptically, comparing it with Samuel and Kings, much as one reads Matthew, Mark, and Luke in synoptic fashion. In this commentary we will attend to the Chronicler's alterations of the older text as he rewrites Israel's history. As we observe his changes to the story, some very obvious, many very subtle, we will notice how his theological perspective differs greatly from the earlier history. One difference is striking: the Deuteronomistic History views the era of the monarchy as a downward spiral leading to the Babylonian exile, and blames the regression on sinful actions of the kings. The Chronicler, on the other hand, presents a far more positive view of kings, especially those of Judah. He implies that their ways of conduct, especially their faith and their attention to God through worship, can lead to bountiful blessings for Israel. For the Chronicler, "Israel" is the Jewish people in Judah in the postexilic era, so the message to his audience is that they can enjoy more blessings if they wholeheartedly dedicate themselves to their God.

Israel's early history is recounted in these books quite differently than in the Pentateuch. 1 Chronicles 1–9 consist of a series of genealogies, which cover time from the creation of the world up to the reign of Saul. While many connections exist between people in the genealogies and persons known from stories elsewhere, Chronicles does not entirely depend on narratives. Rather the story is carried through the genealogical connections. King David's reign constitutes the second part of this book (1 Chr 10–29). Here, the Chronicler repeats much of the material in the books of Samuel and describes David's plans for the temple and its personnel in much greater detail (1 Chr 22–29). Solomon's reign (2 Chr 1–9) was a wonderful time for later Israel to remember and to emulate; it includes his building and dedication of the temple and lacks the negative evaluation of him found in 1 Kings 11:10–22. 2 Chronicles 10–36 narrates the history of the kingdom of Judah, with special focus on the exemplary rule of kings Jehoshaphat, Hezekiah, and Josiah. Chronicles generally omits criticism of kings in the northern kingdom of Israel, so the Chronicler may be seen to favor a reunion of the northern and southern kingdoms. In short, we can say that the Chronicler rewrites the Pentateuch by way of genealogies, and the books of Joshua through 2 Kings by a new version of the history emphasizing David's line.

It is very helpful to keep a copy of the books of Samuel and Kings handy while reading this text, since Chronicles clearly uses these sources. The differences between them will catch our attention and suggest to us important emphases for the Chronicler. In particular, the Chronicler rewrites Kings with subtle and substantial differences (e.g., the story of Solomon, 2 Chr 1–9) and completely omits stories well known from Kings (e.g., the narratives about the prophets Elijah and Elisha, 1 Kgs 17–2 Kgs 9). The Chronicler almost ignores the kings of the North, whereas the author of Kings had evaluated them as consistently evil and guilty of idolatry. Along these lines, the Chronicler omits 2 Kings 17 and 18:9-12, a detailed examination of Israel's various offenses against God and how they fulfill God's word through the prophets.

This commentary will focus on some special themes and expressions in Chronicles that differ from the Deuteronomistic History. The Chronicler's idiosyncrasies show a great interest in how Israel (i.e., Judah in postexilic times) should pray and worship, and ultimately what religious practices can help the divided sectors of Israel come together in unity.

The Book of First Chronicles

I. Genealogical Tables

1 **From Adam to Abraham.** [1]Adam, Seth, Enosh, [2]Kenan, Mahalalel, Jared, [3]Enoch, Methuselah, Lamech, [4]Noah, Shem, Ham, and Japheth. [5]The sons of Japheth were Gomer, Magog, Madai, Javan, Tubal, Meshech, and Tiras. [6]The sons of Gomer were Ashkenaz, Riphath, and Togarmah. [7]The sons of Javan were Elishah, Tarshish, the Kittim, and the Rodanim.

GENEALOGIES

I Chronicles I–9

Genealogies offer people a sense of their identity by linking them to their past, giving them a type of connection to those who gave birth to them and to their ancestors. Frequently we think of building links backwards in a line of ancestry; these we may call linear genealogies. Other genealogies spread out and display all the relations (e.g., siblings) in a certain generation, offering a sense of the breadth of connections; some people call these segmented genealogies. Occasionally, the two mix, with a genealogical line described for one or more members of a broad list of siblings. The manner and order of presentation gives a good idea of what values are most important to the writer. For example, a genealogy might trace a "line" by naming the parental relationships of one to another, going through several generations. If several members of one generation are mentioned, then you may observe which members of the line are carried through, and in what order they are described. Often they save the most important for the last.

For the people of the Chronicler's age, hard questions persisted: how did their identity connect with the twelve tribes of Israel? What happened to the ten lost tribes? How did Israel fit into the whole of the human race? What would be their future: a small group or all Israel (represented by all twelve tribes)? Which tribes and families of Israel were most important to their self-understanding? The genealogies offer subtle answers to these questions.

⁸The sons of Ham were Cush, Mizraim, Put, and Canaan. ⁹The sons of Cush were Seba, Havilah, Sabta, Raama, and Sabteca. The sons of Raama were Sheba and Dedan. ¹⁰Cush became the father of Nimrod, who was the first to be a warrior on the earth. ¹¹Mizraim became the father of the Ludim, Anamim, Lehabim, Naphtuhim, ¹²Pathrusim, Casluhim, and Caphtorim, from whom the Philistines sprang. ¹³Canaan became the father of Sidon, his firstborn, and Heth, ¹⁴and the Jebusites, the Amorites, the Girgashites, ¹⁵the Hivites, the Arkites, the Sinites, ¹⁶the Arvadites, the Zemarites, and the Hamathites.

¹⁷The sons of Shem were Elam, Asshur, Arpachshad, Lud, and Aram. The sons of Aram were Uz, Hul, Gether, and Mash. ¹⁸Arpachshad became the father of Shelah, and Shelah became the father of Eber. ¹⁹Two sons were born to Eber; the first was named Peleg (for in his time the world was divided), and his brother was named Joktan. ²⁰Joktan became the father of Almodad, Sheleph, Hazarmaveth, Jerah, ²¹Hadoram, Uzal, Diklah, ²²Ebal, Abimael, Sheba, ²³Ophir, Havilah, and Jobab; all these were the sons of Joktan.

²⁴Shem, Arpachshad, Shelah, ²⁵Eber, Peleg, Reu, ²⁶Serug, Nahor, Terah, ²⁷Abram, that is, Abraham.

Much of this information can be found in the Pentateuch, interspersed with narratives well known to all Israelites. The genealogical lists in chapters 1–9 call to mind many stories and narratives recounted elsewhere.

1:1–2:2 Descendants of Adam to Israel

This chapter demonstrates that Israel's origins go back to the origins of all peoples—i.e., Abraham's ancestry in Adam and Noah; it places Israel in this wider scope of human history envisaged by the Bible. Verses 1-4 list thirteen names of the ancestors of all human beings, distributed in ten generations. These names differ somewhat from the stories in Genesis 2–5, but they match closely a genealogical list in Genesis 5:1-32. Only in the case of Noah are all the sons listed: Shem, Ham, and Japheth (1:4).

1:5-23 lists the descendants of the sons of Noah, drawing from a genealogy in Genesis 10:1-32. Japheth's fourteen descendants (1:5-7) seemingly relate to Noah's sons' settling in Europe and Asia. Ham's thirty descendants (1:8-16) point to specific peoples and lands in Africa and Syria-Palestine; they include Canaan and other peoples later connected to lands to be dispossessed: Jebusites, Amorites, etc. Then come twenty-six descendants of Shem, the Semites localized in Arabia and Mesopotamia, with some familiar names: Asshur (Assyria) and Aram (Arameans, near Damascus) (1:17-23). Verses 24-27 contain another list of Shem's descendants, in generations from Noah to Abraham, which parallels the genealogy in Genesis 11:10-26. In verse 27, the Chronicler says "Abram, that is, Abraham," the name first

From Abraham to Jacob. [28]The sons of Abraham were Isaac and Ishmael. [29]These were their generations:

Nebaioth, the firstborn of Ishmael, then Kedar, Adbeel, Mibsam, [30]Mishma, Dumah, Massa, Hadad, Tema, [31]Jetur, Naphish, and Kedemah. These were the sons of Ishmael.

[32]The sons of Keturah, Abraham's concubine: she bore Zimran, Jokshan, Medan, Midian, Ishbak, and Shuah. The sons of Jokshan were Sheba and Dedan. [33]The sons of Midian were Ephah, Epher, Hanoch, Abida, and Eldaah. All these were the sons of Keturah.

[34]Abraham begot Isaac. The sons of Isaac were Esau and Israel.

[35]The descendants of Esau were Eliphaz, Reuel, Jeush, Jalam, and Korah. [36]The descendants of Eliphaz were Teman, Omar, Zephi, Gatam, Kenaz, Timna, and Amalek. [37]The descendants of Reuel were Nahath, Zerah, Shammah, and Mizzah.

[38]The sons of Seir were Lotan, Shobal, Zibeon, Anah, Dishon, Ezer, and Dishan. [39]The sons of Lotan were Hori and Homam; Timna was the sister of Lotan. [40]The sons of Shobal were Alian, Manahath, Ebal, Shephi, and Onam. The sons of Zibeon were Aiah and Anah. [41]The sons of Anah: Dishon. The sons of Dishon were Hemdan, Eshban, Ithran, and Cheran. [42]The sons of Ezer were Bilhan, Zaavan, and Jaakan. The sons of Dishan were Uz and Aran.

[43]The kings who reigned in the land of Edom before the Israelites had kings were the following: Bela, son of Beor, the name of whose city was Dinhabah. [44]When Bela died, Jobab, son of Zerah, from Bozrah, succeeded him as king. [45]When Jobab died, Husham, from the land of the Temanites, succeeded him as king. [46]Husham died and Hadad, son of Bedad, succeeded him as king. He overthrew the Midianites on the Moabite plateau, and the name of his city was Avith. [47]Hadad died and Samlah of Masrekah succeeded him as king. [48]Samlah died and Shaul from Rehoboth on the

---

given him in Genesis 17:1. Thus the Chronicler jumps from Genesis 11 to Genesis 17 with a new focus on Abraham, father of Israel. The rest of this chapter lists Abraham's descendants: Ishmael (1:29-31; cf. Gen 25:13-16), Keturah his concubine (1:32-33; cf. Gen 25:1-4 where she is called a "wife"), Isaac his son (1:34), with a long genealogy for Esau (1:35-54; cf. Gen 36:10-42).

Notice how the less-favored descendants (e.g., Ishmael, Keturah, Esau) appear first, followed by the most important line. Chapter 2 begins the line of the twelve sons of Jacob, though the Chronicler never uses the name Jacob, but rather Israel. These are the heads of the twelve tribes of Israel. There are parallel lists in Genesis (35:16-18; 35:22-26; 29:31; 30:24) and Exodus (1:1-4). Although Dan and Zebulun are found in this list (2:1-2), the Chronicler does not give them a genealogy, and Dinah, Jacob's daughter (Gen 34), goes unmentioned in the genealogies.

9

Euphrates succeeded him as king. ⁴⁹When Shaul died, Baalhanan, son of Achbor, succeeded him as king. ⁵⁰Baalhanan died and Hadad succeeded him as king. The name of his city was Pai, and his wife's name was Mehetabel. She was the daughter of Matred, who was the daughter of Mezahab. ⁵¹After Hadad died, there were chiefs in Edom: the chiefs of Timna, Aliah, Jetheth, ⁵²Oholibamah, Elah, Pinon, ⁵³Kenaz, Teman, Mibzar, ⁵⁴Magdiel, and Iram were the chiefs of Edom.

2 ¹These were the sons of Israel: Reuben, Simeon, Levi, Judah, Issachar, Zebulun, ²Dan, Joseph, Benjamin, Naphtali, Gad, and Asher.

Judah. ³The sons of Judah were: Er, Onan, and Shelah; these three Bathshua, a Canaanite woman, bore to him. But Judah's firstborn, Er, was wicked in the sight of the Lord, so he took his life. ⁴Judah's daughter-in-law Tamar bore him Perez and Zerah, so that he had five sons in all.

⁵The sons of Perez were Hezron and Hamul. ⁶The sons of Zerah were Zimri, Ethan, Heman, Calcol, and Darda—five in all. ⁷The sons of Zimri: Carmi. The sons of Carmi: Achar, who brought

2:3–4:23 Descendants of Judah

This is the major tribe of the southern kingdom. Judah's family has the largest genealogy of all, about one hundred verses. It includes several complex genealogies and brings the house of David into immediate prominence.

The genealogies of Judah provide evidence about the occurrence of intermarriage in Israel; this is quite interesting because exogamy, i.e., marrying outside family/tribal lines, is condemned elsewhere (especially in the book of Nehemiah). There are at least six cases of intermarriage in this genealogy: 2:3 ("these three, Bathshua, a Canaanite woman, bore to him"); 2:17 (Abigail, David's sister, bears Amasa, whose father was Jether the Ishmaelite); 2:34-35 (Sheshan has his daughter marry his Egyptian slave Jarha); 3:2 (David's wife Maacah is daughter of King Talmai of Geshur); 4:18 ("sons of Bithiah, the daughter of Pharaoh"); 4:21-22 (Saraph, who marries into Moab). The Chronicler does not critique any of these intermarriages. This may be the way that the Chronicler incorporates marginal figures or clans into the central group. Clearly it is one of the ways for Judah to expand its population.

2:3-55 Judah

This list ultimately focuses on David. For the reader already familiar with other biblical histories, this genealogy recalls several well-known biblical stories, such as Judah and Tamar in Genesis 38 (2:3-4), Samuel's anointing of Jesse's youngest son (cf. 1 Sam 16:1-13), and Ruth (2:5, 9-15; cf. the genealogy in Ruth 4:18-22).

trouble upon Israel by violating the ban. ⁸The sons of Ethan: Azariah. ⁹The sons born to Hezron were Jerahmeel, Ram, and Chelubai.

¹⁰Ram became the father of Amminadab, and Amminadab became the father of Nahshon, a prince of the Judahites. ¹¹Nahshon became the father of Salmah. Salmah became the father of Boaz. ¹²Boaz became the father of Obed. Obed became the father of Jesse. ¹³Jesse became the father of Eliab, his firstborn, of Abinadab, the second son, Shimea, the third, ¹⁴Nethanel, the fourth, Raddai, the fifth, ¹⁵Ozem, the sixth, and David, the seventh. ¹⁶Their sisters were Zeruiah and Abigail. Zeruiah had three sons: Abishai, Joab, and Asahel. ¹⁷Abigail bore Amasa, whose father was Jether the Ishmaelite.

¹⁸By his wife Azubah, Caleb, son of Hezron, became the father of a daughter, Jerioth. Her sons were Jesher, Shobab, and Ardon. ¹⁹When Azubah died, Caleb married Ephrath, who bore him Hur. ²⁰Hur became the father of Uri, and Uri became the father of Bezalel. ²¹Then Hezron had relations with the daughter of Machir, the father of Gilead, whom he married when he was sixty years old. She bore him Segub. ²²Segub became the father of Jair, who possessed twenty-three cities in the land of Gilead. ²³Geshur and Aram took from them the villages of Jair, that is, Kenath and its towns, sixty cities in all, which had belonged to the sons of Machir, the father of Gilead. ²⁴After the death of Hezron, Caleb had relations with Ephrathah, the widow of his father Hezron, and she bore him Ashhur, the father of Tekoa.

²⁵The sons of Jerahmeel, the firstborn of Hezron, were Ram, the firstborn, then Bunah, Oren, and Ozem, his brothers.

²⁶Jerahmeel also had another wife, named Atarah, who was the mother of Onam. ²⁷The sons of Ram, the firstborn of Jerahmeel, were Maaz, Jamin, and Eker. ²⁸The sons of Onam were Shammai and Jada. The sons of Shammai were Nadab and Abishur. ²⁹Abishur's wife, who was named Abihail, bore him Ahban and Molid. ³⁰The sons of Nadab were Seled and Appaim. Seled died childless. ³¹The sons of Appaim: Ishi. The sons of Ishi: Sheshan. The sons of Sheshan: Ahlai. ³²The sons of Jada, the brother of Shammai, were Jether and Jonathan. Jether died childless. ³³The sons of Jonathan were Peleth and Zaza. These were the sons of Jerahmeel. ³⁴Sheshan had no sons, only daughters; he had an Egyptian slave named Jarha. ³⁵Sheshan gave his daughter in marriage to his slave Jarha, and she bore him Attai. ³⁶Attai became the father of Nathan. Nathan became the father of Zabad. ³⁷Zabad became the father of Ephlal. Ephlal became the father of Obed. ³⁸Obed became the father of Jehu. Jehu became the father of Azariah. ³⁹Azariah became the father of Helez. Helez became the father of Eleasah. ⁴⁰Eleasah became the father of Sismai. Sismai became the father of Shallum. ⁴¹Shallum became the father of Jekamiah. Jekamiah became the father of Elishama.

⁴²The sons of Caleb, the brother of Jerahmeel: Mesha his firstborn, who was the father of Ziph. Then the sons of Mareshah, who was the father of Hebron. ⁴³The sons of Hebron were Korah, Tappuah, Rekem, and Shema. ⁴⁴Shema became the father of Raham, who was the father of Jorkeam. Rekem became the father of Shammai. ⁴⁵The son of Shammai: Maon, who was the father of

DAVID
PS: XLVII.
IPSE TANQVAM
SPONSVS,
PROCEDENS
DE THAL
SVO.

Beth-zur. ⁴⁶Ephah, Caleb's concubine, bore Haran, Moza, and Gazez. Haran became the father of Gazez. ⁴⁷The sons of Jahdai were Regem, Jotham, Geshan, Pelet, Ephah, and Shaaph. ⁴⁸Maacah, Caleb's concubine, bore Sheber and Tirhanah. ⁴⁹She also bore Shaaph, the father of Madmannah, Sheva, the father of Machbenah, and the father of Gibea. Achsah was Caleb's daughter.

⁵⁰These were sons of Caleb, sons of Hur, the firstborn of Ephrathah: Shobal, the father of Kiriath-jearim, ⁵¹Salma, the father of Bethlehem, and Hareph, the father of Bethgader. ⁵²The sons of Shobal, the father of Kiriath-jearim, were Reaiah, half of the Manahathites, ⁵³and the clans of Kiriath-jearim: the Ithrites, the Puthites, the Shumathites, and the Mishraites. From these the Zorahites and the Eshtaolites derived. ⁵⁴The sons of Salma were Bethlehem, the Netophathites, Atroth-beth-Joab, half of the Manahathites, and the Zorites. ⁵⁵The clans of the Sopherim dwelling in Jabez were the Tirathites, the Shimeathites, and the Sucathites. They were the Kenites, who descended from Hammath, the ancestor of the Rechabites.

3 ¹These were the sons of David born to him in Hebron: the firstborn, Amnon, by Ahinoam of Jezreel; the second, Daniel, by Abigail of Carmel; ²the third, Absalom, son of Maacah, who was the daughter of Talmai, king of Geshur; the fourth, Adonijah, son of Haggith; ³the fifth, Shephatiah, by Abital; the sixth, Ithream, by his wife Eglah. ⁴Six in all were born to him in Hebron, where he reigned seven years and six months. Then he reigned thirty-three years in Jerusalem. ⁵In Jerusalem the following were born to him: Shimea, Shobab, Nathan, Solomon—four by Bathsheba, the daughter of Ammiel; ⁶Ibhar, Elishua, Eliphelet, ⁷Nogah, Nepheg, Japhia, ⁸Elishama, Eliada, and Eliphelet—nine. ⁹All these were sons of David, in addition to other sons by concubines; and Tamar was their sister.

¹⁰The son of Solomon was Rehoboam, whose son was Abijah, whose son was Asa, whose son was Jehoshaphat, ¹¹whose son was Joram, whose son was Ahaziah, whose son was Joash, ¹²whose son was Amaziah, whose son was Azariah, whose son was Jotham, ¹³whose son was Ahaz, whose son was Hezekiah,

---

3:1-9 David

The genealogy lists names of various mothers of his children and differentiates children born in Hebron from those born in Jerusalem, paralleling 2 Samuel 3:2-5. Another list of his children is in 1 Chronicles 14:3-7.

3:10-24 Solomon

Here is a list of kings of Judah to the Babylonian exile (3:10-16) and their descendants after the exile (3:17-24). This list corresponds to information from the books of Kings up to Josiah (died ca. 609 B.C.), where there is divergence. A post-exilic list of about eight generations shows that for the Chronicler the lineage of David remains important after the return from exile.

13

Statue of King David in the Servite church in Vienna. David points to a book of Psalms, many of which he composed. David's story begins in 1 Chronicles, chapter 11.

whose son was Manasseh, [14]whose son was Amon, whose son was Josiah. [15]The sons of Josiah were: the firstborn Johanan; the second, Jehoiakim; the third, Zedekiah; the fourth, Shallum. [16]The sons of Jehoiakim were: Jeconiah, his son; Zedekiah, his son.

[17]The sons of Jeconiah the captive were: Shealtiel, [18]Malchiram, Pedaiah, Shenazzar, Jekamiah, Hoshama, and Nedabiah. [19]The sons of Pedaiah were Zerubbabel and Shimei. The sons of Zerubbabel were Meshullam and Hananiah; Shelomith was their sister. [20]The sons of Meshullam were Hashubah, Ohel, Berechiah, Hasadiah, Jushab-hesed—five. [21]The sons of Hananiah were Pelatiah, Jeshaiah, Rephaiah, Arnan, Obadiah, and Shecaniah. [22]The sons of Shecaniah were Shemaiah, Hattush, Igal, Bariah, Neariah, Shaphat—six. [23]The sons of Neariah were Elioenai, Hizkiah, and Azrikam—three. [24]The sons of Elioenai were Hodaviah, Eliashib, Pelaiah, Akkub, Johanan, Delaiah, and Anani—seven.

4 [1]The sons of Judah were: Perez, Hezron, Carmi, Hur, and Shobal. [2]Reaiah, the son of Shobal, became the father of Jahath, and Jahath became the father of Ahumai and Lahad. These were the clans of the Zorathites.

[3]These were the sons of Hareph, the father of Etam: Jezreel, Ishma, and Idbash; their sister was named Hazzelelponi. [4]Penuel was the father of Gedor, and Ezer the father of Hushah. These were the sons of Hur, the firstborn of Ephrathah, the father of Bethlehem.

[5]Ashhur, the father of Tekoa, had two wives, Helah and Naarah. [6]Naarah bore him Ahuzzam, Hepher, the Temenites, and the Ahashtarites. These were the sons of Naarah. [7]The sons of Helah were Zereth, Izhar, Ethnan, and Koz. [8]Koz became the father of Anub and Zobebah, as well as of the clans of Aharhel, son of Harum. [9]Jabez was the most distinguished of his brothers. His mother had named him Jabez, saying, "I bore him with pain." [10]Jabez prayed to the God of Israel: "Oh, that you may truly bless me and extend my boundaries! May your hand be with me and make me free of misfortune, without pain!" And God granted his prayer.

[11]Chelub, the brother of Shuhah, became the father of Mehir, who was the father of Eshton. [12]Eshton became the father of Bethrapha, Paseah, and Tehinnah, the father of the city of Nahash. These were the men of Recah.

[13]The sons of Kenaz were Othniel and Seraiah. The sons of Othniel were Hathath and Meonothai; [14]Meonothai became the father of Ophrah. Seraiah became the father of Joab, the father of

---

4:1-23 Judah

This list of his descendants derives from various lists. In 4:9-10 we hear the story of a man named Jabez, whose name is derived from the verb for pain (in childbirth), and who is honored above his brothers. Jabez asks for a sizeable blessing from God, who grants his request. Though consistent with the Chronicler's theology of prayer, this request is more self-referential than most prayers in 1–2 Chronicles.

Geharashim, so called because they were artisans. [15]The sons of Caleb, son of Jephunneh, were Ir, Elah, and Naam. The sons of Elah: Kenaz. [16]The sons of Jehallelel were Ziph, Ziphah, Tiria, and Asarel. [17]The sons of Ezrah were Jether, Mered, Epher, and Jalon. Jether became the father of Miriam, Shammai, and Ishbah, the father of Eshtemoa. [18]Mered's Egyptian wife bore Jered, the father of Gedor, Heber, the father of Soco, and Jekuthiel, the father of Zanoah. These were the sons of Bithiah, the daughter of Pharaoh, whom Mered married. [19]The sons of his Jewish wife, the sister of Naham, the father of Keilah, were Shimon the Garmite and Ishi the Maacathite. [20]The sons of Shimon were Amnon, Rinnah, Benhanan, and Tilon. The son of Ishi was Zoheth and the son of Zoheth. . . .

[21]The sons of Shelah, son of Judah, were: Er, the father of Lecah; Laadah, the father of Mareshah; the clans of the linen weavers' guild in Bethashbea; [22]Jokim; the people of Cozeba; and Joash and Saraph, who held property in Moab, but returned to Bethlehem. (These are events of old.) [23]They were potters and inhabitants of Netaim and Gederah, where they lived in the king's service.

Simeon. [24]The sons of Simeon were Nemuel, Jamin, Jachin, Zerah, and Shaul, [25]whose son was Shallum, whose son was Mibsam, whose son was Mishma. [26]The sons of Mishma were his son Hammuel, whose son was Zaccur, whose son was Shimei. [27]Shimei had sixteen sons and six daughters. His brothers, however, did not have many sons, and as a result all their clans did not equal the number of the Judahites.

[28]They dwelt in Beer-sheba, Moladah, Hazar-shual, [29]Bilhah, Ezem, Tolad, [30]Bethuel, Hormah, Ziklag, [31]Bethmarcaboth, Hazar-susim, Bethbiri, and Shaaraim. Until the reign of David, these were their cities [32]and their villages. Etam, also, and Ain, Rimmon, Tochen, and Ashan—five cities, [33]together with all their outlying villages as far as Baal. Here is where they dwelt, and so it was inscribed of them in their family records.

4:24-43 Descendants of Simeon

Simeon traditionally occupies territory close to Judah, in the south of the land. The list of names in 4:24-27 draws on two sources: Genesis 46:10 and Exodus 6:15. Verse 27 recounts Shimei's offspring, surprisingly mentioning six daughters (plus sixteen sons) and that he has more offspring than his brothers, suggesting a problem with underpopulation in the time of the Chronicler. A list of cities and towns follows, drawing on a list in Joshua 19:1-9 (land allotments after the conquest) but implying that Israelites have been here from time immemorial. Verses 39-43 narrate two events in which Simeon increases its territory, pushing out earlier inhabitants (Meunites and Amalekites) when they needed more space for their flocks. The warlike nature of this group corresponds to their characterization in Genesis 34, 49:5-7 and Judges 9:2.

³⁴Meshobab, Jamlech, Joshah, son of Amaziah, ³⁵Joel, Jehu, son of Joshibiah, son of Seraiah, son of Asiel, ³⁶Elioenai, Jaakobah, Jeshohaiah, Asaiah, Adiel, Jesimiel, Benaiah, ³⁷Ziza, son of Shiphi, son of Allon, son of Jedaiah, son of Shimri, son of Shemaiah— ³⁸these just named were princes in their clans, and their ancestral houses spread out to such an extent ³⁹that they went to the approaches of Gedor, east of the valley, seeking pasture for their flocks. ⁴⁰They found abundant and good pastures, and the land was spacious, quiet, and peaceful—for the Hamites dwelt there formerly. ⁴¹They who have just been listed by name set out during the reign of Hezekiah, king of Judah, and attacked their tents and also the Meunites who were there. They put them under the ban that is still in force to this day and dwelt in their place because they found pasture there for their flocks.

⁴²Five hundred of them (the Simeonites) went to Mount Seir, with Pelatiah, Neariah, Rephaiah, and Uzziel, sons of Ishi, at their head. ⁴³They attacked the surviving Amalekites who had escaped, and have lived there to the present day.

5 Reuben. ¹The sons of Reuben, the firstborn of Israel. (He was indeed the firstborn, but because he defiled the couch of his father his birthright was given to the sons of Joseph, son of Israel, so that he is not listed in the family records according to his birthright. ²Judah, in fact, became powerful among his brothers, so that the ruler came from him, though the birthright had been Joseph's.) ³The sons of Reuben, the firstborn of Israel, were Hanoch, Pallu, Hezron, and Carmi. ⁴His son was Joel, whose son was Shemaiah, whose son was Gog, whose son was Shimei, ⁵whose son was Micah, whose son was Reaiah, whose son was Baal, ⁶whose son was Beerah, whom Tilgath-pileser, the king of Assyria, took into exile; he was a prince of the Reubenites. ⁷His brothers who belonged to his clans, when they were listed in the family records according to their descendants, were: Jeiel, the chief, and Zechariah, ⁸and Bela, son of Azaz, son of Shema, son of Joel. The Reubenites lived in Aroer and as far as Nebo and Baal-meon; ⁹toward the east they dwelt as far as the wilderness which extends from the Euphrates River, for they had much livestock in the land of Gilead. ¹⁰In Saul's time they waged war with the Hagrites, and when they had defeated them they dwelt in their tents throughout the region east of Gilead.

5:1-10 Descendants of Reuben

Reuben occupies territory east of the Jordan River. His four descendants are known also from Genesis 46:8-9, Exodus 6:14, and Numbers 26:5-6. In verses 1-2 Reuben, though firstborn, loses his birthright to the sons of Joseph, since he defiled his father's bed by having sexual relations with Bilhah, his father's concubine (Gen 35:22). Moreover, the real power of the firstborn is exercised by Judah.

Gad. [11]The Gadites lived alongside them in the land of Bashan as far as Salecah. [12]Joel was chief, Shapham was second in command, and Janai was judge in Bashan. [13]Their brothers, according to their ancestral houses, were: Michael, Meshullam, Sheba, Jorai, Jacan, Zia, and Eber—seven. [14]These were the sons of Abihail, son of Huri, son of Jaroah, son of Gilead, son of Michael, son of Jeshishai, son of Jahdo, son of Buz. [15]Ahi, son of Abdiel, son of Guni, was the head of their ancestral houses. [16]They dwelt in Gilead, in Bashan and its towns, and in all the pasture lands of Sirion to the borders. [17]All were listed in the family records in the time of Jotham, king of Judah, and of Jeroboam, king of Israel.

[18]The Reubenites, Gadites, and the half-tribe of Manasseh were warriors, men who bore shield and sword and who drew the bow, trained in warfare—forty-four thousand seven hundred and sixty men fit for military service. [19]When they waged war against the Hagrites and against Jetur, Naphish, and Nodab, [20]they received help so that the Hagrites and all who were with them were delivered into their power. For during the battle they cried out to God, and he heard them because they had put their trust in him. [21]Along with one hundred thousand persons they also captured their livestock: fifty thousand camels, two hundred fifty thousand sheep, and two thousand donkeys. [22]Many were slain and fell; for "From God the victory." They dwelt in their place until the time of the exile.

The Half-tribe of Manasseh. [23]The half-tribe of Manasseh lived in the land of Bashan as far as Baal-hermon, Senir, and Mount Hermon; they were numerous. [24]The following were the heads of their ancestral houses: Epher, Ishi, Eliel, Azriel, Jeremiah, Hodaviah, and Jahdiel—men who were warriors, famous men, and heads over their ancestral houses.

[25]However, they acted treacherously toward the God of their ancestors by prostituting themselves to follow the gods of the peoples of the land, whom God had destroyed before them. [26]Therefore the God of Israel stirred up against them the anger of Pul, king of Assyria, and the anger of Tilgath-pilneser [*sic*], king of Assyria, who deported the Reubenites, the Gadites, and the half-tribe of Manasseh and brought them to Halah, Habor, and Hara, and to the river Gozan, where they have remained to this day.

5:11-17 Descendants of Gad

The names of members of this tribe, situated in northern Transjordan, do not resemble his brief genealogies in Genesis 46:16 and Numbers 26:15.

5:18-26 Descendants of the two-and-a-half tribes

This unusual section describes the situation of the tribes of Reuben, Gad, and the half-tribe of Manasseh, all situated east of the Jordan River. The Chronicler mentions their initial conquests, their sin of idolatry (5:25) which led to their demise, and their (later) exile by the Assyrians ca. 722 B.C.

Levi. [27]The sons of Levi were Gershon, Kohath, and Merari. [28]The sons of Kohath were Amram, Izhar, Hebron, and Uzziel. [29]The children of Amram were Aaron, Moses, and Miriam. The sons of Aaron were Nadab, Abihu, Eleazar, and Ithamar. [30]Eleazar became the father of Phinehas. Phinehas became the father of Abishua. [31]Abishua became the father of Bukki. Bukki became the father of Uzzi. [32]Uzzi became the father of Zerahiah. Zerahiah became the father of Meraioth. [33]Meraioth became the father of Amariah. Amariah became the father of Ahitub. [34]Ahitub became the father of Zadok. Zadok became the father of Ahimaaz. [35]Ahimaaz became the father of Azariah. Azariah became the father of Johanan. [36]Johanan became the father of Azariah, who served as priest in the temple Solomon built in Jerusalem. [37]Azariah became the father of Amariah. Amariah became the father of Ahitub. [38]Ahitub became the father of Zadok. Zadok became the father of Shallum. [39]Shallum became the father of Hilkiah. Hilkiah became the father of Azariah. [40]Azariah became the father of Seraiah. Seraiah became the father of Jehozadak. [41]Jehozadak was one of those who went into the exile which the LORD inflicted on Judah and Jerusalem through Nebuchadnezzar.

6 [1]The sons of Levi were Gershon, Kohath, and Merari. [2]The sons of Gershon were named Libni and Shimei. [3]The sons of Kohath were Amram, Izhar, Hebron, and Uzziel. [4]The sons of Merari were Mahli and Mushi.

These were the clans of Levi, according to their ancestors. [5]Of Gershon: his

---

5:27-41 Descendants of Levi

This is another complex genealogy, which includes various kinds of information about Levites and priests (Aaronites and Zadokites). The passage begins with Levi, mentions three of his sons (Gershon, Kohath, and Merari), and traces the line through his second son, Kohath: Amram, who fathers Aaron, Moses, and Miriam (5:27-41). The Chronicler traces a line through Aaron, Eleazar, Phinehas . . . all the way to Zadok (6:34), a priest in the time of David and Solomon. The line of priests then continues into the post-exilic era (including, incidentally, another Zadok). Zadok seems to be the center of the family—i.e., twelve generations (of forty years) precede him and twelve follow him. So the Chronicler has provided an Aaronite ancestry for Zadok, a fact not mentioned during his more prominent appearances in the books of Samuel (cf. 2 Sam 15–19). The Levi family's antiquity points to the importance of this family to the entire constitution of Israel. This is part of the Chronicler's view.

6:1-15 Another listing of Levi's sons

This list includes Gershon, Kohath, and Merari, with a number of offspring for each of these family groups. Important figures include: Mushi (Moses), son of Merari in verse 4, and Samuel in verse 12 (from Kohath).

son Libni, whose son was Jahath, whose son was Zimmah, ⁶whose son was Joah, whose son was Iddo, whose son was Zerah, whose son was Jetherai.

⁷The sons of Kohath: his son Amminadab, whose son was Korah, whose son was Assir, ⁸whose son was Elkanah, whose son was Ebiasaph, whose son was Assir, ⁹whose son was Tahath, whose son was Uriel, whose son was Uzziah, whose son was Shaul. ¹⁰The sons of Elkanah were Amasai and Ahimoth, ¹¹whose son was Elkanah, whose son was Zophai, whose son was Nahath, ¹²whose son was Eliab, whose son was Jeroham, whose son was Elkanah, whose son was Samuel. ¹³The sons of Samuel were Joel, the firstborn, and Abijah, the second.

¹⁴The sons of Merari: Mahli, whose son was Libni, whose son was Shimei, whose son was Uzzah, ¹⁵whose son was Shimea, whose son was Haggiah, whose son was Asaiah.

¹⁶The following were established by David for the service of song in the LORD's house at the time when the ark had a resting place. ¹⁷They served as singers before the tabernacle of the tent of meeting until Solomon built the house of the LORD in Jerusalem, and they performed their services according to the order prescribed for them. ¹⁸Those who so performed are the following, together with their sons.

Among the Kohathites: Heman, the chanter, son of Joel, son of Samuel, ¹⁹son of Elkanah, son of Jeroham, son of Eliel, son of Toah, ²⁰son of Zuph, son of Elkanah, son of Mahath, son of Amasi, ²¹son of Elkanah, son of Joel, son of Azariah, son of Zephaniah, ²²son of Tahath, son of Assir, son of Ebiasaph, son of Korah, ²³son of Izhar, son of Kohath, son of Levi, son of Israel.

²⁴His brother Asaph stood at his right hand. Asaph was the son of Berechiah, son of Shimea, ²⁵son of Michael, son of Baaseiah, son of Malchijah, ²⁶son of Ethni, son of Zerah, son of Adaiah, ²⁷son of Ethan, son of Zimmah, son of Shimei, ²⁸son of Jahath, son of Gershon, son of Levi.

²⁹Their brothers, the Merarites, stood at the left: Ethan, son of Kishi, son of Abdi, son of Malluch, ³⁰son of Hashabiah, son of Amaziah, son of Hilkiah, ³¹son of Amzi, son of Bani, son of Shemer,

6:16-32 Levites trusted with song

Levites are entrusted with the "service of song in the Lord's house" (6:16), after the ark is installed there. From the house of Kohath are: Heman (6:18), a descendant of Korah (6:22), a name found in several psalm titles. From Gershon, standing at Heman's right, is Asaph (6:24), another name well known from titles of various psalms. Standing on Heman's left are the sons of Merari (6:29). Since Levitical temple singers in the First Temple are mentioned only in Chronicles, their presence here may be a bold move to give Levites in the Second Temple era (516 C.E. ff.) an ancient heritage and function. This link with antiquity, i.e., David and Moses, increases their religious significance for Chronicles. From Merari, again, comes Mushi (Moses in 6:32).

³²son of Mahli, son of Mushi, son of Merari, son of Levi.

³³Their brother Levites were appointed to all the other services of the tabernacle of the house of God. ³⁴However, it was Aaron and his sons who made the sacrifice on the altar for burnt offerings and on the altar of incense; they alone had charge of the holy of holies and of making atonement for Israel, as Moses, the servant of God, had commanded.

³⁵These were the sons of Aaron: his son Eleazar, whose son was Phinehas, whose son was Abishua, ³⁶whose son was Bukki, whose son was Uzzi, whose son was Zerahiah, ³⁷whose son was Meraioth, whose son was Amariah, whose son was Ahitub, ³⁸whose son was Zadok, whose son was Ahimaaz.

³⁹The following were their dwelling places, by encampments in their territories. To the sons of Aaron who belonged to the clan of the Kohathites, since the lot fell to them, ⁴⁰was assigned Hebron in the land of Judah, with its adjacent pasture lands. ⁴¹However, the open country and the villages belonging to the city had been given to Caleb, the son of Jephunneh. ⁴²There were assigned to the sons of Aaron: Hebron a city of refuge, Libnah with its pasture lands, Jattir with its pasture lands, Eshtemoa with its pasture lands, ⁴³Holon with its pasture lands, Debir with its pasture lands, ⁴⁴Ashan with its pasture lands, Jetta with its pasture lands, and Beth-shemesh with its pasture lands. ⁴⁵Also from the tribe of Benjamin: Gibeon with its pasture lands, Geba with its pasture lands, Almon with its pasture

6:33-34 Priestly institutions

These lists portray a traditional view of priestly institutions, i.e., Levite singers (6:16), Levites in charge of "all the other services of the tabernacle of the house of God" (6:33), and priests descended from Aaron, who are responsible for burnt offerings, incense offerings, and all the work of the "holy of holies" (6:34). Service corresponds to our notion of liturgy, so Levites have responsibility for everything but the three tasks assigned to the priests.

6:35-38 Aaronite priests

These verses list Aaronite priests in charge of burnt offerings and incense offerings to make atonement for Israel, according to Moses' commands. This list concludes in the time of David, with Zadok and his son Ahimaaz.

6:39-66 Levite cities

This listing of the cities of the Levites, given to them by all the tribes of Israel, probably derives from Joshua 21:1-42. In order to more closely follow the account in Joshua, the original NAB translators transposed verses 46–50 and the NABRE revisers followed suit. Members of the tribe of Levi receive no allotment of land because they are dedicated to God (Josh 14:4), so the Chronicler clearly indicates the names of their cities.

lands, Anathoth with its pasture lands. In all, they had thirteen cities with their pasture lands. ⁴⁹The Israelites assigned these cities with their pasture lands to the Levites, ⁵⁰designating them by name and assigning them by lot from the tribes of the Judahites, Simeonites, and Benjaminites.

⁴⁶The other Kohathites obtained ten cities by lot for their clans from the tribe of Ephraim, from the tribe of Dan, and from the half-tribe of Manasseh. ⁴⁷The clans of the Gershonites obtained thirteen cities from the tribes of Issachar, Asher, and Naphtali, and from the half-tribe of Manasseh in Bashan. ⁴⁸The clans of the Merarites obtained twelve cities by lot from the tribes of Reuben, Gad, and Zebulun.

⁵¹The clans of the Kohathites obtained cities by lot from the tribe of Ephraim. ⁵²They were assigned cities of refuge: Shechem in the mountain region of Ephraim, with its pasture lands, Gezer with its pasture lands, ⁵³Kibzaim with its pasture lands, and Beth-horon with its pasture lands. ⁵⁴From the tribe of Dan: Elteke with its pasture lands, Gibbethon with its pasture lands, Aijalon with its pasture lands, and Gath-rimmon with its pasture lands. ⁵⁵From the half-tribe of Manasseh: Taanach with its pasture lands and Ibleam with its pasture lands. These belonged to the rest of the Kohathite clan.

⁵⁶The clans of the Gershonites received from the half-tribe of Manasseh:

Golan in Bashan with its pasture lands and Ashtaroth with its pasture lands. ⁵⁷From the tribe of Issachar: Kedesh with its pasture lands, Daberath with its pasture lands, ⁵⁸Ramoth with its pasture lands, and Engannim with its pasture lands. ⁵⁹From the tribe of Asher: Mashal with its pasture lands, Abdon with its pasture lands, ⁶⁰Hilkath with its pasture lands, and Rehob with its pasture lands. ⁶¹From the tribe of Naphtali: Kedesh in Galilee with its pasture lands, Hammon with its pasture lands, and Kiriathaim with its pasture lands.

⁶²The rest of the Merarites received from the tribe of Zebulun: Jokneam with its pasture lands, Kartah with its pasture lands, Rimmon with its pasture lands, and Tabor with its pasture lands. ⁶³Across the Jordan at Jericho (that is, east of the Jordan) they received from the tribe of Reuben: Bezer in the desert with its pasture lands, Jahzah with its pasture lands, ⁶⁴Kedemoth with its pasture lands, and Mephaath with its pasture lands. ⁶⁵From the tribe of Gad: Ramoth in Gilead with its pasture lands, Mahanaim with its pasture lands, ⁶⁶Heshbon with its pasture lands, and Jazer with its pasture lands.

7 Issachar. ¹The sons of Issachar were Tola, Puah, Jashub, and Shimron: four. ²The sons of Tola were Uzzi, Rephaiah, Jeriel, Jahmai, Ibsam, and Shemuel, heads of the ancestral houses of Tola, mighty

7:1-5 Descendants of Issachar

Issachar is a northern tribe, located southwest of the Sea of Galilee. Many of this family are warriors, numbered in a census in David's time. The only biblical parallels for this list are Genesis 46:13 and Numbers 26:23-25, so the Chronicler may have had other sources of information. Here the

warriors in their generations. In the time of David they numbered twenty-two thousand six hundred. ³The sons of Uzzi: Izarahiah. The sons of Izarahiah were Michael, Obadiah, Joel, and Isshiah. All five of these were chiefs. ⁴Along with them, in their generations, according to ancestral houses, were thirty-six thousand men in organized military troops, since they had more wives and children ⁵than their fellow tribesmen. In all the clans of Issachar there was a total of eighty-seven thousand warriors listed in their family records.

Benjamin. ⁶The sons of Benjamin were Bela, Becher, and Jediael—three. ⁷The sons of Bela were Ezbon, Uzzi, Uzziel, Jerimoth, and Iri—five. They were heads of their ancestral houses and warriors. Their family records listed twenty-two thousand and thirty-four. ⁸The sons of Becher were Zemirah, Joash, Eliezer, Elioenai, Omri, Jeremoth, Abijah, Anathoth, and Alemeth—all these were sons of Becher. ⁹Their family records listed twenty thousand two hundred of their kindred who were heads of their ancestral houses and warriors. ¹⁰The sons of Jediael: Bilhan. The sons of Bilhan were Jeush, Benjamin, Ehud, Chenaanah, Zethan, Tarshish, and Ahishahar. ¹¹All these were sons of Jediael, heads of ancestral houses and warriors. They numbered seventeen thousand two hundred men fit for military service . . . ¹²Shupham and Hupham.

Dan, Naphtali and Manasseh. The sons of Dan: Hushim. ¹³The sons of

---

Chronicler only details three of the five Galilean tribes: Issachar, Naphtali, and Asher. Zebulun is missing and so is Dan (except for a possible reference noted in verse 12). Altogether, these tribes merit only sixteen verses. Clearly, the Chronicler was much more interested in southern tribes, especially Judah, and in Levi. But his information on the Galilean tribes suggests his ongoing interest in the return of the lost northern tribes.

7:6-12 Descendants of Benjamin

Benjamin is a small territory, lying north of Judah and south of Ephraim. Parallels include Genesis 46:21 and Numbers 26:38-41. There is a longer genealogy of this family in 1 Chronicles 8:1-28, with many different names. In 7:12, "The sons of Dan: Hushim," Dan is not actually mentioned in the Hebrew text, but many commentators interpret the Hebrew word as another, unnamed brother and think of it as a reference to Dan, who is not mentioned elsewhere in these genealogies.

7:13 Descendants of Naphtali

A single verse, this genealogy draws on parallels in Genesis 46:24 and Numbers 26:48-50. Since it is so brief, scholars think the actual genealogy was lost. Naphtali's territory was north of Issachar, in the region known to us as Galilee.

Naphtali were Jahziel, Guni, Jezer, and Shallum. These were sons of Bilhah. [14]The sons of Manasseh, whom his Aramean concubine bore: she bore Machir, the father of Gilead. [15]Machir took a wife whose name was Maacah; his sister's name was Molecheth. Manasseh's second son was named Zelophehad, who had only daughters. [16]Maacah, Machir's wife, bore a son whom she named Peresh. He had a brother named Sheresh, whose sons were Ulam and Rakem. [17]The sons of Ulam: Bedan. These were the sons of Gilead, the son of Machir, the son of Manasseh. [18]His sister Molecheth bore Ishhod, Abiezer, and Mahlah. [19]The sons of Shemida were Ahian, Shechem, Likhi, and Aniam.

Ephraim. [20]The sons of Ephraim: Shuthelah, whose son was Bered, whose son was Tahath, whose son was Eleadah, whose son was Tahath, [21]whose son was Zabad. Ephraim's son Shuthelah, and Ezer and Elead, who were born in the land, were killed by the inhabitants of Gath because they had gone down to take away their livestock. [22]Their father Ephraim mourned a long time, but after his relatives had come and comforted him, [23]he had relations with his wife, who conceived and bore a son whom he named Beriah, since evil had befallen his house. [24]He had a daughter, Sheerah, who built Lower and Upper Beth-horon and Uzzen-sheerah. [25]Zabad's son was Rephah, whose son was Resheph, whose

7:14-19 Descendants of Manasseh

This territory lies north of Ephraim and south of Issachar, from the Jordan River west to the Mediterranean Sea. Biblical parallels include Numbers 26:29-34 and Joshua 17:1-6. This brief notice mentions more women family members than most others (7:15), including the concubine of Manasseh, wives for his sons, and the name of his sister, Maacah. It also mentions Zelophehad, who had only daughters. Zelophehad's five daughters play an important role in Numbers 27:1-11 and 36:1-12, where they challenge traditional laws of heredity (restricted to sons) and invite Moses to reinterpret law to meet changing circumstances. Here the Chronicler provides a clear reference to their family.

7:20-29 Descendants of Ephraim

This tribe inhabits the central hill country north of Benjamin. The genealogy is somewhat convoluted, but we do learn that Ephraim's sons were killed by the people of Gath and that he and his wife subsequently had a third son, Beriah (7:23). His daughter Sheerah, however, is more prominent. She builds three towns, two of which guard the routes from the coastland up into the hill country (7:24). Joshua appears in this genealogy (7:27), which concludes with a list of famous places inhabited by Ephraimites and Manassites: Bethel, Gezer, Shechem, Beth-shean, Taanach, Megiddo, and Dor.

son was Telah, whose son was Tahan, [26]whose son was Ladan, whose son was Ammihud, whose son was Elishama, [27]whose son was Nun, whose son was Joshua.

[28]Their property and their dwellings were in Bethel and its towns, Naaran to the east, Gezer and its towns to the west, and also Shechem and its towns as far as Ayyah and its towns. [29]Manasseh, however, had possession of Beth-shean and its towns, Taanach and its towns, Megiddo and its towns, and Dor and its towns. In these dwelt the sons of Joseph, the son of Israel.

Asher. [30]The sons of Asher were Imnah, Ishvah, Ishvi, and Beriah; their sister was Serah. [31]Beriah's sons were Heber and Malchiel, who was the father of Birzaith. [32]Heber became the father of Japhlet, Shomer, Hotham, and their sister Shua. [33]The sons of Japhlet were Pasach, Bimhal, and Ashvath; these were the sons of Japhlet. [34]The sons of Shomer were Ahi, Rohgah, Jehubbah, and Aram. [35]The sons of his brother Hotham were Zophah, Imna, Shelesh, and Amal. [36]The sons of Zophah were Suah, Harnepher, Shual, Beri, Imrah, [37]Bezer, Hod, Shamma, Shilshah, Ithran, and Beera. [38]The sons of Jether were Jephunneh, Pispa, and Ara. [39]The sons of Ulla were Arah, Hanniel, and Rizia. [40]All these were sons of Asher, heads of ancestral houses, distinguished men, warriors, and chiefs among the princes. Their family records numbered twenty-six thousand men fit for military service.

8 **Benjamin.** [1]Benjamin became the father of Bela, his firstborn, Ashbel, the second son, Aharah, the third, [2]Nohah, the fourth, and Rapha, the fifth. [3]The sons of Bela were Addar and Gera, the father of Ehud. [4]The sons of Ehud were Abishua, Naaman, Ahoah, [5]Gera, Shephuphan, and Huram. [6]These were

7:30-40 Descendants of Asher

This group's territory is far north, along the coast south of present-day Lebanon. Like the genealogies of Issachar and Benjamin, it focuses on names and references to military leaders (7:4-5, 9, 11, 40). Here are also listed two women: Serah, a daughter of Asher (7:30), and Shua, daughter of Heber, son of Asher (7:32). Biblical parallels are found in Genesis 46:17 and Numbers 26:44-47.

8:1-28 Descendants of Benjamin

Here is a second Benjaminite genealogy (cf. 7:6-12, above). This tribe, just to the north of Jerusalem and Judah, is important because Saul came from it, and after the loss of the ten northern tribes it continued in association with Judah. The five sons of Benjamin found in 8:1-2 differ from three sons in 1 Chronicles 7:6 and larger numbers in Genesis 46:21 and Numbers 26:38-39. The Chronicler lists the sons of Bela in 8:3-7, and in 8:8-14 lists the sons of Shaharaim.

the sons of Ehud, family heads over those who dwelt in Geba and were deported to Manahath. [7]Also Naaman, Ahijah, and Gera. The last, who led them into exile, became the father of Uzza and Ahihud. [8]Shaharaim became a father on the Moabite plateau after he had put away his wives Hushim and Baara. [9]By his wife Hodesh he begot Jobab, Zibia, Mesha, Malcam, [10]Jeuz, Sachia, and Mirmah. These were his sons, family heads. [11]By Hushim he begot Abitub and Elpaal. [12]The sons of Elpaal were Eber, Misham, Shemed (who built Ono and Lod with its nearby towns), [13]and Beriah, and Shema. They were family heads of those who dwelt in Aijalon, and they put the inhabitants of Gath to flight. [14]Their relatives were Elpaal, Shashak, and Jeremoth. [15]Zebadiah, Arad, Eder, [16]Michael, Ishpah, and Joha were the sons of Beriah. [17]Zebadiah, Meshullam, Hizki, Heber, [18]Ishmerai, Izliah, and Jobab were the sons of Elpaal. [19]Jakim, Zichri, Zabdi, [20]Elienai, Zillethai, Eliel, [21]Adaiah, Beraiah, and Shimrath were the sons of Shimei. [22]Ishpan, Eber, Eliel, [23]Abdon, Zichri, Hanan, [24]Hananiah, Elam, Anthothijah, [25]Iphdeiah, and Penuel were the sons of Shashak. [26]Shamsherai, Shehariah, Athaliah, [27]Jaareshiah, Elijah, and Zichri were the sons of Jeroham. [28]These were family heads in their generations, chiefs who dwelt in Jerusalem.

[29]In Gibeon dwelt Jeiel, the founder of Gibeon, whose wife's name was

---

Again, women are featured in the story: Shaharaim's wives Hushim and Baara, whom he "put away" (i.e., divorced) (8:8); his wife Hodesh, by whom he had sons (8:9-10); and a later note that he also had children by Hushim (8:11). Some familiar towns, Lod and Ono, were built by Hushim's descendants, a sign of blessing through a divorcee. Two more families are introduced in verses 13-14: Beriah and Shemah. In 8:15-28, the Chronicler lists a number of families, some members already mentioned, which were said to live in Jerusalem (8:28), which was located on the border of Benjamin and Judah.

8:29-40 Genealogy of Saul

A nearly identical genealogy appears in 1 Chronicles 9:35-44. Saul provides the transition from the period of the judges to the monarchy, described in the books of Judges and 1 Samuel but presented in Chronicles only through genealogies. This genealogy carries Saul's family through approximately ten generations after his death (1 Chr 10), into the eighth century b.c. So Saul's line remains important even after being displaced by David's family. Three names in this list refer to the Canaanite god Baal: Baal (8:30), Eshbaal (8:33), and Meribbaal (8:34). Elsewhere the "baal" in these names is modified, eradicating any reference to Baal, but the Chronicler seems not to be worried about the dangers of such worship in his own day.

Maacah; [30]also his firstborn son, Abdon, and Zur, Kish, Baal, Ner, Nadab, [31]Gedor, Ahio, Zecher, and Mikloth. [32]Mikloth became the father of Shimeah. These, too, dwelt with their relatives in Jerusalem, opposite their fellow tribesmen. [33]Ner became the father of Kish, and Kish became the father of Saul. Saul became the father of Jonathan, Malchishua, Abinadab, and Eshbaal. [34]The son of Jonathan was Meribbaal, and Meribbaal became the father of Micah. [35]The sons of Micah were Pithon, Melech, Tarea, and Ahaz. [36]Ahaz became the father of Jehoaddah, and Jehoaddah became the father of Alemeth, Azmaveth, and Zimri. Zimri became the father of Moza. [37]Moza became the father of Binea, whose son was Raphah, whose son was Eleasah, whose son was Azel. [38]Azel had six sons, whose names were Azrikam, his firstborn, Ishmael, Sheariah, Azariah, Obadiah, and Hanan; all these were the sons of Azel. [39]The sons of Eshek, his brother, were Ulam, his firstborn, Jeush, the second son, and Eliphelet, the third. [40]The sons of Ulam were warriors, skilled with the bow, and they had many sons and grandsons: one hundred and fifty. All these were the sons of Benjamin.

9 [1]Thus all Israel was listed in family lists, and these are recorded in the book of the kings of Israel.

Now Judah had been exiled to Babylon because of its treachery. [2]The first to settle again in their cities and dwell there were certain Israelites, the priests, the Levites, and the temple servants.

Jerusalemites. [3]In Jerusalem lived Judahites and Benjaminites; also Ephraimites and Manassites. [4]Among the Judahites was Uthai, son of Ammihud, son of Omri, son of Imri, son of Bani, one of the sons of Perez, son of Judah. [5]Among the Shelanites were Asaiah, the firstborn, and his sons. [6]Among the Zerahites were Jeuel and six hundred and ninety of their relatives. [7]Among the Benjaminites were Sallu, son of Meshullam, son of Hodaviah, son of Hassenuah, [8]as well as Ibneiah, son of Jeroham; Elah, son of Uzzi, son of Michri; Meshullam, son of Shephatiah, son of Reuel, son of Ibnijah. [9]Their kindred of various families were nine hundred and fifty-six. All those named were heads of their ancestral houses.

[10]Among the priests were Jedaiah; Jehoiarib; Jachin; [11]Azariah, son of Hilkiah, son of Meshullam, son of Zadok, son of Meraioth, son of Ahitub, the ruler of the house of God; [12]Adaiah, son of Jeroham, son of Pashhur, son of Malchijah; Maasai, son of Adiel, son of Jahzerah, son of Meshullam, son of Meshillemith, son of Immer. [13]Their

9:1-44 Inhabitants of Jerusalem

This chapter begins by summarizing the descendants of Israel of chapters 2–8 (9:1-2). Then the Chronicler lists the ancestral houses of Jerusalem (9:3-34), repeating the genealogy of Saul (9:35-44; cf. 8:29-40). The section, 9:3-34, divides itself according to postexilic views of how Israel was constituted: Israel (laity, non-clerics) in verses 3-9 (naming four tribes: Judah, Benjamin, Ephraim, Manasseh); and the clergy—i.e., the priests (9:10-13)

brothers, heads of their ancestral houses, were one thousand seven hundred and sixty, valiant in the work of the service of the house of God.

[14]Among the Levites were Shemaiah, son of Hasshub, son of Azrikam, son of Hashabiah, one of the sons of Merari; [15]Bakbakkar; Heresh; Galal; Mattaniah, son of Mica, son of Zichri, a descendant of Asaph; [16]Obadiah, son of Shemaiah, son of Galal, a descendant of Jeduthun; and Berechiah, son of Asa, son of Elkanah, whose family lived in the villages of the Netophathites.

[17]The gatekeepers were Shallum, Akkub, Talmon, Ahiman, and their brothers; Shallum was the chief. [18]Previously they had stood guard at the king's gate on the east side; now they became gatekeepers for the encampments of the Levites. [19]Shallum, son of Kore, son of Ebiasaph, a descendant of Korah, and his brothers of the same ancestral house of the Korahites had as their assigned task the guarding of the threshold of the tent, just as their fathers had guarded the entrance to the encampment of the LORD. [20]Phinehas, son of Eleazar, had been their chief in times past; the LORD was with him. [21]Zechariah, son of Meshelemiah, guarded the gate of the tent of meeting. [22]In all, those who were chosen for gatekeepers at the threshold were two hundred and twelve. They were inscribed in the family records of their villages. David and Samuel the seer had established them in their position of trust. [23]Thus they and their sons kept guard over the gates of the house of the LORD, the house which was then a tent. [24]The gatekeepers were stationed at the four sides, to the east, the west, the north, and the south. [25]Their brothers who lived in their own villages took turns in assisting them for seven-day periods, [26]while the four chief gatekeepers were on permanent duty. These were the Levites who also had charge of the chambers and treasures of the house of God. [27]They would spend the night near the house of God, for it was in their charge and they had the duty of opening it each morning.

[28]Some of them had charge of the vessels used there, tallying them as they were brought in and taken out. [29]Others were appointed to take care of the utensils and all the sacred vessels, as well as the fine flour, the wine, the oil, the frankincense, and the spices. [30]It was the sons of priests, however, who mixed the spiced ointments. [31]Mattithiah, one of the Levites, the firstborn of Shallum the Korahite, was entrusted with preparing the cakes. [32]Benaiah the Kohathite, one of their brothers, was in charge of setting out the showbread each sabbath.

and the Levites (9:14-34). An unusual section lists the gatekeepers and describes their functions (9:17-32), and there is similar attention to gatekeepers in 1 Chronicles 26:1-19. Singers are mentioned in verse 33. Verse 34 concludes the entire list of Levites, reiterating their habitation in Jerusalem. This chapter shows the social dimensions of Judah's population and concludes with the first ruling family, that of Saul (9:35-44).

³³These were the singers and the gate-keepers, family heads over the Levites. They stayed in the chambers when free of duty, for day and night they had to be ready for service. ³⁴These were the levitical family heads by their generations, chiefs who dwelt in Jerusalem.

II. The History of David

Genealogy of Saul. ³⁵Jeiel, the founder of Gibeon, dwelt in Gibeon; his wife's name was Maacah. ³⁶His firstborn son was Abdon; then came Zur, Kish, Baal, Ner, Nadab, ³⁷Gedor, Ahio, Zechariah, and Mikloth. ³⁸Mikloth became the father of Shimeam. These, too, with their relatives, dwelt opposite their relatives in Jerusalem. ³⁹Ner became the father of Kish, and Kish became the father of Saul. Saul became the father of Jonathan, Malchishua, Abinadab, and Eshbaal. ⁴⁰The son of Jonathan was Meribbaal, and Meribbaal became the father of Micah. ⁴¹The sons of Micah were Pithon, Melech, Tahrea, and Ahaz. ⁴²Ahaz became the father of Jehoaddah, and Jehoaddah became the father of Alemeth, Azmaveth, and Zimri. Zimri became the father of Moza. ⁴³Moza became the father of Binea, whose son was Rephaiah, whose son was Eleasah, whose son was Azel. ⁴⁴Azel had six sons, whose names were Azrikam, his firstborn, Ishmael, Sheariah, Azariah, Obadiah, and Hanan; these were the sons of Azel.

10 Death of Saul and His Sons. ¹Now the Philistines went to war against Israel, and Israel fled before them, and they fell, slain on Mount Gilboa. ²The Philistines pressed hard after Saul and his sons. When the Philistines had struck down Jonathan, Abinadab, and Malchishua, sons of Saul, ³the fury of the battle converged on Saul. Then the archers hit him, and he was severely wounded.

⁴Saul said to his armor-bearer, "Draw your sword and run me through; otherwise these uncircumcised will come and abuse me." But the armor-bearer, badly frightened, refused, so Saul took his own

THE REIGN OF DAVID BEGINS

1 Chronicles 10–14

10:1-14 [cf. 1 Sam 31:1-13] The death of Saul and his sons

Up to this point, the Chronicler has recounted history through detailed genealogies, so this chapter begins the narrative part of the book. Saul's genealogies are in 1 Chronicles 8:29-40 and 9:35-44. This chapter of Chronicles begins abruptly with the death of Saul, who is killed in a battle with the Philistines. The narrator does not call him a king in this narrative, even though he notes that God had "turned his kingdom over to David" (10:14). The Chronicler emphasizes the death of Saul's household because his theological perspective is that David's reign came immediately and completely (10:12). The Chronicler omits some details from the book of Samuel, e.g., the all-night walk of the Jabeshites and the description of hanging corpses

sword and fell upon it. ⁵When the armor-bearer saw that Saul was dead, he too fell upon his sword and died. ⁶Thus Saul, and his three sons, his whole house, died together. ⁷When all the Israelites in the valley saw that Saul and his sons had fled and that they had died, they abandoned their cities and fled. Then the Philistines came and lived in those cities.

⁸On the following day, when the Philistines came to strip the slain, they found Saul and his sons fallen on Mount Gilboa. ⁹They stripped him, and took his head and his armor; these they sent throughout the land of the Philistines to bring the good news to their idols and to the people. ¹⁰They put his armor in the temple of their gods, but his skull they impaled at the temple of Dagon.

Burial of Saul. ¹¹When all the inhabitants of Jabesh-gilead heard all that the Philistines had done to Saul, ¹²all their warriors set out, recovered the corpses of Saul and his sons, and brought them to Jabesh. They buried their bones under the oak of Jabesh, and fasted for seven days.

¹³Thus Saul died because of his treason against the LORD in disobeying his word, and also because he had sought counsel from a ghost, ¹⁴rather than from the LORD. Therefore the LORD took his life, and turned his kingdom over to David, the son of Jesse.

11 David Is Made King. ¹Then all Israel gathered around David in Hebron, and they said: "Look! We are your bone and your flesh. ²In days past, when Saul was still the king, it was you

on the city walls of Beth-shan. Verses 13-14 are additions by the Chronicler which place the kingdom squarely in David's hands. They show that the Chronicler knows stories about Saul which he opts not to narrate, like Saul's consultation with the witch at Endor (1 Sam 28). He mentions Saul's unfaithfulness which leads to his death and the transfer of his kingship to David, all the results of Saul's sin. Neither the book of Samuel nor Chronicles comments on Saul's taking his own life. Saul's sin consisted in consulting a medium rather than consulting God. The kingdom is at God's disposal, and he turns it over to David.

11:1-3 [cf. 2 Sam 5:1-5] David is made king in Israel

In verse 1 "all Israel" suggests an inclusive view of Israel which the Chronicler offers rather than "the tribes of Israel" in 2 Samuel 5:1. The Chronicler does not distinguish between Judah and the northern tribes of Israel. Verse 2 is the one place in Chronicles where Saul is referred to as king. In verse 3 the phrase "in accordance with the word of the Lord given through Samuel" is an addition by the Chronicler. It might refer to 2 Samuel 7:7-8 (cf. 1 Chr 17:6-7), but it might also hearken back to 1 Samuel 15:28 and 16:1-13. It underlines God's choice of David to be king, an important part of the Chronicler's theology.

who led Israel in all its battles. And now the LORD, your God, has said to you: You shall shepherd my people Israel; you shall be ruler over my people Israel." ³Then all the elders of Israel came to the king at Hebron, and at Hebron David made a covenant with them in the presence of the LORD; and they anointed David king over Israel, in accordance with the word of the LORD given through Samuel.

Jerusalem Captured. ⁴Then David and all Israel went to Jerusalem, that is, Jebus, where the inhabitants of the land were called Jebusites. ⁵The inhabitants of Jebus said to David, "You shall not enter here." David nevertheless captured the fortress of Zion, which is the City of David. ⁶David said, "Whoever strikes the Jebusites first shall be made chief and captain." Joab, the son of Zeruiah, was the first to attack; and so he became chief. ⁷David took up residence in the fortress, which therefore was called the City of David. ⁸He built up the city on all sides,

from the Millo all the way around, while Joab restored the rest of the city. ⁹David became ever more powerful, for the LORD of hosts was with him.

David's Warriors. ¹⁰These were David's chief warriors who, together with all Israel, supported him in his reign in order to make him king, according to the LORD's word concerning Israel.

¹¹Here is the list of David's warriors:

Ishbaal, the son of Hachamoni, chief of the Three. He brandished his spear over three hundred, whom he had slain in a single encounter.

¹²Next to him was Eleazar, the son of Dodo the Ahohite, one of the Three warriors. ¹³He was with David at Pasdammim, where the Philistines had massed for battle. There was a plot of land full of barley. The people were fleeing before the Philistines, ¹⁴but he took his stand in the middle of the plot, kept it safe, and cut down the Philistines. Thus the LORD brought about a great victory.

11:4-9 [cf. 2 Sam 5:6-10] David captures Zion

As in Samuel, David's capture of this Canaanite city as capital of his kingdom is an important part of David's military strategy. The Chronicler narrates David's capture of Zion more briefly and less dramatically than Samuel. For the Chronicler, the event has a much more theological tone, showing God's final plan for David and Jerusalem. In verse 4, David "and all Israel" (instead of "the king and his men" of Samuel) furthers the Chronicler's notion of inclusivity, especially regarding the northern tribes. The Chronicler omits the difficult saying about the blind and the lame (2 Sam 5:6, 8). Verse 6 has a play on words: the one who "first" strikes down Jebusites will be chief (i.e., "first"), so Joab becomes the chief ("first"), even though he is not included in the lists of David's supporters (1 Chr 11:10–12:40).

11:10-47 [cf. 2 Sam 23:8-39] David's mighty men

As David's story begins, the Chronicler includes lists of the mighty men who gave him solid support from the very start. Moreover, the Chronicler

¹⁵Three of the Thirty chiefs went down to the rock, to David, who was in the cave of Adullam while the Philistines were encamped in the valley of Rephaim. ¹⁶David was then in the stronghold, and a Philistine garrison was at Bethlehem. ¹⁷David had a strong craving, and said, "If only someone would give me a drink of water from the cistern by the gate of Bethlehem!" ¹⁸Thereupon the Three broke through the encampment of the Philistines, drew water from the cistern by the gate of Bethlehem, and carried it back to David. But David refused to drink it. Instead, he poured it out to the LORD, ¹⁹saying, "God forbid that I should do such a thing! Could I drink the blood of these men who risked their lives? For at the risk of their lives they brought it." So he refused to drink it. Such deeds as these the Three warriors performed.

²⁰Abishai, the brother of Joab, was the chief of the Thirty; he brandished his spear over three hundred, whom he had slain. He made a name beside the Three, ²¹but was twice as famous as any of the Thirty, becoming their leader. However, he did not attain to the Three.

²²Benaiah, son of Jehoiada, a valiant man of mighty deeds, from Kabzeel, killed the two sons of Ariel of Moab. Also, he went down and killed the lion in the cistern on a snowy day. ²³He likewise slew the Egyptian, a huge man five cubits tall. The Egyptian carried a spear that was like a weaver's beam, but Benaiah came against him with a staff; he wrested the spear from the Egyptian's hand, and killed him with that spear. ²⁴Such deeds as these Benaiah, the son of Jehoiada, performed, and he made a name beside the Three warriors, ²⁵but was more famous than any of the Thirty. However, he did not attain to the Three. David put him in charge of his bodyguard.

---

omits all the stories of David's rise to power in 1 Samuel. Therefore, a different portrait of David emerges: a divinely chosen leader with resounding support from various groups in Israel, both north and south.

Verse 10 shows the Chronicler's theology: David was made king according to the word of the Lord concerning Israel. Here and at 12:23, the Chronicler asserts that David's kingship was God's doing, and not David's own accomplishment. Verses 11-47 are drawn mostly from 2 Samuel 23:8-39, except for the last six verses. In 2 Samuel this list of mighty men comes after all the David stories, almost like an appendix. Here the list resembles a list of characters in the great capture of Zion that was just narrated. The "Three" and the "Thirty" are groups of David's elite warriors and officers. One story lies within these lists of warriors: the Three who brought water from the cistern at Bethlehem (11:15-19) demonstrate their great loyalty to David, while he shows his own humility in face of their courage. Verses 41b-47 are drawn from sources other than Samuel. These names, including Uriah the Hittite, refer to locations east of the Jordan River.

²⁶Also these warriors: Asahel, the brother of Joab; Elhanan, son of Dodo, from Bethlehem; ²⁷Shammoth, from En-harod; Helez, from Beth-pelet; ²⁸Ira, son of Ikkesh, from Tekoa; Abiezer, from Anathoth; ²⁹Sibbecai, from Husha; Ilai, from Ahoh; ³⁰Maharai, from Netophah; Heled, son of Baanah, from Netophah; ³¹Ithai, son of Ribai, from Gibeah of Benjamin; Benaiah, from Pirathon; ³²Hurai, from Nahale-gaash; Abiel, from Beth-arabah; ³³Azmaveth, from Bahurim; Eliahba, from Shaalbon; ³⁴Jashen the Gunite; Jonathan, son of Shagee the Hararite; ³⁵Ahiam, son of Sachar the Hararite; Elipheleth, son of ³⁶Ahasbai, from Beth-maacah; Ahijah, from Gilo; ³⁷Hezro, from Carmel; Naarai, the son of Ezbai; ³⁸Joel, brother of Nathan, from Rehob, the Gadite; ³⁹Zelek the Ammonite; Naharai, from Beeroth, the armor-bearer of Joab, son of Zeruiah; ⁴⁰Ira, from Jattir; Gareb, from Jattir; ⁴¹Uriah the Hittite; Zabad, son of Ahlai, ⁴²and, in addition to the Thirty, Adina, son of Shiza, the Reubenite, chief of the tribe of Reuben; ⁴³Hanan, son of Maacah; Joshaphat the Mithnite; ⁴⁴Uzzia, the Ashterathite; Shama and Jeiel, sons of Hotham, from Aroer; ⁴⁵Jediael, son of Shimri, and Joha, his brother, the Tizite; ⁴⁶Eliel the Mahavite; Jeribai and Joshaviah, sons of Elnaam; Ithmah, from Moab; ⁴⁷Eliel, Obed, and Jaasiel the Mezobian.

12 **David's Early Followers.** ¹The following men came to David in Ziklag while he was still under banishment from Saul, son of Kish; they, too, were among the warriors who helped him in his battles. ²They were archers who could use either the right or the left hand, both in slinging stones and in shooting arrows with the bow. They were some of Saul's kinsmen, from Benjamin. ³Ahiezer was their chief, along with Joash, both sons of Shemaah of Gibeah; also Jeziel and Pelet, sons of Azmaveth; Beracah; Jehu, from Anathoth; ⁴Ishmaiah the Gibeonite, a warrior among the Thirty, and over the Thirty; ⁵Jeremiah; Jahaziel; Johanan; Jozabad from Gederah; ⁶Eluzai; Jerimoth; Bealiah; Shemariah;

12:1-23 David's helpers at Ziklag

This section, with no parallel in Samuel, is a composition by the Chronicler. It refers to David's time with the Philistines at Ziklag (cf. 1 Sam 27:6), depicts the widespread support for David, and recalls the time before he was acclaimed king. He has the support of Benjaminites, Saul's own tribe (12:2b-8, 17), of the Gadites (12:9-16; not well known in Deuteronomistic History) and Manassites in the north (12:20-21, a story which summarizes some incidents in 1 Sam 28–30). In verse 19, Amasai, chief of the Thirty, speaks with prophetic inspiration of David's beneficial relationship (peace is mentioned three times) with his supporters. This language of closeness points to the unity that exists when David takes the throne. This feeling of intimate relationship will be sundered in the time of Rehoboam, when the kingdom is divided (2 Chr 10:16).

Shephatiah the Haruphite; [7]Elkanah, Isshiah, Azarel, Joezer, and Jashobeam, who were Korahites; [8]Joelah and Zebadiah, sons of Jeroham, from Gedor.

[9]Some of the Gadites also went over to David when he was at the stronghold in the wilderness. They were valiant warriors, experienced soldiers equipped with shield and spear, fearsome as lions, swift as gazelles on the mountains. [10]Ezer was their chief, Obadiah was second, Eliab third, [11]Mishmannah fourth, Jeremiah fifth, [12]Attai sixth, Eliel seventh, [13]Johanan eighth, Elzabad ninth, [14]Jeremiah tenth, and Machbannai eleventh. [15]These Gadites were army commanders, the lesser over hundreds and the greater over thousands. [16]It was they who crossed over the Jordan in the first month, when it was overflowing both its banks, and chased away all who were in the valleys to the east and to the west.

[17]Some Benjaminites and Judahites also came to David at the stronghold. [18]David went out to meet them and addressed them in these words: "If you come peacefully, to help me, I am of a mind to have you join me. But if you have come to betray me to my enemies though my hands have done no wrong, may the God of our ancestors see and punish you."

[19]Then a spirit clothed Amasai, the chief of the Thirty, and he answered David:

"We are yours, O David,
    we are with you, son of Jesse.
Peace, peace to you,
    and peace to him who helps
        you;
    may your God be your helper!"

So David received them and placed them among the leaders of his troops.

[20]Men from Manasseh also deserted to David when he came with the Philistines to battle against Saul. However, he did not help the Philistines, for their lords took counsel and sent him home, saying, "At the cost of our heads he will desert to his master Saul." [21]As he was returning to Ziklag, therefore, these deserted to him from Manasseh: Adnah, Jozabad, Jediael, Michael, Jozabad, Elihu, and Zillethai, chiefs of thousands of Manasseh. [22]They helped David by taking charge of his troops, for they were all warriors and became commanders of his army. [23]And from day to day men kept coming to David's help until there was a vast encampment, like God's own encampment.

The Assembly at Hebron. [24]This is the muster of the detachments of armed troops that came to David at Hebron to bring Saul's kingdom over to him, as the LORD had ordained. [25]Judahites bearing shields and spears: six thousand eight hundred armed troops. [26]Of the Simeonites, warriors fit for battle: seven thousand one hundred. [27]Of the Levites: four

---

12:24-41 David's army at Hebron

Composed by the Chronicler, this section offers a more inclusive listing of Israel's troops which come to David at Hebron, not just the heads or the commanders. It includes soldiers from all the tribes of Israel (including

thousand six hundred, ²⁸along with Jehoiada, leader of the line of Aaron, with another three thousand seven hundred, ²⁹and Zadok, a young warrior, with twenty-two princes of his father's house. ³⁰Of the Benjaminites, the kinsmen of Saul: three thousand—until this time, most of them had kept their allegiance to the house of Saul. ³¹Of the Ephraimites: twenty thousand eight hundred warriors, men renowned in their ancestral houses. ³²Of the half-tribe of Manasseh: eighteen thousand, designated by name to come and make David king. ³³Of the Issacharites, their chiefs who were endowed with an understanding of the times and who knew what Israel had to do: two hundred chiefs, together with all their kinsmen under their command. ³⁴From Zebulun, men fit for military service, set in battle array with every kind of weapon for war: fifty thousand men rallying with a single purpose. ³⁵From Naphtali: one thousand captains, and with them, armed with shield and lance, thirty-seven thousand men. ³⁶Of the Danites, set in battle array: twenty-eight thousand six hundred. ³⁷From Asher, fit for military service and set in battle array: forty thousand. ³⁸From the other side of the Jordan, of the Reubenites, Gadites, and the half-tribe of Manasseh, men equipped with every kind of weapon of war: one hundred and twenty thousand.

³⁹All these soldiers, drawn up in battle order, came to Hebron with the resolute intention of making David king over all Israel. The rest of Israel was likewise of one mind to make David king. ⁴⁰They remained with David for three days, eating and drinking, for their relatives had prepared for them. ⁴¹Moreover, their neighbors from as far as Issachar, Zebulun, and Naphtali came bringing food on donkeys, camels, mules, and oxen—provisions in great quantity of meal, pressed figs, raisins, wine, oil, oxen, and sheep. For there was rejoicing in Israel.

divisions of Levi, into Zadokites and Aaronites) and the two sons of Joseph (Ephraim and Manasseh as two separate half-tribes) so that the total could be considered fourteen. Verses 39-41 contain language typical of the Chronicler: David's kingdom as "all Israel" drawn up in battle array with "resolute intention," with all the rest of Israel "of one mind," i.e., in agreement. Verses 40-41 mention three days of festive celebration, with much eating and drinking of various delicacies which were brought by donkeys, camels, mules, and oxen by three northern tribes: Issachar, Zebulun, and Naphtali. No wonder there was rejoicing in Israel! This word "rejoicing" (12:41) also appears in 2 Chronicles 30:23, 26 (Hezekiah's Passover festival) and in other post-exilic worship festivals (Neh 8:12, 17, and 12:43). Rejoicing describes a characteristic mood of festive celebration. Joyful eating and drinking characterize most public worship events in Chronicles.

13 **Transfer of the Ark.** ¹After David had taken counsel with his commanders of thousands and of hundreds, that is, with every leader, ²he said to the whole assembly of Israel: "If it seems good to you, and is so decreed by the LORD our God, let us send to the rest of our kindred from all the districts of Israel, and also the priests and the Levites from their cities with pasture lands, that they may join us; ³and let us bring the ark of our God here among us, for in the days of Saul we did not consult it." ⁴And the whole assembly agreed to do it, for it seemed right in the eyes of all the people.

⁵Then David assembled all Israel, from Shihor of Egypt to Lebo-hamath, to bring the ark of God from Kiriath-jearim. ⁶David and all Israel went up to Baalah, that is, to Kiriath-jearim, of Judah, to bring up from there the ark of God, which was known by the name "LORD enthroned upon the cherubim." ⁷They transported the ark of God on a new cart from the house of Abinadab; Uzzah and Ahio were guiding the cart, ⁸while David and all Israel danced before God with all their might, with singing, and with lyres, harps, tambourines, cymbals, and trumpets.

⁹As they reached the threshing floor of Chidon, Uzzah stretched out his hand to steady the ark, for the oxen were tipping it. ¹⁰Then the LORD became angry with Uzzah and struck him, because he had laid his hand on the ark; he died

13:1-4 David proposes to bring the ark to Jerusalem

David's transfer of the ark to Jerusalem continues for four chapters: 1 Chronicles 13:1–16:43. The Chronicler rearranges the story found in 2 Samuel 5–6. David's concern for the ark of God comes first, before he negotiates with Hiram of Tyre and defeats the Philistines, and before the record of his posterity (in 2 Samuel, these events precede his decision to move the ark). For the Chronicler, David's concern for the ark, for Israel's worship of God, is his primary role as chosen king.

In this section, composed by the Chronicler, David consults his commanders, and then the assembly of Israel, about the ark. They all participate in the decision to lead the ark to Jerusalem, since it had been neglected in the days of Saul. All the people demonstrate the correct attitude toward the ark (modeling a proper attitude toward symbols of the Lord in the Chronicler's own day). Special mention of priests and Levites in verse 2 indicates his religious concerns.

13:5-14 [cf. 2 Sam 6:1-11] David goes to bring the ark

The Chronicler follows the source in 2 Samuel, with a few differences. In verse 5 "from Shihor of Egypt to Lebo-hamath," i.e., from Egypt to Lebanon, denotes the widest boundaries ever claimed by Israel and suggests David's total inclusion of all peoples ever considered part of Israel. Next

35

there in God's presence. ¹¹David was angry because the LORD's anger had broken out against Uzzah. Therefore that place has been called Perez-uzzah even to this day.

¹²David was afraid of God that day, and he said, "How can I bring in the ark of God to me?" ¹³Therefore he did not take the ark with him into the City of David, but deposited it instead at the house of Obed-edom the Gittite. ¹⁴The ark of God remained in the house of Obed-edom with his family for three months, and the LORD blessed Obed-edom's household and all that he possessed.

14 **David in Jerusalem.** ¹Hiram, king of Tyre, sent envoys to David along with cedar wood, and masons and carpenters to build him a house. ²David now knew that the LORD had truly established him as king over Israel, for his kingdom was greatly exalted for the sake of his people Israel. ³David took other wives in Jerusalem and became the father of more sons and daughters. ⁴These are the names of those who were born to him in Jerusalem: Shammua, Shobab, Nathan, Solomon, ⁵Ibhar, Elishua, Elpelet, ⁶Nogah, Nepheg, Japhia, ⁷Elishama, Beeliada, and Eliphelet.

the Chronicler follows the story in 2 Samuel: David and all Israel go to bring the ark, which they transport on a cart drawn by oxen to the house of Abinadab, while singing and dancing in great liturgical procession. When the oxen stumble and Uzzah tries to save the ark from falling, God's anger flares forth because of the command not to touch the ark. In anger, David discontinues the journey, leaving the ark at the house of Obed-edom, which is abundantly blessed by its presence.

14:1-2 [cf. 2 Sam 5:11-12] Hiram's recognition of David

The Chronicler follows the Samuel text closely. Hiram of Tyre's international recognition of David occurs after David demonstrates his concern for the ark. Thus, David's concern for worship brings benefits in the political realm.

14:3-7 [cf. 2 Sam 5:13-16; cf. 1 Chr 3:5-9] David's children born at Jerusalem

The Chronicler follows Samuel, though he does not mention David's concubines (2 Sam 5:13). In a comparable genealogical section (1 Chr 3:5-9), the Chronicler does mention David's concubines, as well as Tamar his daughter, whose narrative in 2 Samuel 13 is not reproduced in Chronicles. Theologically, a large household, as here attributed to David, is a blessing from God. This blessing of progeny also follows the king's initiative concerning the ark and worship of God.

The Philistine Wars. ⁸When the Philistines had heard that David was anointed king over all Israel, they marched out in force looking for him. But when David heard of this, he went out against them. ⁹Meanwhile the Philistines had come and raided the valley of Rephaim. ¹⁰David inquired of God, "Shall I attack the Philistines, and will you deliver them into my power?" The Lord answered him, "Attack, for I have delivered them into your power." ¹¹So they attacked, at Baal-perazim, and David defeated them there. Then David said, "By my hand God has broken through my enemies just as water breaks through a dam." Therefore that place was called Baal-perazim. ¹²The Philistines abandoned their gods there, and David ordered them to be burnt.

¹³Once again the Philistines raided the valley, ¹⁴and again David inquired of God. But God answered him: Do not try to pursue them, but go around them and come against them near the balsam trees. ¹⁵When you hear the sound of marching in the tops of the balsam trees, then go forth to battle, for God has already gone before you to strike the army of the Philistines. ¹⁶David did as God commanded him, and they routed the Philistine army from Gibeon to Gezer.

¹⁷Thus David's fame was spread abroad through every land, and the Lord put the fear of him on all the nations.

15 Preparations for Moving the Ark. ¹David built houses for himself in the City of David and prepared a place for the ark of God, pitching a tent for it there. ²At that time he said, "No one may carry the ark of God except the Levites, for the Lord chose them to carry the ark

---

14:8-17 [cf. 2 Sam 5:17-25] David defeats the Philistines

The Chronicler follows 2 Samuel, adding the comment that David's fame spread to all the nations (14:17). This victory again follows David's concern for the ark, suggesting that his military strength depended on his concern for worship.

LITURGY FOR INSTALLING THE ARK

I Chronicles 15–16

These chapters constitute a very important text for the Chronicler, who transforms a brief notice in 2 Samuel 6:12-19a (about David's transfer of the ark to Jerusalem) into a major liturgical festival of transfer and dedication of the ark. It also includes a lengthy psalm of thanksgiving, which portrays the spiritual climate of the celebration.

15:1–16:6 [cf. 2 Sam 6:12-19a] David brings the ark to Jerusalem

In 15:1-24 David prepares for the transfer of the ark, i.e., the arrangement of a grand liturgical action. The Levites should carry the ark in procession

of the LORD and to minister to him forever." ³Then David assembled all Israel to Jerusalem to bring up the ark of the LORD to its place, which he had prepared for it. ⁴David also convened the sons of Aaron and the Levites: ⁵of the sons of Kohath, Uriel, their chief, and one hundred and twenty of his brothers; ⁶of the sons of Merari, Asaiah, their chief, and two hundred and twenty of his brothers; ⁷of the sons of Gershon, Joel, their chief, and one hundred and thirty of his brothers; ⁸of the sons of Elizaphan, Shemaiah, their chief, and two hundred of his brothers; ⁹of the sons of Hebron, Eliel, their chief, and eighty of his brothers; ¹⁰of the sons of Uzziel, Amminadab,

their chief, and one hundred and twelve of his brothers.

¹¹David summoned the priests Zadok and Abiathar, and the Levites Uriel, Asaiah, Joel, Shemaiah, Eliel, and Amminadab, ¹²and said to them: "You heads of the levitical houses, sanctify yourselves along with your brothers to bring up the ark of the LORD, the God of Israel, to the place which I have prepared for it. ¹³Because you were not with us the first time, the LORD our God broke out against us, for we did not seek him aright." ¹⁴Accordingly, the priests and the Levites sanctified themselves to bring up the ark of the LORD, the God of Israel. ¹⁵The Levites carried the ark of

and they must prepare (i.e., "sanctify") themselves for the ceremony. The Levites Obed-edom and Jeiel should be the doorkeepers at the sanctuary after this liturgy. This liturgy seems an example of the kind of worship the Chronicler recommends for people of his day. This unit is an original composition of the Chronicler and it highlights his interest in worship, its texts, its music and song, and its officials.

Levites have prominent roles at the temple and in worship. They carry the ark (15:2). In fact, the first attempt to bring the ark to Jerusalem (13:9-11) had failed because Levites did not carry it (15:13). They carry the ark on their shoulders, as Moses had commanded (15:14-15). They are responsible for song and music—a song of joy. So they appoint their kindred to play musical instruments (e.g., cymbals, harps, lyres) and to sing (15:16-22). Finally, some Levites serve as doorkeepers for the ark (15:23, 24). Priests are appointed to blow trumpets before the ark (15:24). Processions with the ark, music, and song are important parts of this type of worship.

First Chronicles 15:25–16:6 is the second part of this narrative. The Chronicler rewrites 2 Samuel 6:12-19, following the sources fairly closely, but with the following changes. First, when David goes to the house of Obed-edom to bring the ark, he is accompanied by the elders of Israel and the officers of the thousands (15:25). Then, in the next verse, the Chronicler says "God helped the Levites to carry the ark of the covenant" (15:26). The Levites enjoy divine favor in Chronicles.

Top: A corner of the Old City Wall of Jerusalem. Here King David brought the ark of God (1 Chr 15). Bottom: The ark of the covenant is brought to Jerusalem, carried by the Levites (1 Chr 15–16).

God on their shoulders with poles, as Moses had commanded according to the word of the LORD.

[16]David commanded the commanders of the Levites to appoint their brothers as singers and to play on musical instruments, harps, lyres, and cymbals, to make a loud sound of rejoicing. [17]Therefore the Levites appointed Heman, son of Joel, and, among his brothers, Asaph, son of Berechiah; and among the sons of Merari, their brothers, Ethan, son of Kushaiah; [18]and, together with these, their brothers of the second rank: the gatekeepers Zechariah, Uzziel, Shemiramoth, Jehiel, Unni, Eliab, Benaiah, Maaseiah, Mattithiah, Eliphelehu, Mikneiah, Obed-edom, and Jeiel. [19]The singers, Heman, Asaph, and Ethan, sounded brass cymbals. [20]Zechariah, Uzziel, Shemiramoth, Jehiel, Unni, Eliab, Maaseiah, and Benaiah played on harps set to "Alamoth." [21]But Mattithiah, Eliphelehu, Mikneiah, Obed-edom, and Jeiel led the song on lyres set to "sheminith." [22]Chenaniah was the chief of the Levites in the singing; he directed the singing, for he was skillful. [23]Berechiah and Elkanah were gatekeepers before the ark. [24]The priests, Shebaniah, Joshaphat, Nethanel, Amasai, Zechariah, Benaiah, and Eliezer, sounded the trumpets before the ark of God. Obed-edom and Jeiel were also gatekeepers before the ark.

The Ark Comes to Jerusalem. [25]Thus David, the elders of Israel, and the commanders of thousands went to bring up

David's clothing and that of the Levites in 15:27 is also distinctly priestly: fine linen robes, and also the ephod in both Samuel and Chronicles. As in Samuel, Michal (Saul's daughter and David's wife) looks on David's dancing with disgust (15:29). Here her reaction is hard to understand, for she has observed a liturgical procession, not the bawdy, raucous parade of 2 Samuel. She and David's family appear just to be petty. At this point, the Chronicler omits the ugly scene between David and Michal in 2 Samuel 6:20-23.

In 16:1-3 the Chronicler returns to issues of worship. After this procession reaches the tent, the ritual continues as they make burnt offerings and thanksgiving offerings, and David blesses the people and distributes food delicacies to all. As usual in Chronicles, this type of ceremony is conducted with rejoicing. Then, in 16:4-6, the Chronicler further describes duties of Levites. They serve before the ark, appointed to "celebrate, thank, and praise the Lord" (we prefer "invoke" rather than "celebrate" of the NAB). The Chronicler may indicate three types of psalm-prayers found in the book of Psalms: lament-petitions to God, thanksgiving psalms, and hymns of praise. Asaph the Levite and his family receive important musical tasks (interestingly, there are twelve psalms attributed to Asaph: Psalms 50 and 73–83). Two priests are appointed to make music on trumpets.

the ark of the covenant of the LORD with joy from the house of Obed-edom. ²⁶While God helped the Levites to carry the ark of the covenant of the LORD, they sacrificed seven bulls and seven rams. ²⁷David was vested in a robe of fine linen, as were all the Levites who carried the ark, the singers, and Chenaniah, the leader of song; David was also wearing a linen ephod. ²⁸Thus all Israel brought up the ark of the covenant of the LORD with joyful shouting, to the sound of horns, trumpets, and cymbals, and the music of harps and lyres. ²⁹But as the ark of the covenant of the LORD was entering the City of David, Michal, daughter of Saul, looked down from her window, and when she saw King David leaping and dancing, she despised him in her heart.

16 ¹They brought in the ark of God and set it within the tent which David had pitched for it. Then they sacrificed burnt offerings and communion offerings to God. ²When David had finished sacrificing the burnt offerings and communion offerings, he blessed the people in the name of the LORD, ³and distributed to every Israelite, to every man and every woman, a loaf of bread, a piece of meat, and a raisin cake.

David's Directives for the Levites. ⁴He then appointed certain Levites to minister before the ark of the LORD, to celebrate, thank, and praise the LORD, the God of Israel. ⁵Asaph was their chief, and second to him were Zechariah, Uzziel, Shemiramoth, Jehiel, Mattithiah, Eliab, Benaiah, Obed-edom, and Jeiel. These were to play on harps and lyres, while Asaph was to sound the cymbals, ⁶and the priests Benaiah and Jahaziel were to be the regular trumpeters before the ark of the covenant of God.

⁷On that same day, David appointed Asaph and his brothers to sing for the first time these praises of the LORD:

⁸Give thanks to the LORD, invoke
   his name;
   make known among the peoples
      his deeds.
⁹Sing praise, play music;
   proclaim all his wondrous
      deeds.
¹⁰Glory in his holy name;
   rejoice, O hearts that seek the
      LORD!

16:7-36 [cf. Pss 105:1-15; 96:1-13; 106:1, 47-48] David's psalm of thanksgiving

The Chronicler adds this long psalm adapted for the occasion by Asaph and his brothers. It includes verses from several canonical psalms. Psalm 105 praises and thanks God for good deeds done for Israel, especially the covenant. Psalm 96 is a hymn of praise, which claims that the Lord is king and calls the people to worship. Psalm 106 is a thanksgiving psalm, but the Chronicler incorporates only its beginning and ending verses (1 Chr 16:34-36; cf. Ps 106:1, 47-48). Verse 34 repeats a favorite refrain of postexilic Judah: "Give thanks to the Lord, who is good, whose love endures forever." Verse 35 changes tone, petitioning God their savior to gather and deliver them

¹¹Rely on the mighty L, ord;
  constantly seek his face.
¹²Recall the wondrous deeds he has
    done,
  his signs, and his words of judg-
    ment,
¹³You sons of Israel, his servants,
  offspring of Jacob, the chosen
    ones!
¹⁴The Lord is our God;
  who rules the whole earth.
¹⁵He remembers forever his cove-
    nant
  the pact imposed for a thousand
    generations—
¹⁶Which was made with Abraham,
  confirmed by oath to Isaac,
¹⁷And ratified as binding for Jacob,
  an everlasting covenant for Is-
    rael:
¹⁸"To you will I give the land of Ca-
    naan,
  your own allotted heritage."
¹⁹When they were few in number,
  a handful, and strangers there,
²⁰Wandering from nation to nation,
  from one kingdom to another,
²¹He let no one oppress them;
  for their sake he rebuked kings:
²²"Do not touch my anointed,
  to my prophets do no harm."
²³Sing to the Lord, all the earth,
  announce his salvation, day
    after day.
²⁴Tell his glory among the nations;
  among all peoples, his won-
    drous deeds.
²⁵For great is the Lord and highly
  to be praised;

to be feared above all gods.
²⁶For the gods of the nations all do
    nothing,
  but the Lord made the heavens.
²⁷Splendor and majesty go before
    him;
  power and rejoicing are in his
    holy place.
²⁸Give to the Lord, you families of
    nations,
  give to the Lord glory and
    might;
²⁹Give to the Lord the glory due his
    name!
Bring gifts, and come before him;
  bow down to the Lord, splen-
    did in holiness.
³⁰Tremble before him, all the earth;
  the world will surely stand fast,
    never to be moved.
³¹Let the heavens be glad and the
    earth rejoice;
  let them say among the nations:
    The Lord is king.
³²Let the sea and what fills it re-
    sound;
  let the plains be joyful and all
    that is in them!
³³Then let all the trees of the forest
    exult
  before the Lord, who comes,
  who comes to rule the earth.
³⁴Give thanks to the Lord, who is
    good,
  whose love endures forever;
³⁵And say, "Save us, O God, our
    savior,
  gather us and deliver us from
    among the nations,

from the nations. The Chronicler might be reflecting postexilic Judah's desire to be freed of Persian interference and domination. The Chronicler implies that two different kinds of song go together at this point, praise and invocation of God.

That we may give thanks to your
holy name
and glory in praising you."
[36]Blessed be the LORD, the God of
Israel,
from everlasting to everlasting!
Let all the people say, Amen! Halle-
lujah.

[37]Then David left Asaph and his brothers there before the ark of the covenant of the LORD to minister before the ark regularly according to the daily ritual; [38]he also left there Obed-edom and sixty-eight of his brothers, including Obed-edom, son of Jeduthun, and Hosah, to be gatekeepers.

[39]But the priest Zadok and his priestly brothers he left before the tabernacle of the LORD on the high place at Gibeon, [40]to make burnt offerings to the LORD on the altar for burnt offerings regularly, morning and evening, and to do all that is written in the law of the LORD which he commanded Israel. [41]With them were Heman and Jeduthun and the others who were chosen and designated by name to give thanks to the LORD, "whose love endures forever," [42]with trumpets and cymbals for accompaniment, and instruments for sacred song. The sons of Jeduthun kept the gate.

[43]Then all the people departed, each to their own homes, and David returned to bless his household.

17 **The Oracle of Nathan.** [1]After David had taken up residence in his house, he said to Nathan the prophet,

---

16:37-42 Priests and Levites lead worship at Gibeon and Jerusalem

The Chronicler concludes the ceremony by assigning different tasks to priests and Levites at two different sites: Gibeon and Jerusalem. The altar of burnt offering remains at Gibeon, where Zadok and the other priests continue regular sacrificial offerings, and some Levites (Heman and Jeduthun) lead the music and song (16:39-42). At Jerusalem, where the ark is installed in the tent, Asaphite Levites lead the worship (without sacrifices). This sung worship seems to be an innovation of the Chronicler and probably mirrors worship patterns of his day. For the Chronicler, the time of Solomon saw both kinds of worship merge in the first temple, an example for his later era.

GOD'S COVENANT WITH DAVID AND HIS RESULTING SUCCESS

I Chronicles 17–21

17:1-15 [cf. 2 Sam 7:1-16] God's covenant with David

David's concern for worship results in God's promise to establish his house, i.e., Solomon his son, and a lasting temple to be built by him. David's

"See, I am living in a house of cedar, but the ark of the covenant of the LORD is under tentcloth." ²Nathan replied to David, "Whatever is in your heart, go and do, for God is with you."

³But that same night the word of God came to Nathan: ⁴Go and tell David my servant, Thus says the LORD: It is not you who are to build the house for me to dwell in. ⁵For I have never dwelt in a house, from the day I brought Israel up, even to this day, but I have been lodging in tent or tabernacle. ⁶As long as I have wandered about with all Israel, did I ever say a word to any of the judges of Israel whom I commanded to shepherd my people, Why have you not built me a house of cedar? ⁷Now then, speak thus to my servant David, Thus says the LORD of hosts: I took you from the pasture, from following the flock, to become ruler over my people Israel. ⁸I was with you wherever you went, and I cut down all your enemies before you. I will make your name like that of the greatest on the earth. ⁹I will assign a place for my people Israel and I will plant them in it to dwell there; they will never again be disturbed, nor shall the wicked ever again oppress them, as they did at the beginning, ¹⁰and during all the time when I appointed judges over my people Israel. And I will subdue all your enemies. Moreover, I declare to you that the LORD will build you a house: ¹¹when your days have been completed and you must join your ancestors, I will raise up your offspring after you who will be one of your own sons, and I will establish his kingdom. ¹²He it is who shall build me a house, and I will establish his throne forever. ¹³I ▶ will be a father to him, and he shall be a

---

petition (16:35) has a response from God: the "favor" promised to David (17:13). This pattern of petition and response suggests that those who call upon God will find salvation.

The Chronicler's source is 2 Samuel 7, God's promise through Nathan the prophet to establish a lasting dynasty. The Chronicler states some conditions for the behavior of his successors and also changes the story in subtle ways. He omits the warning against sin by David's son (2 Sam 7:14b). Rather he focuses on the promise to confirm Solomon, who will build the temple. The Chronicler shifts the focus from David's dynasty to Solomon's temple. This alteration corresponds with the Chronicler's views on the importance of worship. David's proposal to build a house is transformed into a divine promise: a temple (i.e., house) built by his son, Solomon. Another subtle change of the Chronicler concerns "rest." David as a "man of rest" (2 Sam 7:1, 11) is omitted by the Chronicler in

---

▶ This symbol indicates a cross reference number in the *Catechism of the Catholic Church*. See page 147 for number citations.

son to me, and I will not withdraw my favor from him as I withdrew it from the one who was before you; [14]but I will maintain him in my house and in my kingdom forever, and his throne shall be firmly established forever.

[15]In accordance with all these words and this whole vision Nathan spoke to David.

David's Thanksgiving. [16]Then King David came in and sat in the LORD's presence, and said: "Who am I, LORD God, and what is my house, that you should have brought me so far? [17]And yet, even this is too little in your sight, O God! For you have made a promise regarding your servant's house reaching into the future, and you have looked on me as henceforth the most notable of men, LORD God. [18]What more can David say to you? You have known your servant. [19]LORD, for your servant's sake and in keeping with your purpose, you have done this great thing. [20]LORD, there is no one like you, no God but you, just as we have always heard.

[21]"Is there, like your people Israel, whom you redeemed from Egypt,

favor of Solomon who will be the "man of rest" (1 Chr 22:9). "Rest" in Chronicles seems to be a quality Israel experiences in association with the temple (2 Chr 6:41). Perhaps the Chronicler adjusts the promise to reflect the reality of his day, i.e., a temple without a king. Thus, his community can find a new person of "rest" and a place of "rest" in the temple of their day.

17:16-27 [cf. 2 Sam 7:18-29] David's prayer

David utters a prayer of praise and thanksgiving to God for his "house" (i.e., family, dynasty), for Israel, and for God's promise of a temple. It begins with David's humble question, "Who am I" that I should be here? (17:16), which is also a confession of God's graciousness to him. One of the Chronicler's changes stands out: David claims that God has already blessed his household (17:27), whereas in Samuel God's blessing would be a future event (2 Sam 7:29). The Chronicler's David appears more secure and confident because God has already fulfilled his promises. The fate of David (recipient of God's gracious promise) intertwines with Israel's well-being, and the themes and the mood of David's prayer inspire his descendants, especially those of the Chronicler's era.

God's graciousness and David's receptivity work their way out in the next several chapters (1 Chr 18:1–20:8), where David enjoys overwhelming military success against various foes in surrounding countries: Edom, Moab, Ammon, and Philistia. We readers may wonder whether his victories in battle result from his desire to build God a house to dwell in (ch. 17) or

another nation on earth whom a god went to redeem as his people? You won for yourself a name for great and awesome deeds by driving out the nations before your people. [22]You made your people Israel your own forever, and you, LORD, became their God. [23]Now, LORD, may the promise that you have spoken concerning your servant and his house remain firm forever. Bring about what you have promised, [24]that your name, LORD of hosts, God of Israel, may be great and abide forever, while the house of your servant is established in your presence.

[25]"Because you, my God, have revealed to your servant that you will build him a house, your servant dares to pray before you. [26]Since you, LORD, are truly God and have made this generous promise to your servant, [27]do, then, bless the house of your servant, that it may be in your presence forever—since it is you, LORD, who blessed it, it is blessed forever."

18 David's Victories. [1]After this, David defeated the Philistines and subdued them; and he took Gath and its towns away from the Philistines. [2]He also defeated Moab, and the Moabites became David's subjects, paying tribute.

[3]David then defeated Hadadezer, king of Zobah, toward Hamath, who was on his way to set up his victory stele at the river Euphrates. [4]David captured from him one thousand chariots, seven thousand horsemen, and twenty thousand foot soldiers. David hamstrung all the chariot horses, but left one hundred for his chariots. [5]The Arameans of Damascus came to help Hadadezer, king of Zobah, but David also defeated twenty-two thousand of their men in Aram. [6]Then David set up garrisons in the Damascus region of Aram, and the Arameans became David's subjects, paying tribute. Thus the LORD made David victorious in all his campaigns.

[7]David took the golden shields that were carried by Hadadezer's attendants and brought them to Jerusalem. [8]David likewise took away from Tibhath and Cun, cities of Hadadezer, large quantities of bronze; Solomon later used it to make the bronze sea and the pillars and the vessels of bronze.

[9]When Tou, king of Hamath, heard that David had defeated the entire army

---

from God's pleasure in the great worship ceremony (ch. 15–16). We may view this success as God's promise playing itself out in David's actions. To put it more theologically, David's success in battle demonstrates God's blessings for him.

18:1-13 [cf. 2 Sam 8:1-14; Ps 60:2] David's victories

David defeats Philistines (north and west, especially along the coast), Moabites (east, across the Jordan valley), Hadadezer of Zobah (north and east of Aram), and the Arameans (north and east). These victories demonstrate how God makes David victorious everywhere (18:6b, 13b). The Chronicler

of Hadadezer, king of Zobah, ¹⁰he sent his son Hadoram to wish King David well and to congratulate him on having waged a victorious war against Hadadezer; for Hadadezer had been at war with Tou. He also brought gold, silver and bronze articles of every sort. ¹¹These also King David consecrated to the LORD along with all the silver and gold that he had taken from the nations: from Edom, Moab, the Ammonites, the Philistines, and Amalek.

¹²Abishai, the son of Zeruiah, also defeated eighteen thousand Edomites in the Valley of Salt. ¹³He set up garrisons in Edom, and all the Edomites became David's subjects. Thus the LORD brought David victory in all his undertakings.

David's Officials. ¹⁴David was king over all Israel; he dispensed justice and right to all his people. ¹⁵Joab, son of Zeruiah, was in command of the army; Jehoshaphat, son of Ahilud, was chancellor; ¹⁶Zadok, son of Ahitub, and Ahimelech, son of Abiathar, were priests; Shavsha was scribe; ¹⁷Benaiah, son of Jehoiada, was in command of the Cherethites and the Pelethites; and David's sons were the chief assistants to the king.

19 **Campaigns Against Ammon.** ¹Afterward Nahash, king of the Ammonites, died and his son succeeded him as king. ²David said, "I will show kindness to Hanun, the son of Nahash, for his father showed kindness to me." Therefore he sent envoys to console him over his father. But when David's servants had entered the land of the Ammonites to console Hanun, ³the Ammonite princes said to Hanun, "Do you think David is doing this—sending you these consolers—to honor your father? Have not his servants rather come to you to explore the land, spying it out for its overthrow?" ⁴So Hanun seized David's servants and had them shaved and their garments cut off halfway at the hips. Then he sent them away. ⁵David was told about the men, and he

---

mentions that booty from battle and the bronze taken from battle with Hadadezer are later used by Solomon to construct the bronze sea and other temple vessels. Here in Chronicles David's nephew Abishai, rather than David himself, defeats the Edomites (1 Chr 18:12; cf. 2 Sam 8:13).

18:14-17 [cf. 2 Sam 8:15-18] List of David's officers

The Chronicler's only change is to redefine David's sons as officials rather than priests (2 Sam 8:18). Since they are not of the line of Aaron, the Chronicler presents a more cautious view (18:17).

19:1-19 [cf. 2 Sam 10:1-19] David defeats the Ammonites and Arameans

The Chronicler omits the story of David's graciousness to Meribbaal (2 Sam 9), the crippled son of his friend Jonathan. This story would contra-

sent word for them to be intercepted, for the men had been greatly disgraced. "Remain at Jericho," the king told them, "until your beards have grown again; then come back here."

⁶When the Ammonites realized that they had put themselves in bad odor with David, Hanun and the Ammonites sent a thousand talents of silver to hire chariots and horsemen from Aram Naharaim, from Aram-maacah, and from Zobah. ⁷They hired thirty-two thousand chariots along with the king of Maacah and his army, who came and encamped before Medeba. The Ammonites also assembled from their cities and came out for war.

⁸When David heard of this, he sent Joab and his whole army of warriors against them. ⁹The Ammonites marched out and lined up for battle at the entrance of the city, while the kings who had come to their help remained apart in the open field. ¹⁰When Joab saw that there was a battle line both in front of and behind him, he chose some of the best fighters among the Israelites and lined them up against the Arameans; ¹¹the rest of the army, which he placed under the command of his brother Abishai, then lined up to oppose the Ammonites. ¹²And he said: "If the Arameans prove too strong for me, you must come and save me; and if the Ammonites prove too strong for you, I will save you. ¹³Hold firm and let us show ourselves courageous for the sake of our people and the cities of our God; and may the LORD do what is good in his sight." ¹⁴Joab therefore advanced with his men to engage the Arameans in battle; but they fled before him. ¹⁵And when the Ammonites saw that the Arameans had fled, they too fled before his brother Abishai, and entered their city. Joab then came to Jerusalem.

¹⁶Seeing themselves vanquished by Israel, the Arameans sent messengers to bring out the Arameans from beyond the Euphrates, with Shophach, the commander of Hadadezer's army, at their head. ¹⁷When this was reported to David, he gathered all Israel together, crossed the Jordan, and met them. With the army of David drawn up to fight the Arameans, they gave battle. ¹⁸But the Arameans fled before Israel, and David killed seven thousand of their chariot fighters and forty thousand of their foot soldiers; he also put to death Shophach, the commander of the army. ¹⁹When the vassals of Hadadezer saw themselves vanquished by Israel, they made peace with David and became his subjects. After this, the Arameans refused to come to the aid of the Ammonites.

---

dict the Chronicler's assertion that all of Saul's household died with him at Mount Gilboa (1 Chr 10:6). The Chronicler, unlike Samuel, omits the ongoing power struggle between David and the house of Saul. For the Chronicler, the old order has passed away and a new one begun. In verses 6, 7, and 18, the Chronicler changes some details to magnify David's role, since enemies make peace with David rather than with Israel (2 Sam 10:19).

²⁰ ¹At the turn of the year, the time when kings go to war, Joab led the army out in force, laid waste the land of the Ammonites, and went on to besiege Rabbah; David himself remained in Jerusalem. When Joab had attacked Rabbah and destroyed it, ²David took the crown of Milcom from the idol's head. It was found to weigh a talent of gold, with precious stones on it; this crown David wore on his own head. He also brought out a great amount of spoil from the city. ³He deported the people of the city and set them to work with saws, iron picks, and axes. David dealt thus with all the cities of the Ammonites. Then David and his whole army returned to Jerusalem.

Victories over the Philistines. ⁴Afterward there was another battle with the Philistines, at Gezer. At that time, Sibbecai the Hushathite struck down Sippai, one of the descendants of the Rephaim, and the Philistines were subdued.

20:1-3 [cf. 2 Sam 11:1–12:31] Joab besieges and defeats Rabbah

The Chronicler mentions that Joab besieges and defeats Rabbah (present-day Amman), while David remains behind in Jerusalem. In 2 Samuel 11, David arranges from Jerusalem for the death of Uriah the Hittite, husband of Bathsheba. The stories of David and Bathsheba and Nathan's reproof of David (2 Sam 11–12) are not told in Chronicles.

20:4–21:27 Chronicles Omits the "Court History" of 2 Samuel 11–20

The Chronicler reproduces only eleven verses from ten chapters of 2 Samuel. The stories the Chronicler omitted include many incidents in which David's loyalty and character seem compromised, where he appears weakened by sin that affects him and most of his household negatively. Omitted are: David, Bathsheba, and Uriah; the rape of Tamar (daughter of David) by Amnon; the anger and rebellion of Absalom, son of David; the flight of David from Jerusalem; the death of Absalom; the revolt of Sheba; and the final quelling of the rebellious groups. The Chronicler omits much of the negative portrayal of David ("whitewash"), perhaps to make him appear more religious and saintly. The Chronicler pictures David as the initiator and leader of Israel's worship life at the Jerusalem temple. The Chronicler also includes stories (e.g., battle victories) that demonstrate the blessed outcomes of a life of dedicated worship.

20:4-8 [cf. 2 Sam 21:18-22] Giants slain by David and his men

Like David's victory over the Ammonites (20:1-3), his defeat of Philistines shows how God fulfills his blessings for David. For some reason, the Chronicler omits the beautiful psalm of David's thanksgiving (2 Sam 22:1-51, which is a nearly exact version of Ps 18). Likewise, the Chronicler skips

⁵There was another battle with the Philistines, and Elhanan, the son of Jair, slew Lahmi, the brother of Goliath of Gath, whose spear shaft was like a weaver's beam.

⁶There was another battle, at Gath, and there was a giant, who had six fingers to each hand and six toes to each foot; twenty-four in all. He too was descended from the Rephaim. ⁷He defied Israel, and Jonathan, the son of Shimea, David's brother, slew him. ⁸These were the descendants of the Rephaim of Gath who died at the hands of David and his servants.

21 David's Census; the Plague. ¹A satan rose up against Israel, and he incited David to take a census of Israel. ²David therefore said to Joab and to the other generals of the army, "Go, number the Israelites from Beer-sheba to Dan, and report back to me that I may know their number." ³But Joab replied: "May the LORD increase his people a hundredfold! My lord king, are not all of them my lord's subjects? Why does

David's "last words" in 2 Samuel 23:1-7. Though both poems present magnificent religious and spiritual motifs, they differ from the public liturgical songs of praise and thanksgiving which the Chronicler seems to prefer.

21:1-27 [cf. 2 Sam 24:1-25] David's census of Israel and Judah

This is a pivotal chapter, since the Chronicler presents David's first personal encounter with sin. This story provides an opportunity to select a site for the temple. Theologically, God seems to respond to those who are seeking him, with the temple as symbol of God's readiness to grant mercy. So the Chronicler emphasizes this event, which was merely one of the "miscellaneous" stories in 2 Samuel 21–24.

The Chronicler alters the story significantly. In 2 Samuel 24:1, God's wrath has flared against Israel, so he incites David to sin by ordering the census. The Chronicler says a satan or "an adversary"—and not God—stands against Israel and incites David (21:1). This Satan is like the Satan in Job 1–2, a troublemaker opposed to Job in the heavenly court. The Chronicler thus removes from God any responsibility for tempting David to this sinful action. Next, where 2 Samuel speaks of the threshing floor, the Chronicler changes it to "the place" (21:22, 25), signifying that it would be a site of something special. Some Jewish writings use "the place" as a synonym for the temple, and even refer it to God.

This section comprises four parts. First comes a census, i.e., a military draft (21:1-7); the story implies that all these soldiers belong to David, rather than to God. Second, the prophecy of Gad occurs when David becomes aware of his sin and asks for forgiveness (21:8-13). Through Gad God presents David with three options: famine, enemy attack, or pestilence. David

my lord seek to do this thing? Why should he bring guilt upon Israel?" ⁴However, the king's command prevailed over Joab, who departed and traversed all of Israel, and then returned to Jerusalem. ⁵Joab reported the census figures to David: of men capable of wielding a sword, there were in all Israel one million one hundred thousand, and in Judah four hundred and seventy thousand. ⁶Levi and Benjamin, however, he did not include in the census, for the king's command was repugnant to Joab. ⁷This command was evil in the sight of God, and he struck Israel. ⁸Then David said to God, "I have sinned greatly in doing this thing. Take away your servant's guilt, for I have acted very foolishly."

⁹Then the LORD spoke to Gad, David's seer, in these words: ¹⁰Go, tell David: Thus says the LORD: I am laying out three options; choose one of them, and I will inflict it on you. ¹¹Accordingly, Gad went to David and said to him: "Thus says the LORD: Decide now— ¹²will it be three years of famine; or three months of fleeing your enemies, with the sword of your foes ever at your back; or three days of the LORD's own sword, a plague in the land, with the LORD's destroying angel in every part of Israel? Now consider: What answer am I to give him who sent me?" ¹³Then David said to Gad: "I am in serious trouble. But let me fall into the hand of the LORD, whose mercy is very great, rather than into hands of men."

¹⁴Therefore the LORD sent a plague upon Israel, and seventy thousand Israelites died. ¹⁵God also sent an angel to Jerusalem to destroy it; but as the angel

chooses the third, presuming it comes directly from God (whom he offended) and leaves open possibility of divine compassion (21:13). Third, the plague results in the death of seventy thousand (21:14-17). Afterwards, God sends a divine messenger to destroy Jerusalem, but at the last moment the Lord sees and repents, telling the messenger to stop the slaughter. This messenger is standing at the threshing floor of Ornan the Jebusite (Araunah, in 2 Sam), between earth and heaven with his drawn sword in his hand (21:16). This terrible sight symbolizes only a lull in the killing, for the sword is still drawn. So David and the elders make a gesture of penitence, and David confesses his sin—his alone—and begs mercy for his people, "these sheep" (21:17). Fourth, David purchases the threshing floor and the plague ends (21:18-27). Afterwards, David offers sacrifices (21:23, 27) together with his prayer of petition. When fire descends from heaven on the offerings, it demonstrates God's favor, just as at other key moments in biblical tradition (Lev 9:24, the beginning of Aaron's priesthood; 1 Kgs 18:38, Elijah on Mt. Carmel. Later in 2 Chr 7:1 fire will descend on offerings in Solomon's temple, showing divine acceptance of sacrifices and divine hostility coming to an end).

was on the point of destroying it, the LORD saw and changed his mind about the calamity, and said to the destroying angel, "Enough now! Stay your hand!"

Ornan's Threshing Floor. The angel of the LORD was then standing by the threshing floor of Ornan the Jebusite. [16]When David raised his eyes, he saw the angel of the LORD standing between earth and heaven, drawn sword in hand stretched out against Jerusalem. David and the elders, clothed in sackcloth, fell face down, [17]and David prayed to God: "Was it not I who ordered the census of the people? I am the one who sinned, I did this wicked thing. But these sheep, what have they done? O LORD, my God, strike me and my father's family, but do not afflict your people with this plague!"

[18]Then the angel of the LORD commanded Gad to tell David to go up and set up an altar to the LORD on the threshing floor of Ornan the Jebusite. [19]David went up at the word of Gad, which he spoke in the name of the LORD. [20]Ornan turned around and saw the king; his four sons who were with him hid themselves, but Ornan kept on threshing wheat. [21]But as David came toward Ornan, he looked up and saw that it was David, and left the threshing floor and bowed down before David, his face to the ground. [22]David said to Ornan: "Sell me the site of this threshing floor, that I may build on it an altar to the LORD. Sell it to me at its full price, that the plague may be withdrawn from the people." [23]But Ornan said to David: "Take it as your own, and let my lord the king do what is good in his sight. See, I also give you the oxen for the burnt offerings, the threshing sledges for the wood, and the wheat for the grain offering. I give it all to you." [24]But King David replied to Ornan: "No! I will buy it from you properly, at its full price. I will not take what is yours for the LORD, nor bring burnt offerings that cost me nothing." [25]So David paid Ornan six hundred shekels of gold for the place.

Altar for Burnt Offerings. [26]David then built an altar there to the LORD, and sacrificed burnt offerings and communion offerings. He called upon the LORD, who answered him by sending down fire from heaven upon the altar for burnt offerings. [27]Then the LORD gave orders to the angel to return his sword to its sheath.

[28]Once David saw that the LORD had answered him at the threshing floor of Ornan the Jebusite, he continued to offer

21:28–22:1 The site for the temple

The Chronicler points to this "place" for a continuing encounter with God in the temple, for David sacrifices at the threshing floor of Ornan the Jebusite. The key point is in 22:1: "This is the house of the Lord God, and this is the altar for burnt offerings for Israel." This verse points to the ultimate religious symbol in this place, the temple to be built by Solomon, with its altar of burnt offering. But for the present (and until Solomon), the tabernacle and altar for offerings are still at the high place at Gibeon. Even though David will not build the temple, he prepares the site for construction.

Overview of Jerusalem with the site of the Temple at the high domed structure in the center of the photo.

sacrifices there. ²⁹The tabernacle of the LORD, which Moses had made in the wilderness, and the altar for burnt offerings were at that time on the high place at Gibeon. ³⁰But David could not go into his presence to inquire of God, for he was fearful of the sword of the angel of the LORD.

22 ¹Thus David said, "This is the house of the LORD God, and this is the altar for burnt offerings for Israel." ²David then ordered that the resident aliens in the land of Israel should be brought together, and he appointed them stonecutters to hew out stone blocks for building the house of God.

For the Chronicler, worship of God in the temple was the final goal of David's reign.

PREPARING FOR THE TEMPLE

I Chronicles 22–29

These chapters have no parallel source elsewhere in the Bible, so they highlight the Chronicler's concern with the temple, its construction, and all its personnel. All these events occur during David's reign instead of Solomon's, while some verses in Kings about Solomon constructing the temple are omitted. Thus, the Chronicler's goal seems clear: to show that David really planned the temple and its worship. Chapters 22, 28, and 29 contain narratives about David's actions, while chapters 23–27 contain lists of personnel for the temple. These chapters give detailed lists of priests and Levites (chs. 23–24), musicians (ch. 25), gatekeepers and overseers (ch. 26), and officials of the kingdom (ch. 27). The Chronicler portrays David positively, showing him as a good king, worthy to be remembered by Israel and by God.

22:2–23:1 David's preparations for the temple

In verses 2-4, David gathers stones, iron, bronze, and cedar for temple building because Solomon is still "young and inexperienced" (22:5). Then he addresses Solomon privately, telling him to build the temple (22:6-16). David cannot do so because he has shed so much blood (22:8). It seems that waging war disqualifies David from enacting his religious program. But Solomon is a "peaceful man," so he will bring Israel peace and quiet all his days (22:9). Some of the language in this speech reflects Nathan's message to David in 1 Chronicles 17:1-15. In 1 Chronicles 22:17-19 David instructs Israel's leaders to help Solomon in this task. Next, in 1 Chronicles

³David also laid up large stores of iron to make nails for the doors of the gates, and clamps, together with so much bronze that it could not be weighed, ⁴and cedar trees without number. The Sidonians and Tyrians brought great stores of cedar logs to David. ⁵David said: "My son Solomon is young and inexperienced; but the house that is to be built for the LORD must be made so magnificent that it will be renowned and glorious in all lands. Therefore I will make preparations for it." Thus before his death David laid up materials in abundance.

Charge to Solomon. ⁶Then he summoned his son Solomon and commanded him to build a house for the LORD, the God of Israel. ⁷David said to Solomon: "My son, it was my purpose to build a house myself for the name of the LORD, my God. ⁸But this word of the LORD came to me: You have shed much blood, and you have waged great wars. You may not build a house for my name, because you have shed too much blood upon the earth in my sight. ⁹However, a son will be born to you. He will be a peaceful man, and I will give him rest from all his enemies on every side. For Solomon shall be his name, and in his time I will bestow peace and tranquility on Israel. ¹⁰It is he who shall build a house for my name; he shall be a son to me, and I will be a father to him, and I will establish the throne of his kingship over Israel forever.

¹¹"Now, my son, the LORD be with you, and may you succeed in building the house of the LORD your God, as he has said you shall. ¹²But may the LORD give you prudence and discernment when he gives you command over Israel, so that you keep the law of the LORD, your God. ¹³Only then shall you succeed, if you are careful to observe the statutes and ordinances which the LORD commanded Moses for Israel. Be strong and steadfast; do not fear or be dismayed. ¹⁴See, with great effort I have laid up for the house of the LORD a hundred thousand talents of gold, a million talents of silver, and bronze and iron in such great quantities that they cannot be weighed. I have also laid up wood and stones, to which you must add. ¹⁵Moreover, you have available workers, stonecutters, masons, carpenters, and experts in every craft, ¹⁶without number, skilled with gold, silver, bronze, and iron. Set to work, therefore, and the LORD be with you!"

Charge to the Officials. ¹⁷David also commanded all of the officials of Israel to help his son Solomon: ¹⁸"Is not the LORD your God with you? Has he not

---

23:1, David makes Solomon king. In Samuel–Kings, there are many struggles in David's family over the succession to the throne, including an attempt to usurp it by his elder son Adonijah while David is lying on his deathbed. Here, in Chronicles, political intrigue and infighting evaporate, just as the struggles between David and Saul have vanished.

given you rest on every side? Indeed, he has delivered the inhabitants of the land into my power, and the land is subdued before the LORD and his people. [19]Therefore, devote your hearts and souls to seeking the LORD your God. Proceed to build the sanctuary of the LORD God, that the ark of the covenant of the LORD and God's sacred vessels may be brought into the house built for the name of the LORD."

23 **The Levitical Divisions.** [1]When David had grown old and was near the end of his days, he made his son Solomon king over Israel. [2]He then gathered together all the officials of Israel, along with the priests and the Levites.

[3]The Levites thirty years old and above were counted, and their total number was found to be thirty-eight thousand. [4]Of these, twenty-four thousand were to direct the service of the house of the LORD, six thousand were to be officials and judges, [5]four thousand were to be gatekeepers, and four thousand were to praise the LORD with the instruments which [David] had devised

for praise. [6]David apportioned them into divisions according to the sons of Levi: Gershon, Kohath, and Merari.

[7]To the Gershonites belonged Ladan and Shimei. [8]The sons of Ladan: Jehiel the chief, then Zetham and Joel; three in all. [9]The sons of Shimei were Shelomoth, Haziel, and Haran; three. These were the heads of the families of Ladan. [10]The sons of Shimei were Jahath, Zizah, Jeush, and Beriah; these were the sons of Shimei, four in all. [11]Jahath was the chief and Zizah was second to him; but Jeush and Beriah had few sons, and therefore they were classed as a single family, exercising a single office.

[12]The sons of Kohath: Amram, Izhar, Hebron, and Uzziel; four in all. [13]The sons of Amram were Aaron and Moses. Aaron was set apart to be consecrated as most holy, he and his sons forever, to offer sacrifice before the LORD, to minister to him, and to bless in his name forever. [14]As for Moses, however, the man of God, his sons were counted as part of the tribe of Levi. [15]The sons of Moses were Gershom and Eliezer. [16]The sons of Gershom: Shubael

---

23:2-32 Division and duties of Levites

David assigns 38,000 Levites to four different tasks: 24,000 for service of the temple; 6,000 as officers and judges; 4,000 as gatekeepers; and 4,000 for choral music and song (23:3-5). The divisions of Levites correspond to the sons of Levi: Gershon (23:7-11); Kohath (23:12-20); and Merari (23:21-23). David then outlines Levitical duties (23:26-32). They do not carry the tabernacle or its instruments (23:26), but they do assist the priests for the service in the temple (23:28-29). They sing thanks and praise at morning and evening worship and whenever the priests offer burnt offerings, especially at sabbaths, new moons, and festivals (23:30-31). Levites also oversee the tent of meeting and the sanctuary (23:32). The responsibilities and rights of Levites all depend on decisions made by King David.

the chief. [17]The sons of Eliezer were Rehabiah the chief—Eliezer had no other sons, but the sons of Rehabiah were very numerous. [18]The sons of Izhar: Shelomith the chief. [19]The sons of Hebron: Jeriah, the chief, Amariah, the second, Jahaziel, the third, and Jekameam, the fourth. [20]The sons of Uzziel: Micah, the chief, and Isshiah, the second.

[21]The sons of Merari: Mahli and Mushi. The sons of Mahli: Eleazar and Kish. [22]Eleazar died leaving no sons, only daughters; the sons of Kish, their kinsmen, married them. [23]The sons of Mushi: Mahli, Eder, and Jeremoth; three in all.

[24]These were the sons of Levi according to their ancestral houses, the family heads as they were enrolled one by one according to their names. They performed the work of the service of the house of the LORD beginning at twenty years of age.

[25]David said: "The LORD, the God of Israel, has given rest to his people, and has taken up his dwelling in Jerusalem forever. [26]Henceforth the Levites need not carry the tabernacle or any of the equipment for its service." [27]For by David's last words the Levites were enlisted from the time they were twenty years old. [28]Their duty is to assist the sons of Aaron in the service of the house of the LORD, having charge of the courts, the chambers, and the preservation of everything holy: they take part in the service of the house of God. [29]They also have charge of the showbread, of the fine flour for the grain offering, of the wafers of unleavened bread, and of the baking and mixing, and of all measures of quantity and size. [30]They are to be present every morning to offer thanks and to praise the LORD, and likewise in the evening; [31]and at every sacrifice of burnt offerings to the LORD on sabbaths, new moons, and feast days, in such numbers as are prescribed, they must always be present before the LORD [32]and observe what is prescribed for them concerning the tent of meeting, the sanctuary, and the sons of Aaron, their kinsmen, in the service of the house of the LORD.

24 **The Priestly Divisions.** [1]There were also divisions for the sons of Aaron. The sons of Aaron were Nadab, Abihu, Eleazar, and Ithamar. [2]Nadab and Abihu died before their father, leaving no sons; therefore only Eleazar and Ithamar served as priests. [3]David, with Zadok, a descendant of Eleazar, and

---

24:1-31 Divisions and duties of priests and of additional Levites

The postexilic priests are divided up into twenty-four courses or groups, which take turns officiating at the Jerusalem temple, alternating week after week. These are listed as deriving from Aaron's surviving sons, Eleazar and Ithamar, since Nadab and Abihu died in the desert (cf. Lev 10:1-3; Num 3:4). The Chronicler depicts priests of the line of Eleazar as superior, with Zadok listed among them (24:3-4). Shemaiah the Levite writes down this list in the presence of King David and some prominent priests (24:6). There follows another list of Levites (24:20-30), who cast lots for their positions, just like priests (24:31).

Ahimelech, a descendant of Ithamar, apportioned them their offices in the priestly service. ⁴But since the sons of Eleazar were found to be more numerous by male heads than those of Ithamar, the former were divided into sixteen groups, and the latter into eight groups, each under its family heads. ⁵Their functions were assigned impartially by lot, for there were officers of the holy place, and officers of God, descended both from Eleazar and from Ithamar. ⁶The scribe Shemaiah, son of Nethanel, a Levite, recorded them in the presence of the king, and of the officials, of Zadok the priest, and of Ahimelech, son of Abiathar, and of the heads of the ancestral houses of the priests and of the Levites, listing two successive family groups from Eleazar before each one from Ithamar.

⁷The first lot fell to Jehoiarib, the second to Jedaiah, ⁸the third to Harim, the fourth to Seorim, ⁹the fifth to Malchijah, the sixth to Mijamin, ¹⁰the seventh to Hakkoz, the eighth to Abijah, ¹¹the ninth to Jeshua, the tenth to Shecaniah, ¹²the eleventh to Eliashib, the twelfth to Jakim, ¹³the thirteenth to Huppah, the fourteenth to Ishbaal, ¹⁴the fifteenth to Bilgah, the sixteenth to Immer, ¹⁵the seventeenth to Hezir, the eighteenth to Happizzez, ¹⁶the nineteenth to Pethahiah, the twentieth to Jehezkel, ¹⁷the twenty-first to Jachin, the twenty-second to Gamul, ¹⁸the twenty-third to Delaiah, the twenty-fourth to Maaziah. ¹⁹This was the appointed order of their service when they functioned in the house of the LORD according to the precepts given them by Aaron, their father, as the LORD, the God of Israel, had commanded him.

Other Levites. ²⁰Of the remaining Levites, there were Shubael, of the sons of Amram, and Jehdeiah, of the sons of Shubael; ²¹Isshiah, the chief, of the sons of Rehabiah; ²²Shelomith of the Izharites, and Jahath of the sons of Shelomith. ²³The sons of Hebron were Jeriah, the chief, Amariah, the second, Jahaziel, the third, Jekameam, the fourth. ²⁴The sons of Uzziel were Micah; Shamir, of the sons of Micah; ²⁵Isshiah, the brother of Micah; and Zechariah, a descendant of Isshiah. ²⁶The sons of Merari were Mahli, Mushi, and the sons of his son Uzziah. ²⁷The sons of Merari through his son Uzziah: Shoham, Zaccur, and Ibri. ²⁸The sons of Mahli were Eleazar, who had no sons, ²⁹and Jerahmeel, of the sons of Kish. ³⁰The sons of Mushi were Mahli, Eder, and Jerimoth.

These were the sons of the Levites according to their ancestral houses. ³¹They too, in the same manner as their kinsmen, the sons of Aaron, cast lots in the presence of King David, Zadok, Ahimelech, and the heads of the priestly and levitical families; the more important family did so in the same way as the less important one.

The Singers. ¹David and the leaders of the liturgy set apart for the

25:1–26:32 Additional Levitical officers: musicians, gatekeepers, and overseers

David and his army officers set up the families of Asaph, Heman, and Jeduthun as musicians for the temple (25:1, 6) and divide them by lot into

service the sons of Asaph, Heman, and Jeduthun, who prophesied to the accompaniment of lyres and harps and cymbals.

This is the list of those who performed this service: ²Of the sons of Asaph: Zaccur, Joseph, Nethaniah, and Asharelah, sons of Asaph, under the direction of Asaph, who prophesied under the guidance of the king. ³Of Jeduthun, these sons of Jeduthun: Gedaliah, Zeri, Jeshaiah, Shimei, Hashabiah, and Mattithiah; six, under the direction of their father Jeduthun, who prophesied to the accompaniment of a lyre, to give thanks and praise to the Lord. ⁴Of Heman, these sons of Heman: Bukkiah, Mattaniah, Uzziel, Shubael, and Jerimoth; Hananiah, Hanani, Eliathah, Giddalti, Romamti-ezer, Joshbekashah, Mallothi, Hothir, and Mahazioth. ⁵All these were the sons of Heman, the king's seer for divine matters; to exalt him God gave Heman fourteen sons and three daughters. ⁶All these, whether of Asaph, Jeduthun, or Heman, were under their fathers' direction in the singing in the house of the Lord to the accompaniment of cymbals, harps and lyres, serving in the house of God, under the guidance of the king. ⁷Their number, together with that of their kinsmen who were trained in singing to the Lord, all of them skilled men, was two hundred and eighty-eight. ⁸They cast lots for their functions equally, young and old, master and pupil alike.

⁹The first lot fell to Asaph, to the family of Joseph; he and his sons and his kinsmen were twelve. Gedaliah was the second; he and his kinsmen and his sons were twelve. ¹⁰The third was Zaccur, his sons, and his kinsmen: twelve. ¹¹The fourth fell to Izri, his sons, and his kinsmen: twelve. ¹²The fifth was Nethaniah, his sons, and his kinsmen: twelve. ¹³The sixth was Bukkiah, his sons, and his kinsmen: twelve. ¹⁴The seventh was Jesarelah, his sons, and his kinsmen: twelve. ¹⁵The eighth was Jeshaiah, his sons, and his kinsmen: twelve. ¹⁶The ninth was Mattaniah, his sons, and his kinsmen: twelve. ¹⁷The tenth was Shimei, his sons, and his kinsmen: twelve. ¹⁸The eleventh was Uzziel, his sons, and his kinsmen: twelve. ¹⁹The twelfth fell to Hashabiah, his sons, and his kinsmen: twelve. ²⁰The thirteenth was Shubael, his sons, and his kinsmen: twelve. ²¹The fourteenth was Mattithiah, his sons, and his kinsmen: twelve. ²²The fifteenth fell

---

twenty-four divisions of Levites, paralleling the priests in chapter 24. These Levites prophesy on lyres, harps, and cymbals (25:1). So the music ministry of Levites has a prophetic character, which indicates high regard for their work. David, then, is also responsible for the twenty-four courses of Levite singers with prophetic powers. Moreover, in 2 Chronicles 20 an important Levite will prophesy to King Jehoshaphat in time of grave danger from enemy armies. Chapter 26 lists those Levites serving as gatekeepers and overseers of finances and other civil matters.

to Jeremoth, his sons, and his kinsmen: twelve. ²³The sixteenth fell to Hananiah, his sons, and his kinsmen: twelve. ²⁴The seventeenth fell to Joshbekashah, his sons, and his kinsmen: twelve. ²⁵The eighteenth fell to Hanani, his sons, and his kinsmen: twelve. ²⁶The nineteenth fell to Mallothi, his sons, and his kinsmen: twelve. ²⁷The twentieth fell to Eliathah, his sons, and his kinsmen: twelve. ²⁸The twenty-first fell to Hothir, his sons, and his kinsmen: twelve. ²⁹The twenty-second fell to Giddalti, his sons, and his kinsmen: twelve. ³⁰The twenty-third fell to Mahazioth, his sons, and his kinsmen: twelve. ³¹The twenty-fourth fell to Romamti-ezer, his sons, and his kinsmen: twelve.

26 Divisions of Gatekeepers.

¹As for the divisions of gatekeepers: Of the Korahites was Meshelemiah, the son of Kore, one of the sons of Abiasaph. ²Meshelemiah's sons: Zechariah, the firstborn, Jediael, the second son, Zebadiah, the third, Jathniel, the fourth, ³Elam, the fifth, Jehohanan, the sixth, Eliehoenai, the seventh. ⁴Obed-edom's sons: Shemaiah, the firstborn, Jehozabad, a second son, Joah, the third, Sachar, the fourth, Nethanel, the fifth, ⁵Ammiel, the sixth, Issachar, the seventh, Peullethai, the eighth, for God blessed him. ⁶To his son Shemaiah were born sons who ruled over their family, for they were warriors. ⁷The sons of Shemaiah were Othni, Rephael, Obed, and Elzabad; also his kinsmen who were men of substance, Elihu and Semachiah. ⁸All these were the sons of Obed-edom, who, together with their sons and their kinsmen, were men of substance, fit for the service. Of Obed-edom, sixty-two.

⁹Of Meshelemiah, eighteen sons and kinsmen, men of substance.

¹⁰Hosah, a descendant of Merari, had these sons: Shimri, the chief (for though he was not the firstborn, his father made him chief), ¹¹Hilkiah, the second son, Tebaliah, the third, Zechariah, the fourth. All the sons and kinsmen of Hosah were thirteen.

¹²To these divisions of the gatekeepers, by their chief men, were assigned watches for them to minister in the house of the LORD, for each group in the same way. ¹³They cast lots for each gate, small and large families alike. ¹⁴When the lot was cast for the east side, it fell to Meshelemiah. Then they cast lots for his son Zechariah, a prudent counselor, and the north side fell to his lot. ¹⁵To Obed-edom fell the south side, and to his sons the storehouse. ¹⁶To Hosah fell the west side with the Shallecheth gate at the ascending highway. For each family, watches were established. ¹⁷On the east, six watched each day, on the north, four each day, on the south, four each day, and at the storehouse they were two and two; ¹⁸as for the large building on the west, there were four at the highway and two at the large building. ¹⁹These were the classes of the gatekeepers, sons of Korah and Merari.

Treasurers. ²⁰Their brother Levites had oversight of the treasuries of the house of God and the treasuries of votive offerings. ²¹Among the sons of Ladan the Gershonite, the family heads were sons of Jehiel: ²²the sons of Jehiel, Zetham and his brother Joel, who oversaw the treasures of the house of the LORD. ²³Of the Amramites, Izharites, Hebronites, and Uzzielites, ²⁴Shubael, son of Gershom, son of Moses, was principal overseer of the treasures. ²⁵His associate was of the line of Eliezer, whose son was Rehabiah, whose son was Jeshaiah, whose son was Joram, whose son was Zichri, whose son was Shelomith. ²⁶This Shelomith and his kinsmen oversaw all the treasures of the votive offerings dedicated by King David, the heads of the families, the commanders of thousands and of hundreds, and the commanders of the army; ²⁷what came from wars and from spoils, they dedicated for the support of the house of the Lord. ²⁸Also, whatever Samuel the seer, Saul, son of Kish, Abner, son of Ner, Joab, son of Zeruiah, and all others had consecrated, was under the charge of Shelomith and his kinsmen.

Magistrates. ²⁹Among the Izharites, Chenaniah and his sons were in charge of Israel's civil affairs as officials and judges. ³⁰Among the Hebronites, Hashabiah and his kinsmen, one thousand seven hundred men of substance, had the administration of Israel on the western side of the Jordan for all the work of the Lord and the service of the king. ³¹Among the Hebronites, Jerijah was their chief according to their family records. In the fortieth year of David's reign search was made, and there were found among them warriors at Jazer of Gilead. ³²His kinsmen were also men of substance, two thousand seven hundred heads of families. King David appointed

them to the administration of the Reubenites, the Gadites, and the half-tribe of Manasseh for everything pertaining to God and to the king.

27 Army Commanders. ¹This is the list of the Israelite family heads, commanders of thousands and of hundreds, and other officers who served the king in all that pertained to the divisions, of twenty-four thousand men each, that came and went month by month throughout the year.

²Over the first division for the first month was Ishbaal, son of Zabdiel, and in his division were twenty-four thousand men; ³a descendant of Perez, he was chief over all the commanders of the army for the first month. ⁴Over the division of the second month was Eleazar, son of Dodo, from Ahoh, and in his division were twenty-four thousand men. ⁵The third army commander, for the third month, was Benaiah, son of Jehoiada the chief priest, and in his division were twenty-four thousand men. ⁶This Benaiah was a warrior among the Thirty and over the Thirty. His son Ammizabad was over his division. ⁷Fourth, for the fourth month, was Asahel, brother of Joab, and after him his son Zebadiah, and in his division were twenty-four thousand men. ⁸Fifth, for the fifth month, was the commander Shamhuth, a descendant of Zerah, and in his division were twenty-four

---

27:1-34 Officers of the kingdom

David now lists other officials, not Levites, associated with the king: military leaders (27:1-15), tribal leaders (27:16-24), stewards of the king's property (27:25-31), and members of the royal cabinet (27:32-34). He lists 24,000 workers for each month (27:1-15), and then mentions some well-known advisors

thousand men. ⁹Sixth, for the sixth month, was Ira, son of Ikkesh, from Tekoa, and in his division were twenty-four thousand men. ¹⁰Seventh, for the seventh month, was Hellez, from Beth-pelet, of the Ephraimites, and in his division were twenty-four thousand men. ¹¹Eighth, for the eighth month, was Sibbecai the Hushathite, a descendant of Zerah, and in his division were twenty-four thousand men. ¹²Ninth, for the ninth month, was Abiezer from Anathoth, of Benjamin, and in his division were twenty-four thousand men. ¹³Tenth, for the tenth month, was Maharai from Netophah, a descendant of Zerah, and in his division were twenty-four thousand men. ¹⁴Eleventh, for the eleventh month, was Benaiah the Pirathonite, of the Ephraimites, and in his division were twenty-four thousand men. ¹⁵Twelfth, for the twelfth month, was Heldai the Netophathite, of the family of Othniel, and in his division were twenty-four thousand men.

Tribal Leaders. ¹⁶Over the tribes of Israel, for the Reubenites the leader was Eliezer, son of Zichri; for the Simeonites, Shephatiah, son of Maacah; ¹⁷for Levi, Hashabiah, son of Kemuel; for Aaron, Zadok; ¹⁸for Judah, Eliab, one of David's brothers; for Issachar, Omri, son of Michael; ¹⁹for Zebulun, Ishmaiah, son of Obadiah; for Naphtali, Jeremoth, son of Azriel; ²⁰for the Ephraimites, Hoshea, son of Azaziah; for the half-tribe of Manasseh, Joel, son of Pedaiah; ²¹for the half-tribe of Manasseh in Gilead, Iddo, son of Zechariah; for Benjamin, Jaasiel, son of Abner; ²²for Dan, Azarel, son of Jeroham. These were the commanders of the tribes of Israel.

²³David did not count those who were twenty years of age or younger, for the LORD had promised to multiply Israel like the stars of the heavens. ²⁴Joab, son of Zeruiah, began to take the census, but he did not complete it, for because of it wrath fell upon Israel. Therefore the number was not recorded in the book of chronicles of King David.

Overseers. ²⁵Over the treasuries of the king was Azmaveth, the son of Adiel. Over the treasuries in the country, the cities, the villages, and the towers was Jonathan, son of Uzziah. ²⁶Over the farm workers who tilled the soil was Ezri, son of Chelub. ²⁷Over the vineyards was Shimei from Ramah, and over their produce for the wine cellars was Zabdi the Shiphmite. ²⁸Over the olive trees and sycamores of the Shephelah was Baal-hanan the Gederite, and over the stores of oil was Joash. ²⁹Over the cattle that grazed in Sharon was Shitrai the Sharonite, and over the cattle in the valleys was Shaphat, the son of Adlai; ³⁰over the camels was Obil the Ishmaelite; over the donkeys was Jehdeiah the Meronothite; ³¹and over the flocks was Jaziz the Hagrite. All these were the overseers of King David's possessions.

---

of the king: Ahitophel, Hushai, Jehoiada son of Benaiah, Abiathar, and Joab. Many names in this list mirror names in 1 Chronicles 11–12 (i.e., David's supporters from the time of the monarchy), but they mix with new names that may come from the Persian era, the time of the Chronicler.

David's Court. ³²Jonathan, David's uncle and a man of intelligence, was counselor and scribe; he and Jehiel, the son of Hachmoni, attended the king's sons. ³³Ahithophel was also the king's counselor, and Hushai the Archite was the king's friend. ³⁴After Ahithophel came Jehoiada, the son of Benaiah, and Abiathar. The commander of the king's army was Joab.

28 The Assembly at Jerusalem. ¹David assembled at Jerusalem all the commanders of Israel, the tribal commanders, the commanders of the divisions who were in the service of the king, the commanders of thousands and of hundreds, those in command of all the king's estates and possessions, and his sons, together with the courtiers, the warriors, and every person of substance. ²King David rose to his feet and said: "Hear me, my kinsmen and my people. It was my purpose to build a house of repose myself for the ark of the covenant of the LORD, the footstool for the feet of our God; and I was preparing to build it. ³But God said to me, You may not build a house for my name, for you are a man who waged wars and shed blood. ⁴However, the LORD, the God of Israel, chose me from all my father's family to be king over Israel forever. For he chose Judah as leader, then one family of Judah, that of my father; and finally, among all the sons of my father, it pleased him to make me king over all Israel. ⁵And of all my sons—for the LORD has given me many sons—he has chosen my son Solomon to sit on the throne of the LORD's kingship over Israel. ⁶For he said to me: It is your son Solomon who shall build my house and my courts, for I have chosen him for my son, and I will be a father to him. ⁷I will establish his kingdom forever, if he perseveres in carrying out my commandments and ordinances as he does now. ⁸Therefore, in the sight of all Israel, the assembly of the LORD, and in the hearing of our God: keep and carry out all the commandments of the LORD, your God, that you may continue to possess this good land and afterward leave it as an inheritance to your children forever.

⁹"As for you, Solomon, my son, know the God of your father and serve him with a whole heart and a willing soul, for the LORD searches all hearts and understands all the mind's thoughts. If

---

28:1–29:9 David entrusts temple building to Solomon

In verses 2-10, David addresses an assembly of all royal and civil officials of Israel in a speech that pulls together all the motifs and themes of chapters 22–27. This speech reflects many issues from David's private address to Solomon in 22:6-16, including God's promise to David through Nathan the prophet (1 Chr 17). Solomon would build the temple (28:6-10) and be blessed with a dynasty if he would remain faithful to God's commands (28:7). David exhorts the leaders to study all God's commands and ordinances; then they will receive the divine blessing (28:8). David turns next to say to Solomon: "know the God of your father and serve him with a whole heart" because God "searches all hearts and understands all the mind's thoughts" (28:9).

you search for him, he will be found; but if you abandon him, he will cast you off forever. ¹⁰See, then! The Lᴏʀᴅ has chosen you to build a house as his sanctuary. Be strong and set to work."

Temple Plans Given to Solomon. ¹¹Then David gave to his son Solomon the design of the portico and of the house itself, with its storerooms, its upper rooms and inner chambers, and the shrine containing the cover of the ark. ¹²He provided also the design for all else that he had in mind by way of courts for the house of the Lᴏʀᴅ, with the surrounding compartments for the treasuries of the house of God and the treasuries for the votive offerings, ¹³as well as for the divisions of the priests and Levites, for all the work of the service of the house of the Lᴏʀᴅ, and for all the liturgical vessels of the house of the Lᴏʀᴅ. ¹⁴He specified the weight of gold to be used in the golden vessels for the various services and the weight of silver to be used in the silver vessels for the various services;

¹⁵likewise for the golden menorahs and their lamps he specified the weight of gold for each menorah and its lamps, and for the silver menorahs he specified the weight of silver for each menorah and its lamps, depending on the use to which each menorah was to be put. ¹⁶He specified the weight of gold for each table that was to hold the showbread, and the silver for the silver tables; ¹⁷the pure gold for the forks, basins, and pitchers; the weight of gold for each golden bowl and the weight of silver for each silver bowl; ¹⁸the refined gold, and its weight, to be used for the altar of incense; and, finally, gold to fashion the chariot: the cherubim spreading their wings and covering the ark of the covenant of the Lᴏʀᴅ. ¹⁹All this he wrote down, by the hand of the Lᴏʀᴅ, to make him understand it—the working out of the whole design.

²⁰Then David said to his son Solomon: "Be strong and steadfast, and go to work; do not fear or be dismayed, for the Lᴏʀᴅ God, my God, is with you. He

---

God's knowledge of human hearts echoes language used before the Flood (Gen 6:5). There God knows human hearts, especially their evil inclinations, and this grieves God. But here the Chronicler takes an optimistic turn: the phrase "perfect heart" shows up several times in Chronicles to describe total devotion to God (e.g., 1 Chr 12:38; 28:9; 29:9, 19; 2 Chr 15:17; 16:9; 19:9; 25:2). It probably comes from Deuteronomy 6:5 ("You shall love the Lord, your God, with all your heart"). This spiritual stance leads to a hopeful saying in verse 9: "If you search for him, he will be found." David concludes: since God has chosen you, Solomon, to build the temple, you must act on it.

In verses 11-19 David transfers to Solomon the temple plans (of the building, of the priests and Levites, of the vessels and decorations), which he had received in writing from God (28:19). He then exhorts Solomon to be courageous and not fearful, for God is with him and will support him, even with all the human assistants he may need (28:20-21).

will not fail you or abandon you before you have completed all the work for the service of the house of the LORD. [21]The divisions of the priests and Levites are ready for all the service of the house of God; they will be with you in all the work with all those who are eager to show their skill in every kind of craftsmanship. Also the commanders and all the people will do everything that you command."

29 **Offerings for the Temple.** [1]King David then said to the whole assembly: "My son Solomon, whom alone God has chosen, is still young and inexperienced; the work, however, is great, for this palace is not meant for human beings, but for the LORD God. [2]For this reason I have stored up for the house of my God, as far as I was able, gold for what will be made of gold, silver for what will be made of silver, bronze for what will be made of bronze, iron for what will be made of iron, wood for what will be made of wood, onyx stones and settings for them, carnelian and mosaic stones, every other kind of precious stone, and great quantities of marble. [3]But now, because of the delight I take in the house of my God, in addi-

tion to all that I stored up for the holy house, I give to the house of my God my personal fortune in gold and silver: [4]three thousand talents of Ophir gold, and seven thousand talents of refined silver, for overlaying the walls of the rooms, [5]for the various utensils to be made of gold and silver, and for every work that is to be done by artisans. Now, who else will contribute generously and consecrate themselves this day to the LORD?"

[6]Then the heads of the families, the tribal commanders of Israel, the commanders of thousands and of hundreds, and those who had command of the king's affairs came forward willingly [7]and contributed for the service of the house of God five thousand talents and ten thousand darics of gold, ten thousand talents of silver, eighteen thousand talents of bronze, and one hundred thousand talents of iron. [8]Those who had precious stones gave them into the keeping of Jehiel the Gershonite for the treasury of the house of the LORD. [9]The people rejoiced over these free-will offerings, for they had been contributed to the LORD wholeheartedly. King David also rejoiced greatly.

In 29:1-9 David delivers a third farewell speech (cf. 22:6-16 and 28:2-10) to the assembly, admonishing them to cooperate with Solomon. David lists his generous gifts (29:2-5) and those of others in his administration (29:6-8). All these gifts lead to great rejoicing (29:9), for "[the offerings] had been contributed to the Lord wholeheartedly." Recounting all those donations is probably intended to challenge the hearers to respond generously themselves. Verse 9 begins and ends with the notion of joy (joyful celebration), while the notion of a whole heart stands in the center of this verse. For the Chronicler total devotion to God leads to joyful celebration.

David's Prayer. ¹⁰Then David blessed the LORD in the sight of the whole assembly. David said:

"Blessed are you, LORD,
  God of Israel our father,
    from eternity to eternity.
¹¹Yours, LORD, are greatness and
  might,
    majesty, victory, and splendor.
For all in heaven and on earth is
  yours;
  yours, LORD, is kingship;
    you are exalted as head over all.
¹²Riches and glory are from you,
  and you have dominion over all.
In your hand are power and might;
  it is yours to give greatness and
    strength to all.

¹³Therefore, our God, we give you
  thanks
    and we praise the majesty of
      your name.

¹⁴"But who am I, and who are my people, that we should have the means to contribute so freely? For everything is from you, and what we give is what we have from you. ¹⁵For before you we are strangers and travelers, like all our ancestors. Our days on earth are like a shadow, without a future. ¹⁶LORD our God, all this wealth that we have brought together to build you a house for your holy name comes from you and is entirely yours. ¹⁷I know, my God, that you put hearts to the test and that you take pleasure in integ-

29:10-22a David's farewell liturgy

Here the Chronicler articulates the lofty theology of his postexilic age. He begins with praise and thanksgiving for the God of Israel, expressed in expansive and abstract terms like greatness, power, and glory; and he acknowledges that the kingdom belongs to the Lord (29:11). This language, by the way, resembles the final doxology in the Lord's Prayer: "For the kingdom, the power, and the glory are yours, now and forever." God has the power to make everything strong and lasting. Therefore, David and everyone with him join in praising and thanking God (29:12-13). All is gift from God, so David and his people are grateful recipients of divine grace, as he says, aliens and guests before God (29:14-15). David changes from praising God (29:10-13) to confessing utter dependence on God (29:14-17). His prayer concludes with two petitions: keep your people strong in this spirituality (29:18) and give Solomon a "wholehearted desire" so that he can obey your commands and build the temple (29:19).

These same three elements characterize David's prayer in 1 Chronicles 16:8-36: confession of our sad state as landless patriarchs (16:8-22); praise of God as king (16:23-33); and a petition (16:35). These two prayers (in chs. 16 and 29) pull together key elements of David's ministry for Israel: installing the ark of God at its place in Jerusalem and passing on the reign and temple-building to his son Solomon. The Chronicler's audience should

rity. With a whole heart I have willingly given all these things, and now with joy I have seen your people here present also giving to you generously. [18]LORD, God of our ancestors Abraham, Isaac, and Israel, keep such thoughts in the hearts and minds of your people forever, and direct their hearts toward you. [19]Give to my son Solomon a wholehearted desire to keep your commandments, precepts, and statutes, that he may carry out all these plans and build the palace for which I have made preparation."

[20]Then David told the whole assembly, "Now bless the LORD your God!" And the whole assembly blessed the LORD, the God of their ancestors, bowing down in homage before the LORD and before the king. [21]On the following day they brought sacrifices and burnt offerings to the LORD, a thousand bulls, a thousand rams, and a thousand lambs, together with their libations and many other sacrifices for all Israel; [22]and on that day they ate and drank in the LORD's presence with great rejoicing.

Solomon Anointed. Then for a second time they proclaimed David's son Solomon king, and they anointed him for the LORD as ruler, and Zadok as priest. [23]Thereafter Solomon sat on the throne of the LORD as king succeeding his father David; he prospered, and all Israel obeyed him. [24]All the commanders and warriors, and also all the other sons of King David, swore allegiance to King Solomon. [25]And the LORD exalted Solomon greatly in the eyes of all Israel, giving him a glorious reign such as had not been enjoyed by any king over Israel before him.

David's Death. [26]Thus David, the son of Jesse, had reigned over all Israel. [27]He was king over Israel for forty years: he was king seven years in Hebron and thirty-three years in Jerusalem. [28]He died at a ripe old age, rich in years and wealth and glory, and his son Solomon succeeded him as king.

---

always be able to discern the influence of King David in his views of the temple and its worship.

Afterwards, David invites the others to participate in vocal prayer (praising God, 29:20a) and in gesture (prostration, 29:20b), and in the offering of sacrifices (29:21). This ceremony concludes with "great rejoicing," i.e., with the entire congregation eating and drinking joyfully. Joyful worship, not political intrigue and infighting, are King David's final legacy, as the Chronicler retells this story for his Jewish community.

29:22b-30 [1 Kgs 2:10-12] Solomon becomes king after David's death

In 23:1 David had declared Solomon king, but here the Chronicler repeats it, mentioning the appointment of Zadok as priest (29:22). We learn in advance that Solomon will receive the allegiance of all David's sons, as well as countless riches and blessings. Then follow the basic statistics of David's reign (forty years: seven years in Hebron and thirty-three years in Jerusalem) and the simple statement that David has died (29:27-28). This

²⁹Now the deeds of King David, first and last, are recorded in the history of Samuel the seer, the history of Nathan the prophet, and the history of Gad the seer, ³⁰together with the particulars of his reign and valor, and of the events that affected him and all Israel and all the kingdoms of the earth.

---

chapter concludes with a typical note about the sources of the Chronicler's information: Chronicles of Samuel the seer, of Nathan the prophet, and of Gad the seer (29:29).

The Book of Second Chronicles

I. The Reign of Solomon

1 **Solomon at Gibeon.** [1]Solomon, son of David, strengthened his hold on the kingdom, for the LORD, his God, was with him, making him ever greater. [2]Solomon summoned all Israel, the commanders of thousands and of hundreds, the judges, the princes of all Israel, and the family heads; [3]and, accompanied by the whole assembly, Solomon went to the high place at Gibeon, because the tent of meeting of God, made in the wilderness by Moses, the LORD's servant, was there. [4]David had, however, brought up the ark of God from Kiriath-jearim to Jerusalem, where he had provided a

SOLOMON

2 Chronicles 1–9

Acclaimed as king by all Israel (1 Chr 29:20-25), Solomon was not the candidate of any particular group. Like David, his father, he proved to be an avid patron of divine worship at the temple, which he constructed and dedicated, following David's instructions. Solomon's role in worship overshadows his wise actions, so strong in 1 Kings and in other biblical traditions. The Chronicler makes a very significant change in his portrayal of Solomon. Here he is not a man of sin, as in 1 Kings 11, where his many wives and concubines lead him astray. The Chronicler simply omitted all the offending sections of 1 Kings, just as he skipped over most of David's sins and problems in 2 Samuel 11–20. Here is an idyllic picture of national solidarity and prosperity.

1:1-13 [cf. 1 Kgs 2:12b; 2:46b; 3:1-15; 4:1a]
Solomon prays for wisdom at Gibeon

In this version Solomon took hold of royal power unhindered, since the Lord supported him (1:1; cf. 1 Kgs 2:12b, 46b). The Chronicler omits information in Kings about the king's political marriage with the daughter of Pharaoh (1 Kgs 3:1). He journeys to Gibeon (1:2-6), the great high place

69

place and pitched a tent for it; [5]the bronze altar made by Bezalel, son of Uri, son of Hur, he put in front of the tabernacle of the LORD. There Solomon and the assembly sought out the LORD, [6]and Solomon offered sacrifice in the LORD's presence on the bronze altar at the tent of meeting; he sacrificed a thousand burnt offerings upon it.

[7]That night God appeared to Solomon and said to him: Whatever you ask, I will give you. [8]Solomon answered God: "You have shown great favor to David my father, and you have made me king to succeed him. [9]Now, LORD God, may your word to David my father be confirmed, for you have made me king over a people as numerous as the dust of the earth. [10]Give me, therefore, wisdom and knowledge to govern this people, for otherwise who could rule this vast people of yours?" [11]God then replied to Solomon: Because this has been your wish—you did not ask for riches, treasures, and glory, or the life of those who hate you, or even for a long life for yourself, but you have asked for wisdom and knowledge in order to rule my people over whom I have made you king—[12]wisdom and knowledge are

where the tent of meeting (with the ark) and the bronze altar were located (1:3-5). Solomon and all the people go in procession to Gibeon (2 Chr 3:3).

The ark of God was the central religious symbol in the books of Joshua and Samuel, while the tent was the major religious symbol of priestly traditions in the Pentateuch; here the Chronicler joins them all together. Since 1 Kings waged a verbal campaign against worship at the high places, the writer needed to justify Solomon's trip there—i.e., the temple had not yet been built. The Chronicler has a more complex view of Israel's worship during the time of Solomon. The tabernacle built by Moses in the wilderness, with its altar for sacrifices, was still at Gibeon, where they conducted full worship ceremonies: sacrifices and song. After David moved to Jerusalem, the ark and the tent were symbols of another religious movement: music and song.

The Chronicler solves two problems of Israel's worship. First, he shows why Solomon could go to Gibeon to pray; second, he provides a smooth transition between the older pattern of worship, established by Moses and practiced by the priests in the desert, and the newer worship which also includes choral music and song by the Levites, representing David's liturgical innovations. This story in Chronicles helped people of the Chronicler's day appreciate worship with both sacrifice and song at their temple.

Solomon goes to Gibeon, offers sacrifices, and then makes his famous prayer (1:8-12; cf. 1 Kgs 3:6-15). The Chronicler reduces the content in 1 Kings by about half, especially by omitting some of the typical Deuteronomistic language (e.g., 1 Kgs 3:6-8, 10). Here Solomon asks for gifts more closely resembling those God gives him, "wisdom and knowledge"; in

given you. I will also give you riches, treasures, and glory, such as kings before you never had, nor will those who come after you.

Solomon's Wealth. ¹³Solomon returned to Jerusalem from the high place at Gibeon, from before the tent of meeting, and became king over Israel. ¹⁴Solomon amassed chariots and horses: he had one thousand four hundred chariots and twelve thousand horses; these he allocated among the chariot cities and to the king's service in Jerusalem. ¹⁵The king made silver and gold as common in Jerusalem as stones, and cedars as numerous as the sycamores of the Shephelah. ¹⁶Solomon's horses were imported from Egypt and Cilicia, where the king's agents purchased them at the prevailing price. ¹⁷A chariot imported from Egypt cost six hundred shekels of silver, a horse one hundred and fifty shekels; so they were exported to all the Hittite and Aramean kings.

Preparations for the Temple. ¹⁸Solomon gave orders for the building of a house for the name of the LORD and also a king's house for himself.

---

1 Kings 3:9 he had requested an "understanding heart to judge your people." In Chronicles, Solomon wants these gifts so that he can lead this people and govern appropriately. As in Kings, Solomon receives more gifts than he asks for: wisdom, knowledge, riches, treasures, and glory (1:11-12). But the Chronicler omits verses in Kings which demonstrate Solomon's wisdom: the story of Solomon's judgment between the two harlots and the one living child (1 Kgs 3:16-28), and the lists of Solomon's administrators and officials, which demonstrated his wisdom at governance (1 Kgs 4:1-19).

1:14-17 [cf. 1 Kgs 4:20–5:14; 2 Chr 9:25-28; 1 Kgs 10:26-29] The wealth of Solomon

The Chronicler describes Solomon's wealth: chariots, horsemen, horses, silver and gold, and cedar for (temple) construction. Mentioning them right after Solomon's prayer shows how God's gift of wisdom also resulted in wealth. Information about Solomon's wealth, wisdom, and horses is repeated in 2 Chronicles 9:25-28. By repeating this information, the Chronicler shows that Solomon's wisdom and wealth do not fail him (unlike 1 Kgs 11, where his reign ends disgracefully, in sin).

1:18–2:17 [cf. 1 Kgs 5:15-32] Solomon's treaty with King Huram

This story shows that Gentile kings now recognize Solomon. The decision to build a temple is Solomon's first action after receiving the gift of wisdom (1:18). Here, unlike Kings, Solomon initiated correspondence with Huram of Tyre (Hiram in Kings), which gives him a bit more stature. Since the Chronicler has more interest in worship than the book of Kings, he

2 ¹Solomon conscripted seventy thousand men to carry stones and eighty thousand to cut the stones in the mountains, and over these he placed three thousand six hundred overseers. ²Moreover, Solomon sent this message to Huram, king of Tyre: "As you dealt with David my father, and sent him cedars to build a house for his dwelling— ³now I am going to build a house for the name of the LORD, my God, and to consecrate it to him, for the burning of fragrant incense in his presence, for the perpetual display of the showbread, for burnt offerings morning and evening, and for the sabbaths, new moons, and festivals of the LORD, our God: such is Israel's perpetual obligation. ⁴And the house I am going to build must be great, for our God is greater than all other gods. ⁵Yet who is really able to build him a house, since the heavens and even the highest heavens cannot contain him? And who am I that I should build him a house, unless it be to offer incense in his presence? ⁶Now, send me men skilled at work in gold, silver, bronze, and iron, in purple, crimson, and violet fabrics, and who know how to do engraved work, to join the skilled craftsmen who are with me in Judah and Jerusalem, whom David my father appointed. ⁷Also send me boards of cedar, cypress and cabinet wood from Lebanon, for I realize that your servants know how to cut the wood of Lebanon. My servants will work with yours ⁸in order to prepare for me a great quantity of wood, since the house I intend to build must be great and wonderful. ⁹I will furnish as food for your servants, the woodcutters, twenty thousand kors of wheat, twenty thousand kors of barley, twenty thousand baths of wine, and twenty thousand baths of oil."

¹⁰Huram, king of Tyre, wrote an answer which he sent to Solomon: "Because

describes temple vessels, furnishings, and rituals not mentioned in Kings: incense and bread offerings for daily morning and evening sacrifice, and for Sabbaths, new moons, and appointed festivals. Each of these practices is known from the Pentateuch, but the Chronicler implies that all should take place in the temple of his day. Later kings will be judged by their fidelity to these criteria (e.g., 2 Chr 13; 28; 29–31).

All these negotiations with Huram of Tyre focus on building and equipping the temple, as Huram's response emphasizes in his letter to Solomon (2:10-15). He realizes that the Lord loves Solomon and ought to be blessed for appointing Solomon to such a task, so he will send to him a skilled helper, Huram-abi. In 2 Chronicles 2:16-17 Solomon counts as workers all the aliens, probably the Hittites, Amorites, Perizzites, Hivites, and the Jebusites not from Israel (2 Chr 8:7). By speaking of aliens [resident aliens], he implies that they are no longer foreigners but are still not incorporated into Israel. Here is another occasion where the Chronicler includes all the various groups in the land in Israel.

the LORD loves his people, he has placed you over them as king." [11]He added: "Blessed be the LORD, the God of Israel, who made heaven and earth, for having given King David a wise son of intelligence and understanding, who will build a house for the LORD and also his own royal house. [12]I am now sending you a craftsman of great skill, Huram-abi, [13]son of a Danite woman and of a father from Tyre; he knows how to work with gold, silver, bronze, and iron, with stone and wood, with purple, violet, fine linen, and crimson, and also how to do all kinds of engraved work and to devise every type of design that may be given him and your craftsmen and the craftsmen of my lord David your father. [14]And now, let my lord send to his servants the wheat, barley, oil, and wine which he has promised. [15]For our part, we will cut trees on Lebanon, as many as you need, and send them down to you in rafts to the port of Joppa, whence you may take them up to Jerusalem."

[16]Thereupon Solomon took a census of all the alien men resident in the land of Israel (following the census David his father had taken of them); they were found to number one hundred fifty-three thousand six hundred. [17]Of these he made seventy thousand carriers and eighty thousand cutters in the mountains, and three thousand six hundred overseers to keep the people working.

Building of the Temple. [1]Then Solomon began to build the house of the LORD in Jerusalem on Mount Moriah, which had been shown to David his father, in the place David had prepared, the threshing floor of Ornan the Jebusite. [2]He began to build in the second month of the fourth year of his reign. [3]These were the specifications laid down by Solomon for building the house of God: the length was sixty cubits according to the old measure, and the width was twenty cubits; [4]the front porch along the width of the house was also twenty

---

3:1-14 [cf. 1 Kgs 6:1-31] Solomon builds a house for the Lord

Now Solomon accomplishes his plan; this description is about half as long as its counterpart in Kings. The Chronicler omits completely 1 Kings 6:4-18; 29-38; and 7:1-12. Curiously, the Chronicler abbreviates descriptions of the temple, its construction and furnishings, even though he puts more emphasis on worship and the temple. Apparently the Chronicler has more interest in what went on in the temple than in its furnishings. Also, many details mentioned in Kings may not have existed in the second, rebuilt temple of the Chronicler's era.

Solomon chooses to locate the temple at the site of David's sacrifice (1 Chr 22:1). The Chronicler also names the site Moriah, the place of Abraham's offering of Isaac (Gen 22:2, 14), so this may be the first witness to an ancient tradition that the temple stands on Mount Moriah, site of Abraham's sacrifice. Thus the Chronicler connects traditions about Abraham and Isaac with those about David's sacrifice and plan for the temple.

cubits, and it was twenty cubits high. He covered its interior with pure gold. ⁵The nave he overlaid with cypress wood and overlaid that with fine gold, embossing on it palms and chains. ⁶He also covered the house with precious stones for splendor; the gold was from Parvaim. ⁷The house, its beams and thresholds, as well as its walls and its doors, he overlaid with gold, and he engraved cherubim upon the walls. ⁸He also made the room of the holy of holies. Its length corresponded to the width of the house, twenty cubits, and its width was also twenty cubits. He overlaid it with fine gold to the amount of six hundred talents. ⁹The weight of the nails was fifty gold shekels. The upper chambers he likewise overlaid with gold.

¹⁰For the room of the holy of holies he made two cherubim of carved workmanship, which were then covered with gold. ¹¹The wings of the cherubim spanned twenty cubits: one wing of each cherub, five cubits in length, extended to a wall of the house, while the other wing, also five cubits in length, touched the corresponding wing of the other cherub. ¹²The wing of the cherub, five cubits, touched the wall of the house, and the other wing, five cubits, was joined to the wing of the other cherub.

¹³The combined wingspread of the two cherubim was thus twenty cubits. They stood upon their own feet, facing toward the nave. ¹⁴He made the veil of violet, purple, crimson, and fine linen, and had cherubim embroidered upon it.

¹⁵In front of the house he set two columns thirty-five cubits high; the capital of each was five cubits. ¹⁶He devised chains in the form of a collar with which he encircled the capitals of the columns, and he made a hundred pomegranates which he set on the chains. ¹⁷He set up the columns to correspond with the nave, one for the right side and the other for the left, and he called the one to the right Jachin and the one to the left Boaz.

4 ¹Then he made a bronze altar twenty cubits long, twenty cubits wide and ten cubits high. ²He also made the molten sea. It was made with a circular rim, and measured ten cubits across, five in height, and thirty in circumference. ³Under the brim a ring of figures of oxen encircled it for ten cubits, all the way around the compass of the sea; there were two rows of oxen cast in one mold with the sea. ⁴This rested on twelve oxen, three facing north, three facing west, three facing south, and three facing east, with their haunches all toward the center; upon

---

3:15–5:1 [cf. 1 Kgs 7:15-51; 2 Kgs 25:17; Jer 52:21-23]
The work in the temple

Many details about the physical construction and appearance of the temple derive from Kings, but much of that is not reproduced here, esp. 1 Kings 7:27-37. The Chronicler describes the two columns, Jachin and Boaz (3:15-17), which are also known from 2 Kings 25:17 and Jeremiah 52:21-22. He then describes the bronze altar (4:1), the molten sea (4:2-5), ten basins (4:6), ten menorahs of gold (4:7), the ten tables (4:8), the courtyards for priests and the great court (4:9), pots, shovels, and bowls (4:11) and then

The scale model of the Temple of Herod in Jerusalem.

them was set the sea. [5]It was a hand-breadth thick, and its brim resembled that of a cup, being lily-shaped. It had a capacity of three thousand baths.

[6]Then he made ten basins for washing, placing five of them to the right and five to the left. In these the victims for the burnt offerings were washed; but the sea was for the priests to wash in.

[7]He made the menorahs of gold, ten of them as was prescribed, and placed them in the nave, five to the right and five to the left. [8]He made ten tables and had them set in the nave, five to the right and five to the left; and he made a hundred golden bowls. [9]He made the court of the priests and the great courtyard and the gates of the courtyard; the gates he covered with bronze. [10]The sea he placed off to the southeast from the south side of the house.

[11]When Huram had made the pots, shovels, and bowls, he finished all his work for King Solomon in the house of God: [12]two columns; two nodes for the capitals on top of the columns; and two pieces of netting covering the two nodes for the capitals on top of the columns; [13]four hundred pomegranates in double rows on both pieces of netting that covered the two nodes of the capitals on top

of the columns. [14]He made the stands, and the basins on the stands; [15]one sea, and the twelve oxen under it; [16]pots, shovels, forks, and all the articles Huram-abi made for King Solomon for the house of the LORD; they were of burnished bronze. [17]The king had them cast in the neighborhood of the Jordan, between Succoth and Zeredah, in thick clay molds. [18]Solomon made all these vessels, so many in number that the weight of the bronze could not be determined.

[19]Solomon made all the articles that were for the house of God: the golden altar, the tables on which the showbread lay, [20]the menorahs and their lamps of pure gold which were to burn as prescribed before the inner sanctuary, [21]flowers, lamps, and gold tongs (this was of purest gold), [22]snuffers, bowls, cups, and firepans of pure gold. As for the entrance to the house, its inner doors to the holy of holies, as well as the doors to the nave of the temple, were of gold.

5 **Dedication of the Temple.** [1]When all the work undertaken by Solomon for the house of the LORD was completed, he brought in the votive offerings of David his father, putting the silver, the gold, and other articles in the treasuries of the house of God. [2]Then

---

describes the placement of all these sacred objects (4:11-16). Then he describes Solomon's work with all these sacred objects (4:17-22) and says that Solomon put them all in the temple treasuries (5:1). The only object here that is not found in Kings is the bronze altar (4:1), though it does appear elsewhere in the source (1 Kgs 8:64; 2 Kgs 16:14).

5:2-14 [cf. 1 Kgs 8:1-11] Solomon brings the ark into the temple

In the seventh month Solomon summons all Israel to bring the ark into the temple (5:2-3). The elders enter along with the Levites, who carry the

Solomon assembled the elders of Israel and all the heads of the tribes, the princes in the ancestral houses of the Israelites, to Jerusalem to bring up the ark of the LORD's covenant from the City of David, which is Zion. ³All the people of Israel assembled before the king during the festival of the seventh month. ⁴When all the elders of Israel had arrived, the Levites took up the ark; ⁵and they brought up the ark and the tent of meeting with all the sacred vessels that were in the tent. The levitical priests brought them up.

⁶King Solomon and the entire community of Israel, gathered for the occasion before the ark, sacrificed sheep and oxen too many to number or count. ⁷The priests brought the ark of the covenant of the LORD to its place: the inner sanctuary of the house, the holy of holies, beneath the wings of the cherubim. ⁸The cherubim had their wings spread out over the place of the ark, covering the ark and its poles from above. ⁹The poles were so long that their ends could be seen from the holy place in front of the inner sanctuary. (They cannot be seen from outside, but they remain there to this day.) ¹⁰There was nothing in the ark but the two tablets which Moses had put there at Horeb when the LORD made a covenant with the Israelites after they went forth from Egypt.

¹¹When the priests left the holy place (all the priests who were present had

ark to the tent, while priests help to carry the sacred vessels and solemnize the ritual with animal sacrifices (5:4-6). In a solemn assembly of all Israel, they carry the ark to its place, "the inner sanctuary of the house, the holy of holies, beneath the wings of the cherubin" (5:7).

Three times during this worship service the Chronicler mentions sacred song: in 5:11-14 (esp. 5:13); in 7:1-3; and in 7:4-6. Song does not appear in the parallel passages in Kings. The Chronicler emphasizes that David established sacred song and he fashioned the musical instruments. It was sung by Levites and priests, and presumably all the people. The Chronicler also notes how huge public sacrifices were accompanied by song with joy, contrary to some scholars who think that Israel's sacrifice was always a silent affair.

A different kind of liturgy occurs in 5:11-14: the priests exit from the shrine and are joined east of the altar by large numbers of Levites singing along with the one hundred and twenty priests making music on trumpets. Then a cloud fills the temple as a sign of divine presence (5:14); smoking incense may have carried this meaning in the Chronicler's community. The Chronicler creates this liturgy of choral song (5:11-14), just like his other two descriptions of sung worship within the temple dedication service. Levites sing "praise to the Lord, who is so good, whose love endures forever" (5:13).

purified themselves regardless of the rotation of their various divisions), [12]the Levites who were singers, all who belonged to Asaph, Heman, Jeduthun, and their sons and brothers, clothed in fine linen, with cymbals, harps, and lyres, stood east of the altar, and with them a hundred and twenty priests blowing trumpets.

[13]When the trumpeters and singers were heard as a single voice praising and giving thanks to the LORD, and when they raised the sound of the trumpets, cymbals, and other musical instruments to "Praise the LORD, who is so good, whose love endures forever," the cloud filled the house of the LORD. [14]The priests could no longer minister because of the cloud, since the glory of the LORD had filled the house of God.

6 [1]Then Solomon said:

"The LORD intends to dwell in the dark cloud;
[2]I have built you a princely house,
the base for your enthronement forever."

[3]The king turned and blessed the whole assembly of Israel, while the whole assembly of Israel stood. [4]He said: "Blessed be the LORD, the God of Israel, who with his own mouth spoke a promise to David my father and by his hand fulfilled it, saying: [5]Since the day I brought my people out of the land of Egypt, I have not chosen a city out of any tribe of Israel for the building of a house, that my name might be there; nor have I

This antiphon is very characteristic of postexilic texts. It already appeared in the psalm of thanksgiving at the worship ceremony in David's era (1 Chr 16:34). In general it praises the Lord's ongoing goodness and steadfastness in language that reminds us of the covenant with Moses. We may imagine a cantor and a choir singing this antiphonally, like Psalm 118, reminding us of the covenant and praising God wholeheartedly in grateful acceptance. The Chronicler redefines the style of worship for this moment by introducing Levites and their choirs as a central element. Finally, the cloud that fills the temple reminds Israel of God's presence (5:14), a symbol drawn from old priestly traditions: Exodus 24:17; 40:34; and Numbers 17:7.

6:1–7:10 [cf. 1 Kgs 8:12-66; Ps 132:1, 8-10; Ps 136:1] Temple dedication

This long, complicated ceremony owes much to the Chronicler's source in Kings, but there are significant changes. Israel's heritage in Egypt is downplayed. When speaking of the ark "of the covenant," the Chronicler fails to mention their ancestors coming out of Egypt as God's covenant partners (as in 1 Kgs 8:21). At the end of this prayer, the Chronicler omits the verse in Kings describing Israel as a people brought out of Egypt and set apart by God, as Moses the prophet had proclaimed (1 Kgs 8:53).

chosen any man to be ruler of my people Israel; ⁶but now I have chosen Jerusalem, that my name may be there, and I have chosen David to rule my people Israel. ⁷When David my father wished to build a house for the name of the LORD, the God of Israel, ⁸the LORD said to him: In wishing to build a house for my name, you did well. ⁹But it is not you who will build the house, but your son, who comes from your loins: he shall build the house for my name.

¹⁰"Now the LORD has fulfilled the word he spoke. I have succeeded David my father, and I sit on the throne of Israel, as the LORD has said, and I have built this house for the name of the LORD, the God of Israel. ¹¹I have placed there the ark, in which is the covenant of the LORD that he made with the Israelites."

Solomon's Prayer. ¹²Then he stood before the altar of the LORD in the presence of the whole assembly of Israel and stretched forth his hands. ¹³Solomon had made a bronze platform five cubits long, five cubits wide, and three cubits high, which he had placed in the middle of the courtyard. Having ascended it, Solomon knelt in the presence of the whole assembly of Israel and stretched forth his hands toward heaven. ¹⁴He said: "LORD, God of Israel, there is no God like you in heaven or on earth; you keep the covenant and love toward your servants who walk before you with their whole heart, ¹⁵the covenant that you kept toward your servant, David my father. That which you promised him, your mouth has spoken and your hand has fulfilled this very day. ¹⁶And now, LORD, God of Israel, keep toward your servant, David my father, what you promised: There shall never be wanting someone from your line to sit before me on the throne of Israel, provided that your descendants keep to their way, walking by my law, as you have. ¹⁷Now, LORD, God of Israel, may the words which you spoke to David your servant be confirmed.

¹⁸"Is God indeed to dwell with human beings on earth? If the heavens and the highest heavens cannot contain you, how much less this house which I have built! ¹⁹Regard kindly the prayer and petition of your servant, LORD, my God, and listen to the cry of supplication

---

Solomon's prayer (6:12-42) is the centerpiece of the service in both Kings and Chronicles, but the Chronicler introduces changes. In 1 Kings the king was simply standing before the altar at prayer (1 Kgs 8:22), but here he was standing on a bronze platform (6:13), possibly the liturgical practice of the Chronicler's era.

Solomon's long prayer (6:13-42) highlights the temple as a house of prayer (as in 1 Kgs 8:22-54), a place for petition to God for God's people Israel, especially when they suffer distress. This prayer petitions God, as do psalms of lament, and it seems to fulfill a task that the Chronicler assigns to Levites, to "invoke" God in petitions. Here Levites also fulfill their role in choral song, and later they give thanks. The prayer refers to seven

which I, your servant, utter before you. [20]May your eyes be open day and night toward this house, the place where you have decreed your name shall be; listen to the prayer your servant makes toward this place. [21]Listen to the petition of your servant and of your people Israel which they offer toward this place. Listen, from the place of your enthronement, heaven, and listen and forgive.

[22]"If someone sins against a neighbor and is required to take an oath sanctioned by a curse, and comes and takes the oath before your altar in this house, [23]listen in heaven: act and judge your servants. Condemn the wicked, requiting their ways; acquit the just, rewarding their justice. [24]When your people Israel are defeated by an enemy because they have sinned against you, and then they turn, praise your name, pray to you, and entreat you in this house, [25]listen from heaven and forgive the sin of your people Israel, and bring them back to the land you gave them and their ancestors. [26]When the heavens are closed so that there is no rain, because they have sinned against you, but they pray toward this place and praise your name, and turn from their sin because you have afflicted them, [27]listen in heaven and forgive the sin of your servants, your people Israel. (For you teach them the good way in which they should walk.) Give rain upon this land of yours which you have given to your people as their heritage.

[28]"If there is famine in the land or pestilence; or if blight comes, or mildew, or locusts swarm, or caterpillars; when their enemies besiege them at any of their gates; whatever plague or sickness there may be; [29]whatever prayer of petition any may make, any of your people Israel, who know affliction and pain and stretch out their hands toward this house, [30]listen from heaven, the place of your enthronement, and forgive. Render to each and all according to their ways, you who know every heart; for it is you alone who know the heart of every human being. [31]So may they revere you and walk in your ways as long as they live on the land you gave our ancestors.

[32]"To the foreigners, likewise, who are not of your people Israel, but who come from a distant land for the sake of your great name, your mighty hand and outstretched arm, and come in prayer to

occasions for the people Israel to approach God, so it is often called a Prayer of the People. The crises that call for such prayer are: improper oaths (6:22-23); defeat in war (6:24-25); drought (6:26-27); famine and pestilence (6:28-31); a foreigner praying to God in the temple (6:32-33); God's people going out to battle (6:34-35); and God's people sinning against God (6:36-39).

In the postexilic context one petition stands out: foreigners (e.g., Gentiles) coming to pray in the temple characterizes the Chronicler but contradicts views of Gentiles in other postexilic books (e.g., Ezra and Nehemiah). The second and sixth occasions for prayer concern Israel at war or battle, praying here in the temple for divine help. After the time of Solomon, the Chronicler will show the effectiveness of such prayer in seven different

this house, ³³listen from heaven, the place of your enthronement. Do all that the foreigner asks of you, that all the peoples of the earth may know your name, may revere you as do your people Israel, and may know that your name has been invoked upon this house that I have built.

³⁴"When your people go out to war against their enemies, by whatever way you send them, and they pray to you toward the city you have chosen and the house I have built for your name, ³⁵listen from heaven to their prayer and petition, and uphold their cause. ³⁶When they sin against you (for there is no one who does not sin), and in your anger against them you deliver them to an enemy, so that their captors carry them off to another land, far or near, ³⁷and they have a change of heart in the land of their captivity and they turn and entreat you in the land of their captors and say, 'We have sinned and done wrong; we have been wicked,' ³⁸if with all their heart and soul they turn back to you in the land of those who took them captive, and pray toward their land which you gave their ancestors, the city you have chosen, and the house which I have built for your name, ³⁹listen from heaven, the place of your enthronement, to their prayer and petitions, and uphold their cause. Forgive your people who have sinned against you. ⁴⁰Now, my God, may your eyes be open and your ears be attentive to the prayer of this place. ⁴¹And now:

"Arise, LORD God, come to your
resting place,
you and your majestic ark.
Your priests, LORD God, will be
clothed with salvation,
your faithful ones rejoice in
good things.
⁴²LORD God, do not reject the plea
of your anointed,
remember the devotion of
David, your servant."

---

situations. Each time God saves Israel (Judah) against their enemies: Egypt (12:1-8); the northern kingdom of Israel (13:13-16); Zerah of Cush (14:11-12); the Aramaeans (18:31-32); Moab and Ammon (20:5-17); Edom (25:7-11); and Assyria (32:20-22). This lesson of history shows proper recourse to God in times of crisis.

The Chronicler continues Solomon's prayer with words drawn from Psalm 132, an ancient psalm for processions with the ark. This psalm glorifies David as he brings the ark to Jerusalem, and it celebrates God's choice of David, of the temple, and of the ark. It suggests that Israel—after the exile, in the Chronicler's era—should return to their ancient style of worship, bringing the ark to the temple and singing Psalm 132. In verse 41 the words "Arise, Lord God" come from an ancient song Israel sang when they carried the ark into battle (Num 10:35). This song's theology envisions God's presence moving into the temple. This is a more priestly theology than that in Kings, which describes the temple as the place where God's name dwells.

7 ¹When Solomon had ended his prayer, fire came down from heaven and consumed the burnt offerings and the sacrifices, and the glory of the LORD filled the house. ²But the priests could not enter the house of the LORD, for the glory of the LORD filled the house of the LORD. ³All the Israelites looked on while the fire came down and the glory of the LORD was upon the house, and they fell down upon the pavement with their faces to the earth and worshiped, praising the LORD, "who is so good, whose love endures forever." ⁴The king and all the people offered sacrifices before the LORD. ⁵King Solomon offered as sacrifice twenty-two thousand oxen, and one hundred twenty thousand sheep.

End of the Dedication. Thus the king and all the people dedicated the house of God. ⁶The priests were standing at their stations, as were the Levites, with the musical instruments of the LORD which King David had made to give thanks to the LORD, "whose love endures forever," when David offered praise through them. The priests opposite them blew the trumpets and all Israel stood.

⁷Then Solomon consecrated the middle of the court facing the house of the LORD; he offered there the burnt offerings and the fat of the communion offerings, since the bronze altar which Solomon had made could not hold the burnt offering, the grain offering, and the fat.

⁸On this occasion Solomon and with him all Israel, a great assembly from Lebo-hamath to the Wadi of Egypt, celebrated the festival for seven days. ⁹On the eighth day they held a solemn assembly, for they had celebrated the dedication of the altar for seven days and the feast for seven days. ¹⁰On the twenty-third day of the seventh month he dismissed the people to their tents, rejoicing

---

The Chronicler changes other words of Psalm 132. Priests should clothe themselves with salvation (i.e., saving, delivering properties) rather than with clothing of righteousness (1 Kgs). This small change suggests a desire for God's decisive military aid in the Chronicler's era. The Chronicler says that God's priests should rejoice in goodness (they sing out in Kings). "Rejoice" is a technical word for festive worship, which the Chronicler recommends. The Chronicler's use of Psalm 132 gives the sense of solemn procession and worship.

In 2 Chronicles 7:1-11, like his source in Kings, the Chronicler describes the consecration of the middle court (7:7), the seven-day festival and consecration of the altar (probably the Feast of Booths/Tabernacles, the harvest festival in autumn), and an additional seven days (7:8-9). They rejoiced because of all the good the Lord did for them. This liturgical celebration leads to great benefit and blessing from God, so the Chronicler shows the proper response of the people: sacrifice and also song, always expressed with great joy.

and glad of heart because of all the blessings the LORD had given to David, to Solomon, and to his people Israel. [11]Solomon finished building the house of the LORD, the house of the king, and everything else he wanted to do in regard to the house of the LORD and his own house.

God's Promise to Solomon. [12]The LORD appeared to Solomon during the night and said to him: I have heard your prayer, and I have chosen this place for my house of sacrifice. [13]If I close heaven so that there is no rain, if I command the locust to devour the land, if I send pestilence among my people, [14]if then my people, upon whom my name has been pronounced, humble themselves and pray, and seek my face and turn from their evil ways, I will hear them from heaven and pardon their sins and heal their land. [15]Now, therefore, my eyes shall be open and my ears attentive to the prayer of this place; [16]now I have chosen and consecrated this house that my name may be there forever; my eyes and my heart shall be there always.

[17]As for you, if you walk before me as David your father did, doing all that I have commanded you and keeping my statutes and ordinances, [18]I will establish the throne of your kingship as I covenanted with David your father when I said, There shall never be wanting someone from your line as ruler in Israel. [19]But if ever you turn away and forsake my commandments and statutes which I set before you, and proceed to serve other gods, and bow down to them, [20]I will uproot the people from the land I gave and repudiate the house I have consecrated for my name. I will make it a proverb and a byword among all nations. [21]And this house which is so exalted—every passerby shall be horrified and ask: "Why has the LORD done such things to this land and to this house?" [22]And the answer will come: "Because they abandoned the LORD, the God of their ancestors, who brought them out of the land of Egypt, and they embraced other gods, bowing down to them and serving them. That is why he has brought upon them all this evil."

7:11-22 [cf. 1 Kgs 9:1-9]
God responds to Solomon's temple dedication

God appears to Solomon during the night after he dedicates the temple (7:12), concluding the dedication liturgy. God has heard the prayer of the temple and confirms the power of Solomon's prayers of petition (6:13-39). God promises Solomon an enduring kingly line if he will walk faithfully according to God's commands, as David his father did (7:17-18). Then God challenges Israel: if you turn aside from me and my commands then I will pluck you up, and the fate of your temple will shock everyone who sees it (7:19-22). Although the Chronicler follows the words of 1 Kings closely, the tone is different after the exile. The Chronicler focuses more on God's promise of blessing than on warnings.

8 **Public Works.** ¹After the twenty years during which Solomon built the house of the LORD and his own house, ²he built up the cities which Huram had given him, and settled Israelites there. ³Then Solomon went to Hamath of Zoba and conquered it. ⁴He built Tadmor in the wilderness and all the supply cities, which he built in Hamath. ⁵He built Upper Beth-horon and Lower Beth-horon, fortified cities with walls, gates, and bars; ⁶also Baalath, all the supply cities belonging to Solomon, and all the cities for the chariots, the cities for horses, and whatever else Solomon desired to build in Jerusalem, in Lebanon, and in the entire land under his dominion. ⁷All the people who were left of the Hittites, Amorites, Perizzites, Hivites, and Jebusites who were not Israelites— ⁸those of their descendants who were left in the land and whom the Israelites had not destroyed—Solomon conscripted as forced laborers, as they are to this day. ⁹But Solomon made none of the Israelites forced laborers for his works, for they were his fighting force, commanders, adjutants, chariot officers, and cavalry. ¹⁰They were also King Solomon's two hundred and fifty overseers who directed the people.

Solomon's Piety. ¹¹Solomon brought the daughter of Pharaoh up from the City of David to the house which he had built for her, for he said, "No wife of mine shall dwell in the house of David, king of Israel, for the places where the ark of the LORD has come are holy."

¹²In those times Solomon sacrificed burnt offerings to the LORD upon the

---

8:1-18 [cf. I Kgs 9:10-28] Solomon's further activities

The Chronicler surveys Solomon's accomplishments on a more political front, i.e., the cities which he captured, controlled, built, and fortified. One telltale change by the Chronicler is the following: in 1 Kings 9:11 Solomon seems to hand over to Hiram (Huram in Chronicles) twenty cities in Galilee, but the Chronicler does not mention Solomon's subservience to Huram, so he suggests that Huram actually gave these twenty cities to Solomon (8:2). Solomon needs "forced labor" for his extravagant building projects, but the Chronicler points out that he enlisted descendants of the land's original inhabitants—Hittites, Amorites, Perizzites, Hivites and Jebusites—for this work, but not native Israelites (8:7-9).

Solomon marries Pharaoh's daughter, but the Chronicler abandons Kings' interpretation of this marriage (as evidence of Solomon's wisdom and wealth). For the Chronicler her presence in the city where the temple now stands presents a problem; his wife cannot reside in the palace because of its sacred precincts (8:11). Some think that these verses suggest Jerusalem is to be a sex-free zone, as the temple scroll from Qumran indicates, but others propose a more likely view: she must reside outside the zone of holiness if she keeps worshiping her ancestral gods.

altar of the LORD which he had built in front of the porch, [13]as was required to be done day by day according to the command of Moses, especially on the sabbaths, at the new moons, and on the fixed festivals three times a year: on the feast of the Unleavened Bread, the feast of Weeks, and the feast of Booths.

[14]And according to the ordinance of David his father he appointed the various divisions of the priests for their service, and the Levites according to their functions of praise and attendance upon the priests, as the daily duty required. The gatekeepers by their divisions stood guard at each gate, since such was the command of David, the man of God. [15]There was no deviation from the king's command in whatever related to the priests and Levites or the treasuries. [16]All of Solomon's work was carried out successfully from the day the foundation of the house of the LORD was laid until its completion. The house of the LORD was finished.

Glories of the Court. [17]In those times Solomon went to Ezion-geber and to Elath on the seashore of the land of Edom. [18]Huram had his servants send him ships and his own servants, expert seamen; they went with Solomon's servants to Ophir, and obtained there four hundred and fifty talents of gold and brought it to King Solomon.

9 The Queen of Sheba. [1]The queen of Sheba, having heard a report of Solomon's fame, came to Jerusalem to test him with subtle questions, accompanied by a very numerous retinue and by camels bearing spices, a large amount of gold, and precious stones. She came to Solomon and spoke to him about everything that she had on her mind. [2]Solomon explained to her everything she asked about, and there was nothing so obscure that Solomon could not explain it to her.

The Chronicler gives more details about Israel's worship practices at the temple (8:12-16). Kings mentions three annual festivals with burnt offerings, peace offerings, and incense offerings (1 Kgs 9:25). Here Solomon arranges the proper sacrificial system (8:12) with its worship calendar: daily offerings, Sabbaths, new moons, and three annual festivals, as Moses commanded (8:13). He also arranges the divisions and work of the priests, Levites, and gatekeepers. Here Solomon finalizes the worship arrangements given by his father David.

9:1-12 [cf. 1 Kgs 10:1-13] Visit of the queen of Sheba

In this popular story she travels a long way to visit Solomon and her goal is to test him with riddles, to see if his wisdom matches his reputation (9:1). His correct answers demonstrate his wisdom, just as the wealth and beneficence of his house and temple give signs of wisdom (9:2-4). She praises his wisdom and acclaims him as king appointed to administer "right and justice" (9:8), further signs of wisdom. She brings magnificent gifts to Solomon, who uses them to furnish both his palace and the temple. Solomon

³When the queen of Sheba witnessed Solomon's great wisdom, the house he had built, ⁴the food at his table, the seating of his ministers, the attendance and dress of his waiters, his cupbearers and their dress, and the burnt offerings he sacrificed in the house of the LORD, it took her breath away. ⁵"The report I heard in my country about your deeds and your wisdom is true," she told the king. ⁶"I did not believe the report until I came and saw with my own eyes that not even the half of your great wisdom had been told me. You have surpassed the report I heard. ⁷Happy your servants, happy these ministers of yours, who stand before you always and listen to your wisdom. ⁸Blessed be the LORD, your God, who was pleased to set you on his throne as king for the LORD, your God. In the love your God has for Israel, to establish them forever, he has made you king over them to carry out judgment and justice." ⁹Then she gave the king one hundred and twenty gold talents, a very large quantity of spices, and precious stones. Never again did anyone bring such an abundance of spices as the queen of Sheba gave to King Solomon.

¹⁰The servants of Huram and of Solomon who brought gold from Ophir also brought cabinet wood and precious stones. ¹¹With the cabinet wood the king made stairs for the house of the LORD and the house of the king, and harps and lyres for the chanters. The like of these had not been seen before in the land of Judah.

¹²King Solomon gave the queen of Sheba everything she desired and asked for, more than she had brought to the king. Then she returned with her servants to her own country.

¹³The gold that came to Solomon in one year weighed six hundred and sixty-six gold talents, ¹⁴in addition to what

---

even uses some of the precious cabinet wood he receives to make lyres and harps for temple singers (9:9-11). In the view that wisdom begets the good life—especially opulence—his wisdom is being recognized. Since wisdom crosses boundaries, it seems fitting that Solomon's wisdom is tested and proclaimed by someone from another country. That this person is a woman and a queen adds to the perennial appeal of the story.

The Chronicler shows how Solomon's greatness was recognized by Gentiles both at the start (ch. 2) and end (ch. 9) of his story. The final sentence (9:12) claims that Solomon gave her all that she desired, more than she brought to him. His largesse is appropriate for a great and wise king.

9:13-28 [cf. 1 Kgs 10:14-29] Wisdom and happiness of Solomon

The opulence of this golden era of Israel's life is a measure of Solomon's wisdom, how he was gifted by God (9:22-23). Solomon's horses and stables and his trade in horses with rulers in Egypt, Aram, and the Hittites (9:25-28) again remind us of his wisdom. Often the horse with chariot is the equivalent of a modern war machine. The Chronicler ends the story of Solomon

came from the tolls on travelers and what the merchants brought. All the kings of Arabia also, and the governors of the country, brought gold and silver to Solomon.

[15]King Solomon made two hundred large shields of beaten gold (six hundred shekels of gold went into each shield) [16]and three hundred bucklers of beaten gold (three hundred shekels of gold went into each buckler); and the king put them in the house of the Forest of Lebanon.

[17]The king made a large ivory throne, and overlaid it with fine gold. [18]The throne had six steps; a footstool of gold was fastened to the throne, and there was an arm on each side of the seat, with two lions standing next to the arms, [19]and twelve other lions standing there on the steps, two to a step. Nothing like this was made in any other kingdom. [20]All King Solomon's drinking vessels were gold, and all the utensils in the house of the Forest of Lebanon were pure gold. There was no silver, for in Solomon's time silver was reckoned as nothing. [21]For the king had ships that went to Tarshish with the servants of Huram. Once every three years the fleet of Tarshish ships would come with a cargo of gold, silver, ivory, apes, and monkeys.

Solomon's Renown. [22]Thus King Solomon surpassed all the kings of the earth in riches and wisdom.

[23]All the kings of the earth sought audience with Solomon, to hear the wisdom God had put into his heart. [24]They all brought their tribute: vessels of silver and gold, garments, weapons, spices, horses, and mules—what was due each year. [25]Solomon had four thousand stalls for horses, chariots, and twelve thousand horses; these he allocated among the chariot cities and to the king's service in Jerusalem. [26]He was ruler over all the kings from the River to the land of the Philistines and down to the border of Egypt. [27]The king made silver as common in Jerusalem as stones, and cedars as numerous as the sycamores of the Shephelah. [28]Solomon's horses were imported from Egypt and from all the lands.

---

just as he began it, with his great wealth and riches (1:1-17). The comment here about his horses recalls 1:14-17; this is a literary repetition and it binds the entire Solomon section together and alerts readers to see what the Chronicler considers to be most important in Solomon's story.

The Chronicler omits from the older story of Solomon (1 Kgs 11:1-40) a description of the sin and errors of Solomon's life, especially all his wives and concubines. In Kings this chapter sets the theological stage for the division of the kingdom after his death; it also contains much historical information about opposition faced by Solomon, both external and internal. All that is absent in Chronicles. Solomon's faults and sins have vanished, and he emerges as the most faultless of the kings of Israel (even more so than David).

The Death of Solomon. ²⁹ The remainder of the acts of Solomon, first and last, are recorded in the acts of Nathan the prophet, in the prophecy of Ahijah the Shilonite, and in the visions of Iddo the seer concerning Jeroboam, son of Nebat. ³⁰Solomon was king in Jerusalem over all Israel for forty years. ³¹Solomon rested with his ancestors and was buried in the City of David, his father, and Rehoboam his son succeeded him as king.

II. The Post-Solomonic Monarchy of Judah

10 **Division of the Kingdom.** ¹Rehoboam went to Shechem, where all Israel had come to make him king. ²When Jeroboam, son of Nebat, heard about it, he was in Egypt where he had fled from King Solomon; and he returned from Egypt. ³They sent for him; Jeroboam and all Israel came and said to Rehoboam: ⁴"Your father put on us a heavy yoke. If you now lighten the harsh servitude and the heavy yoke your father imposed on us, we will be your servants." ⁵He answered them, "Come back to me in three days," and the people went away.

⁶King Rehoboam asked advice of the elders who had been in his father Solomon's service while he was still alive, and asked, "How do you advise me to answer this people?" ⁷They replied, "If you will deal kindly with this people and please them, giving them a favorable reply, they will be your servants forever." ⁸But he ignored the advice the elders had

---

9:29-31 [cf. I Kgs 11:41-43] The death of Solomon

The Chronicler narrates Solomon's death and Rehoboam's succession to the throne with only minor changes to the account in Kings. In verse 29, the Chronicler omits Solomon's wisdom (1 Kgs 11:41) as a topic of discussion. For the Chronicler there were three additional prophetic sources of information to consult for further information: the acts of Nathan the prophet, the prophecy of Ahijah, and the visions of Iddo the seer. Only Nathan and Ahijah are mentioned elsewhere. For the Chronicler, telling history becomes another of the tasks of the prophets.

THE DIVIDED MONARCHY

2 Chronicles 10–28

10:1–11:4 [cf. I Kgs 12:1-24] Israel's revolt

After Solomon's death Rehoboam goes north to Shechem to be made king, so Jeroboam returns home from Egypt to confront Rehoboam. Since the Chronicler skipped 1 Kings 11 with its justifications for rebelliousness against Solomon, he can blame this rebellion on Jeroboam and his followers. Jeroboam and his northern companions ask Rehoboam for lighter treatment than they received from Solomon.

given him and asked advice of the young men who had grown up with him and were in his service. ⁹He said to them, "What answer do you advise us to give this people, who have told me, 'Lighten the yoke your father imposed on us'?" ¹⁰The young men who had grown up with him replied: "This is what you must say to this people who have told you, 'Your father laid a heavy yoke on us; lighten it for us.' You must say, 'My little finger is thicker than my father's loins. ¹¹My father put a heavy yoke on you; I will make it heavier. My father beat you with whips; I will use scorpions!'"

¹²On the third day, Jeroboam and the whole people came back to King Rehoboam as the king had instructed them: "Come back to me in three days." ¹³Ignoring the advice the elders had given him, King Rehoboam gave the people a harsh answer. ¹⁴He spoke to them as the young men had advised: "My father laid a heavy yoke on you; I will make it heavier. My father beat you with whips; I will use scorpions." ¹⁵The king did not listen to the people, for this turn of events was from God: the LORD fulfilled the word he had spoken through Ahijah the Shilonite to Jeroboam, the son of Nebat.

¹⁶ When all Israel saw that the king did not listen to them, the people answered the king:

"What share have we in David?
We have no heritage in the son of Jesse.
Everyone to your tents, Israel!
Now look to your own house, David!"

So all Israel went off to their tents, ¹⁷but the Israelites who lived in the cities of Judah had Rehoboam as their king. ¹⁸King Rehoboam then sent out Hadoram, who was in charge of the forced

---

Rehoboam consults first with his elders. They understand that a kingdom united North and South as under David and Solomon depends on the good will of all parties, but especially on Rehoboam's style of rule. They recommend a kindly approach in negotiations to render the Israelites generous (10:7). But Rehoboam also consults his impetuous younger advisors, who counsel forceful and harsh actions to make the northerners submit (10:10-11), and they insult their northern brothers. Unfortunately, Rehoboam prefers their advice, so he reacts harshly to the northerners and alienates them. Israel's rebellion against the house of David begins here (10:19).

Later, the Chronicler has King Abijah summarize this view of Jeroboam as a rebel (1 Chr 13:6-7). But Rehoboam, indecisive son of Solomon, could not stand up against his young counselors, so the Chronicler also hints that the rebellion was due to Rehoboam's ineptitude. But the Chronicler still follows Kings in explaining Rehoboam's rejection of advice as somehow intended by God (10:15; cf. 1 Kgs 12:15). Thus, the Chronicler remains ambivalent: the rebellion and division were brought about by God, but the willfulness of Jeroboam was responsible for its continuation.

labor, but the Israelites stoned him to death. King Rehoboam, however, managed to mount his chariot and flee to Jerusalem. [19]And so Israel has been in rebellion against the house of David to this day.

11 [1]On his arrival in Jerusalem, Rehoboam assembled the house of Judah and Benjamin—one hundred and eighty thousand elite warriors—to wage war against Israel and restore the kingdom to Rehoboam. [2]However, the word of the LORD came to Shemaiah, a man of God: [3]Say to Rehoboam, son of Solomon, king of Judah, and to all the Israelites in Judah and Benjamin: [4]"Thus says the LORD: You must not go out to war against your kinsmen. Return home, each of you, for it is I who have brought this about." They obeyed the word of the LORD and turned back from going against Jeroboam.

Rehoboam's Works. [5]Rehoboam took up residence in Jerusalem and built fortified cities in Judah. [6]He built up Bethlehem, Etam, Tekoa, [7]Beth-zur, Soco, Adullam, [8]Gath, Mareshah, Ziph, [9]Adoraim, Lachish, Azekah, [10]Zorah, Aijalon, and Hebron; these were fortified cities in Judah and Benjamin. [11]Then he strengthened the fortifications and put commanders in them, along with supplies of food, oil, and wine. [12]In every city were shields and spears, and he made them very strong. Thus Judah and Benjamin remained his.

Refugees from the North. [13]Now the priests and Levites throughout Israel

---

The Chronicler changes the picture in Kings because he cannot admit a hint that Jeroboam's reign was legitimate. The Chronicler omits Kings' statement that all Israel went out to meet Jeroboam when he returned in order to make "him king over all Israel" (1 Kgs 12:20). In Chronicles, "all Israel" is the entire people, though it refers only to the North in Kings. In 11:4 Rehoboam and "all Israel" obey the words of the Lord by deciding not to go against Jeroboam. Now Rehoboam demonstrates a sensitivity to God's word (as in 11:17 and 12:5-6), a change from before.

11:5-23 The prosperity of Rehoboam

The Chronicler here paints a positive portrait of King Rehoboam. His building projects symbolize divine blessing on his reign (11:5-12). These projects demonstrate his prosperity and suggest a sound strategy: cities for defense, fortified with ample supplies of food, oil, wine, and weapons. Religious matters and reforms come up when the Chronicler speaks of Levites who had lived and worked in the northern kingdom of Israel but were prevented by Jeroboam from being priests to the Lord. Many decide to move south after being deprived of office by Jeroboam, who reforms northern religion by appointing his own priests. This detail, not found in Kings, proves quite interesting, since many scholars think that northern

presented themselves to him from all parts of their land, [14]for the Levites left their assigned pasture lands and their holdings and came to Judah and Jerusalem, because Jeroboam and his sons rejected them as priests of the LORD. [15]In their place, he himself appointed priests for the high places as well as for the satyrs and calves he had made. [16]After them, all those, of every tribe of Israel, who set their hearts to seek the LORD, the God of Israel, came to Jerusalem to sacrifice to the LORD, the God of their ancestors. [17]Thus they strengthened the kingdom of Judah and made Rehoboam, son of Solomon, prevail for three years; for they walked in the way of David and Solomon three years.

Rehoboam's Family. [18]Rehoboam married Mahalath, daughter of Jerimoth, son of David and of Abihail, daughter of Eliab, son of Jesse. [19]She bore him sons: Jehush, Shemariah, and Zaham. [20]After her, he married Maacah, daughter of Absalom, who bore him Abijah, Attai, Ziza, and Shelomith. [21]Rehoboam loved Maacah, daughter of Absalom, more than all his other wives and concubines; he had taken eighteen wives and sixty concubines, and he fathered twenty-eight sons and sixty daughters. [22]Rehoboam put Abijah, son of Maacah, first among his brothers, as leader, for he intended to make him king. [23]He acted prudently, distributing his various sons throughout all the districts of Judah and Benjamin, in all the fortified cities; and he gave them generous provisions and sought an abundance of wives for them.

12 Rehoboam's Apostasy. [1]Once Rehoboam had established himself

---

Levites moved south to Judah, bringing with them the Moses traditions which comprise the core of the book of Deuteronomy. The Chronicler describes the spirituality of those who joined Israel in the South. They had "set their hearts to seek the Lord, the God of Israel" (11:16), so they came to Jerusalem to make sacrifices there to God.

Altogether Rehoboam had eighteen wives, sixty concubines, twenty-eight sons, and sixty daughters (11:21). These statistics show God's blessings for Rehoboam. Rehoboam also appoints Ahijah as crown prince (11:22) and then distributes his sons to every region of the country, a very strategic move. This information is unique to Chronicles. Comparing this section with the book of Kings is instructive. The Chronicler omits the long account of Jeroboam in 1 Kings 12:25–14:20, so his account of Rehoboam is unique and seems designed to present a story parallel to Jeroboam in Kings. This king will set a pattern for viewing later kings in Judah.

12:1-16 [cf. 1 Kgs 14:21-31]
Rehoboam's demise as Shishak invades Judah

Then Rehoboam and all Israel forsake God's law (12:1), so the Egyptian King Shishak attacks Jerusalem in his fifth year. Shemaiah the prophet

as king and was firmly in charge, he abandoned the law of the LORD, and so did all Israel with him. ²So in the fifth year of King Rehoboam, Shishak, king of Egypt, attacked Jerusalem, for they had acted treacherously toward the LORD. ³He had twelve hundred chariots and sixty thousand horsemen, and there was no counting the army that came with him from Egypt—Libyans, Sukkites, and Ethiopians. ⁴They captured the fortified cities of Judah and came as far as Jerusalem. ⁵Then Shemaiah the prophet came to Rehoboam and the commanders of Judah who had gathered at Jerusalem because of Shishak, and said to them: "Thus says the LORD: You have abandoned me, and so I have abandoned you to the power of Shishak."

⁶Then the commanders of Israel and the king humbled themselves saying, "The LORD is in the right." ⁷When the LORD saw that they had humbled themselves, the word of the LORD came to Shemaiah: Because they have humbled themselves, I will not destroy them; I will give them some deliverance, and my wrath shall not be poured out upon Jerusalem through Shishak. ⁸But they shall be his servants. Then they will know what it is to serve me and what it is to serve the kingdoms of the earth. ⁹Thereupon Shishak, king of Egypt, attacked Jerusalem and took away the treasures of the house of the LORD and the treasures of the house of the king. He took everything, including the gold shields that Solomon had made. ¹⁰To replace them, King Rehoboam made bronze shields, which he entrusted to the officers of the attendants on duty at the entrance of the king's house. ¹¹Whenever the king visited the house of the LORD, the attendants would carry them, and then return them to the guardroom. ¹²Because he had humbled himself, the anger of the LORD turned from him so as not to destroy him completely; in Judah, moreover, there was some good. ¹³King Rehoboam was firmly in power in Jerusalem and continued to rule. Rehoboam was forty-one years old when he became king, and he reigned seventeen years in Jerusalem, the city in

---

delivers a warning to Israel (12:5-6): since they have abandoned the Lord, so the Lord will abandon them. This kind of speech can be used either to evaluate the past or prepare for the future. Here the prophet warns people to change their future behavior. They humble themselves so that God determines not to destroy them but rather to provide a means of escape, even though they must serve Shishak (12:6-7). Servitude to Shishak is intended to teach Israel the difference between serving others and serving God (12:8). Rehoboam humbles himself by agreeing to hand over significant wealth and taxes to the Egyptians, so God's wrath turns away from total destruction of Judah. But the Chronicler's final assessment of Rehoboam is fairly negative; it concludes with an ominous remark about continuing wars between Rehoboam and Jeroboam.

which, out of all the tribes of Israel, the LORD chose to set his name. His mother's name was Naamah, the Ammonite. ¹⁴He did evil, for he had not set his heart to seek the LORD. ¹⁵ The acts of Rehoboam, first and last, are recorded in the history of Shemaiah the prophet and of Iddo the seer (his family record). There were wars between Rehoboam and Jeroboam all their days. ¹⁶Rehoboam rested with his ancestors; he was buried in the City of David. His son Abijah succeeded him as king.

13 War Between Abijah and Jeroboam. ¹In the eighteenth year of King Jeroboam, Abijah became king of Judah; ²he reigned three years in Jerusalem. His mother was named Micaiah, daughter of Uriel of Gibeah. There was war between Abijah and Jeroboam.

³Abijah joined battle with a force of four hundred thousand picked warriors, while Jeroboam lined up against him in battle with eight hundred thousand picked and valiant warriors. ⁴Abijah stood on Mount Zemaraim, which is in the highlands of Ephraim, and said: "Listen to me, Jeroboam and all Israel! ⁵Do you not know that the LORD, the God of Israel, has given David kingship over Israel forever, to him and to his sons, by a covenant of salt? ⁶Yet Jeroboam, son of Nebat, the servant of Solomon, son of David, arose and rebelled against his lord! ⁷Worthless men, scoundrels, joined him and overcame Rehoboam, son of Solomon, when Rehoboam was young and inexperienced, and no match for them. ⁸But now, do you think you are a match for the kingdom of the LORD led by the descendants of David, simply because you are a huge multitude and have with you the golden calves which Jeroboam made you for

13:1-23 [cf. I Kgs 15:1-8] The reign of Abijah (Abijam)

The Chronicler expands the eight verses in Kings to twenty-three verses for this three-year reign, but also omits the negative conclusion in 1 Kings 15:3-5. The Chronicler's fairly positive account focuses on a battle with Jeroboam not included in Kings. Although greatly outnumbered, Abijah stands on a mountain slope in southern Israel (Ephraim) and delivers a long theological speech to his opponents, Jeroboam and Israel (13:4-12). His speech develops these points. God established a covenant with King David, but Jeroboam opposed him, and worthless young men surrounded Rehoboam, who was too young and inexperienced to stand up to them. He challenges the northerners: you cannot oppose David, God's choice. You banished the priests of the House of Aaron and the Levites and set up your own priesthood. Remember that we are faithful, that our priests and Levites continue to perform their duties—burnt offerings morning and evening, spicy incense, the rows of bread, and the lamp they light each evening (13:10-11). God is with us Judeans, so you Israelites should not fight us, or the Lord. You will not succeed!

gods? ⁹Have you not expelled the priests of the LORD, the sons of Aaron, and the Levites, and made for yourselves priests like the peoples of other lands? Everyone who comes to consecrate himself with a young bull and seven rams becomes a priest of no-gods. ¹⁰But as for us, the LORD is our God, and we have not abandoned him. The priests ministering to the LORD are sons of Aaron, and the Levites also have their offices. ¹¹They sacrifice burnt offerings to the LORD and fragrant incense morning after morning and evening after evening; they set out the showbread on the pure table, and the lamps of the golden menorah burn evening after evening; for we observe our duties to the LORD, our God, but you have abandoned him. ¹²See, God is with us, at our head, and his priests are here with trumpets to sound the attack against you. Israelites, do not fight against the LORD, the God of your ancestors, for you will not succeed!"

¹³But Jeroboam had an ambush go around them to come at them from the rear; so that while his army faced Judah, his ambush lay behind them. ¹⁴When Judah turned and saw that they had to battle on both fronts, they cried out to the LORD and the priests sounded the trumpets. ¹⁵Then the Judahites shouted; and when they shouted, God struck down Jeroboam and all Israel before Abijah and Judah. ¹⁶The Israelites fled before Judah, and God delivered them into their power. ¹⁷Abijah and his people inflicted a severe defeat upon them; five hundred thousand picked men of Israel fell slain. ¹⁸The Israelites were humbled on that occasion, while the Judahites were victorious because they relied on the LORD, the God of their ancestors. ¹⁹Abijah pursued Jeroboam and seized cities from him: Bethel and its dependencies, Jeshanah and its dependencies, and Ephron and its dependencies. ²⁰Jeroboam did not regain power during Abijah's time; the LORD struck him down and he died, ²¹while Abijah continued to grow stronger. He married fourteen wives and fathered twenty-two sons and sixteen daughters.

Death of Abijah. ²²The rest of the acts of Abijah, his deeds and his words, are recorded in the midrash of the prophet Iddo. ²³Abijah rested with his ancestors; they buried him in the City of David and his son Asa succeeded him as king. During his time, the land had ten years of peace.

This speech does not persuade Jeroboam, so he sets out for battle and surrounds the southerners. But the Judahites cry out to God while the priests blow their horns (13:14). As is normal for those who cry out to God, the Lord responds: Jeroboam and his men are routed, the northerners flee and many thousands are killed. Theologically speaking, the Israelites are humbled, while the Judahites prevail because they rely on the God of their ancestors (13:18). Abijah's fortunes include fourteen wives, twenty-two sons, and sixteen daughters, signals of a blessed life. The witness to his success is evident.

14

Asa's Initial Reforms. ¹Asa did what was good and right in the sight of the LORD, his God. ²He removed the illicit altars and the high places, smashed the sacred pillars, and cut down the asherahs. ³He told Judah to seek the LORD, the God of their ancestors, and to observe the law and the commandment. ⁴He removed the high places and incense stands from all the cities of Judah, and under him the kingdom had peace. ⁵He built fortified cities in Judah, for the land had peace and no war was waged against him during these years, because the LORD had given him rest. ⁶He said to Judah: "Let us build these cities and surround them with walls, towers, gates and bars. The land is still ours, for we have sought the LORD, our God; we sought him, and he has given us rest on every side." So they built and prospered.

The Ethiopian Invasion. ⁷Asa had an army of three hundred thousand shield- and lance-bearers from Judah, and from Benjamin two hundred and eighty thousand who carried bucklers and were archers, all of them valiant warriors. ⁸Zerah the Ethiopian advanced against them with a force of one million men and three hundred chariots, and he came as far as Mareshah. ⁹Asa went out to meet him and they drew up for battle in the valley of Zephathah, near Mareshah. ¹⁰Asa called upon the LORD, his God: "LORD, there is none like you to help the powerless against the strong. Help us, LORD, our God, for we rely on you, and in your name we have come against this multitude. You are the LORD, our God; do not let men prevail against you." ¹¹And so the LORD defeated the Ethiopians before Asa and Judah, and the Ethiopians fled. ¹²Asa and those with him pursued them as far as Gerar, and the Ethiopians fell until there were no survivors, for they were crushed before the LORD and his army, which carried away enormous spoils. ¹³Then the Judahites conquered all the cities around Gerar, for the fear of the LORD was upon them; they plundered all the cities, for there was much plunder in them. ¹⁴They also attacked the tents of the cattle-herders and carried off a great number of sheep

---

14:1–17:1 [cf. 1 Kgs 15:9-24] The reign of Asa

Asa begins well, calling Judah to seek the Lord, so they prosper. When King Zerah and the Cushites (Ethiopians) attack Judah, Asa cries to the Lord. He professes reliance on God, so they defeat the Ethiopians and other peoples around Gerar. Still Azariah son of Oded receives "the spirit of God" (15:1) and he urges Asa in a type of sermon to seek God (15:2-7). The message is: God is found by those who seek him. Therefore, do not weaken, do not give up, but seek God and persevere. Asa responds by reforming worship in Jerusalem and gathering the people of Judah, Benjamin, and sojourners from the North to celebrate Weeks/Shabuot (15:8-15). Three times the Chronicler says the people sought God (15:12, 13, 15). Here is the key to his auspicious beginning: no war (with Israel) for his first thirty-five years (15:19).

and camels. Then they returned to Jerusalem.

15 **Further Reforms.** [1]The spirit of God came upon Azariah, son of Oded. [2]He went forth to meet Asa and said to him: "Hear me, Asa and all Judah and Benjamin! The LORD is with you when you are with him, and if you seek him he will be found; but if you abandon him, he will abandon you. [3]For a long time Israel was without a true God, without a priest-teacher, without instruction, [4]but when in their distress they turned to the LORD, the God of Israel, and sought him, he was found by them. [5]At that time there was no peace for anyone to go or come; rather, there were many terrors upon the inhabitants of the lands. [6]Nation crushed nation and city crushed city, for God overwhelmed them with every kind of distress. [7]But as for you, be strong and do not slack off, for there shall be a reward for what you do."

[8]When Asa heard these words and the prophecy (Oded the prophet), he was encouraged to remove the detestable idols from the whole land of Judah and Benjamin and from the cities he had taken in the highlands of Ephraim, and to restore the altar of the LORD which was before the vestibule of the LORD. [9]Then he gathered all Judah and Benjamin, together with those of Ephraim, Manasseh, and Simeon who were resident with them; for many had defected to him from Israel when they saw that the LORD, his God, was with him. [10]They gathered at Jerusalem in the third month of the fifteenth year of Asa's reign, [11]and sacrificed to the LORD on that day seven hundred oxen and seven thousand sheep from the spoils they had brought. [12]They entered into a covenant to seek the LORD, the God of their ancestors, with all their heart and soul; [13]and everyone who would not seek the LORD, the God of Israel, was to be put to death, from least to greatest, man or woman. [14]They swore an oath to the LORD with a loud voice, with shouting and with trumpets and horns. [15]All Judah rejoiced over the oath, for they had sworn it with their whole heart and sought him with complete desire. The LORD was found by them, and gave them rest on every side.

[16]He also deposed Maacah, the mother of King Asa, from her position as queen mother because she had made an obscene object for Asherah; Asa cut

In his latter years, Asa responds poorly to the menacing of Baasha, King of Israel (16:1-10). Asa seeks an alliance with the king of Aram instead of renewing the covenant with God; this leads to initial success (16:2-6). Then Hanani the seer excoriates Asa for relying on Ben-hadad rather than on God, reminding him that he overcame the Ethiopians by relying on God (16:7-9). Asa is angered and imprisons the seer and oppresses many others. When he contracts a serious foot disease, he seeks the help of physicians rather than God (16:12). Asa had sought and trusted God in his earlier years, but he changes in his later years. This turn of events challenges the audience to persevere in seeking God.

down this object, smashed it, and burnt it in the Wadi Kidron. ¹⁷The high places did not disappear from Israel, yet Asa's heart was undivided as long as he lived. ¹⁸He brought into the house of God his father's and his own votive offerings: silver, gold, and vessels. ¹⁹There was no war until the thirty-fifth year of Asa's reign.

16 **Asa's Infidelity.** ¹In the thirty-sixth year of Asa's reign, Baasha, king of Israel, attacked Judah and fortified Ramah to block all movement for Asa, king of Judah. ²Asa then brought out silver and gold from the treasuries of the house of the LORD and the house of the king and sent them to Ben-hadad, king of Aram, who ruled in Damascus. He said: ³"There is a treaty between you and me, as there was between your father and my father. I am sending you silver and gold. Go, break your treaty with Baasha, king of Israel, that he may withdraw from me." ⁴Ben-hadad agreed with King Asa and sent the leaders of his troops against the cities of Israel. They attacked Ijon, Dan, Abel-maim, besides all the store cities of Naphtali. ⁵When Baasha heard of it, he left off fortifying Ramah, putting an end to his work. ⁶Then King Asa commandeered all Judah and they carried away the stones and beams with which Baasha was fortifying Ramah. With them he fortified Geba and Mizpah.

⁷At that time Hanani the seer came to Asa, king of Judah, and said to him: "Because you relied on the king of Aram and did not rely on the LORD, your God, the army of the king of Aram has escaped your power. ⁸Were not the Ethiopians and Libyans a vast army, with great numbers of chariots and horses? And yet, because you relied on the LORD, he delivered them into your power. ⁹The eyes of the LORD roam over the whole earth, to encourage those who are devoted to him wholeheartedly. You have acted foolishly in this matter, for from now on you will have wars." ¹⁰But Asa became angry with the seer and imprisoned him in the stocks, so greatly was he enraged at him over this. Asa also oppressed some of his people at this time.

¹¹Now the acts of Asa, first and last, are recorded in the book of the kings of Judah and Israel. ¹²In the thirty-ninth year of his reign, Asa contracted disease in his feet; it became worse, but even with this disease he did not seek the LORD, only physicians. ¹³Asa rested with his ancestors; he died in the forty-first year of his reign. ¹⁴They buried him in the tomb he had hewn for himself in the City of David, after laying him on a couch that was filled with spices and various kinds of aromatics compounded into an ointment; and they kindled a huge fire for him.

The Chronicler moves on to the reign of King Jehoshaphat, passing over without mention several kings of Israel (Nadab, Baasha, Elah, Zimri, Omri, Ahab), plus Elijah and Elisha the prophets (1 Kgs 15:25–21:29). The Chronicler normally omits the history of northern kings, all of whom were evaluated very negatively in the book of Kings.

17 **Jehoshaphat's Zeal for the Law.** [1]His son Jehoshaphat succeeded him as king and strengthened his position against Israel. [2]He placed armed forces in all the fortified cities of Judah, and set garrisons in the land of Judah and in the cities of Ephraim which Asa his father had taken. [3]The LORD was with Jehoshaphat, for he walked in the earlier ways of David his father, and did not seek the Baals. [4]Rather, he sought the God of his father and walked in his commands, and not the practices of Israel. [5]Through him, the LORD made the kingdom secure, and all Judah gave Jehoshaphat gifts, so that great wealth and glory was his. [6]Thus he was encouraged to follow the LORD's ways, and once again he removed the high places and the asherahs from Judah.

[7]In the third year of his reign he sent his officials, Ben-hail, Obadiah, Zechariah, Nethanel, and Micaiah, to teach in the cities of Judah. [8]With them he sent the Levites Shemaiah, Nethaniah, Zebadiah, Asahel, Shemiramoth, Jehonathan, Adonijah, and Tobijah, together with Elishama and Jehoram the priests. [9]They taught in Judah, having with them the book of the law of the LORD; they traveled through all the cities of Judah and taught among the people.

His Power. [10]Now the fear of the LORD was upon all the kingdoms of the countries surrounding Judah, so that they did not war against Jehoshaphat. [11]Some of the Philistines brought Jehoshaphat gifts and a tribute of silver; the Arabians also brought him a flock of seven thousand seven hundred rams and seven thousand seven hundred he-goats.

[12]Jehoshaphat grew ever greater. He built strongholds and store cities in Judah. [13]He carried out many works in the cities of Judah, and he had soldiers, valiant warriors, in Jerusalem. [14]This was their mustering according to their ancestral houses. From Judah, the commanders of thousands: Adnah the commander, and with him three hundred thousand valiant warriors. [15]Next to him, Jehohanan the commander, and with him

---

17:2–21:1 [cf. I Kgs 22:1-51] The reign of Jehoshaphat

The Chronicler expands Jehoshaphat's story from one chapter in Kings to four chapters in Chronicles. Chapter 17 has no parallel in Kings. Jehoshaphat begins positively: he does not seek the Baals but the God of his fathers, and he avoids the practices of Israel. The result is predictable: Jehoshaphat's reign is firmly established and he receives tribute and wealth (17:5). As proof of his piety (17:6), he sends officials and Levites throughout Judah to teach the Torah, so the people can live according to God's law (17:7-9). The Chronicler lists this king's projects, his success in international relations, and the numerical strength of his warrior allies (17:10-19). This data sets the stage for his alliance with Ahab in chapter 18 and it raises an intriguing question: why does a king so devoted to the Lord align himself with Ahab through a marriage alliance (18:1)?

two hundred eighty thousand. ¹⁶Next to him, Amasiah, son of Zichri, who offered himself to the LORD, and with him two hundred thousand valiant warriors. ¹⁷From Benjamin: Eliada, a valiant warrior, and with him two hundred thousand armed with bow and buckler. ¹⁸Next to him, Jehozabad, and with him one hundred and eighty thousand equipped for war. ¹⁹These attended the king; in addition to those whom the king had stationed in the fortified cities throughout all Judah.

18 Alliance with Israel. ¹Jehoshaphat therefore had wealth and glory in abundance; but he became related to Ahab by marriage. ²After some years he went down to Ahab at Samaria; Ahab slaughtered numerous sheep and oxen for him and for the people with him, and incited him to go up against Ramoth-gilead. ³Ahab, king of Israel, asked Jehoshaphat, king of Judah, "Will you come with me to Ramoth-gilead?" He answered, "You and I are as one, and your people and my people as well. We will be with you in the battle." ⁴Jehoshaphat also said to the king of Israel, "Seek the word of the LORD at once."

Prophets in Conflict. ⁵The king of Israel assembled the prophets, four hundred of them, and asked, "Shall we go to fight against Ramoth-gilead, or shall I refrain?" They said, "Attack. God will give it into the power of the king." ⁶But Jehoshaphat said, "Is there no other prophet of the LORD here we might consult?" ⁷The king of Israel answered, "There is one other man through whom we may consult the LORD; but I hate him, because he prophesies not good but always evil about me. He is Micaiah, son of Imlah." Jeshoshaphat said, "Let not the king say that." ⁸So the king of Israel called an official, and said to him, "Get Micaiah, son of Imlah, at once." ⁹The king of Israel and Jehoshaphat, king of Judah, were seated, each on his throne, clothed in their robes of state in the square at the entrance of the gate of Samaria, and all the prophets were prophesying before them.

¹⁰Zedekiah, son of Chenaanah, made himself two horns of iron and said: "The LORD says: With these you shall gore Aram until you have destroyed them." ¹¹The other prophets prophesied in the same vein, saying: "Attack Ramoth-gilead, and conquer! The LORD will give it into the power of the king." ¹²Meanwhile the messenger who had gone to call Micaiah said to him: "Look now, the words of the prophets are as one in speaking good for the king. Let your word be at one with theirs; speak a good word." ¹³Micaiah said, "As the LORD

In chapter 18 Jehoshaphat and Ahab of Israel conspire to battle against Aram. Seeking God's word (18:4) will be tricky, especially since Ahab hates his own prophet by whom he has sought God's word; Micaiah ben Imlah has spoken words that displease Ahab (18:7). Asked about Ahab's proposal to go to battle at Ramoth-gilead, Micaiah describes a terrifying image: Israel will be scattered on the mountains, with no shepherd to guide or guard them, so that all the sheep return home alone (18:16). In the ancient near

lives, I shall speak whatever my God says."

¹⁴When he came to the king, the king said to him, "Micah, shall we go to fight at Ramoth-gilead, or shall I refrain?" He said, "Attack and conquer! They will be delivered into your power." ¹⁵But the king answered him, "How many times must I adjure you to tell me nothing but the truth in the name of the LORD?" ¹⁶So Micaiah said:

"I see all Israel
scattered on the mountains,
like sheep without a shepherd,
And the LORD saying,
These have no masters!
Let each of them go back home
in peace."

¹⁷The king of Israel said to Jehoshaphat, "Did I not tell you, he does not prophesy good about me, but only evil?" ¹⁸Micaiah continued: "Therefore hear the word of the LORD. I saw the LORD seated on his throne, with the whole host of heaven standing to his right and to his left. ¹⁹The LORD asked: Who will deceive Ahab, king of Israel, so that he will go up and fall on Ramoth-gilead? And one said this, another that, ²⁰until this spirit came forth and stood before the LORD, saying, 'I will deceive him.' The LORD asked: How? ²¹He answered, 'I will go forth and become a lying spirit in the mouths of all his prophets.' The LORD replied: You

shall succeed in deceiving him. Go forth and do this. ²²So now the LORD has put a lying spirit in the mouths of these prophets of yours; but the LORD himself has decreed evil against you."

²³Thereupon Zedekiah, son of Chenaanah, came up and struck Micaiah on the cheek, saying, "Has the spirit of the LORD, then, passed from me to speak with you?" ²⁴Micaiah said, "You shall find out on the day you go into an innermost room to hide." ²⁵The king of Israel then said: "Seize Micaiah and take him back to Amon, prefect of the city, and to Joash the king's son, ²⁶and say, 'This is the king's order: Put this man in prison and feed him scanty rations of bread and water until I come back in safety!'" ²⁷But Micaiah said, "If ever you return in safety, the LORD has not spoken through me." (He also said, "Hear, O peoples, all of you!")

Ahab's Death. ²⁸The king of Israel and Jehoshaphat, king of Judah, went up to Ramoth-gilead, ²⁹and the king of Israel said to Jehoshaphat, "I will disguise myself and go into battle. But you, put on your own robes." So the king of Israel disguised himself and they entered the battle. ³⁰In the meantime, the king of Aram had given his chariot commanders the order, "Fight with no one, great or small, except the king of Israel alone." ³¹When the chariot commanders

---

East the shepherds symbolize kings, so Micaiah effectively says that Israel will be without its king, i.e., that Ahab will die in battle. Ahab disregards this unpleasant word, goes to battle, and dies of combat wounds. But Jehoshaphat cries out, so God helps him by luring away his attackers. Once again, crying out to God brings success. The Chronicler's message is: trust more in God than in human means, including political alliances.

100

saw Jehoshaphat, they thought, "There is the king of Israel!" and wheeled to fight him. But Jehoshaphat cried out and the LORD helped him; God induced them to leave him alone. ³²The chariot commanders, seeing that he was not the king of Israel, turned away from him. ³³But someone drew his bow at random and hit the king of Israel between the joints of his breastplate. He ordered his charioteer, "Rein about and take me out of the ranks, for I am wounded." ³⁴The battle grew fierce during the day, and the king of Israel braced himself up in his chariot facing the Arameans until evening. He died as the sun was setting.

19 Jehoshaphat Rebuked. ¹Jehoshaphat king of Judah returned in safety to his house in Jerusalem. ²Jehu the seer, son of Hanani, went out to meet King Jehoshaphat and said to him: "Should you help the wicked and love those who hate the LORD? For this reason, wrath is upon you from the LORD. ³Yet some good has been found in you, since you have removed the asherahs from the land and have set your heart to seek God."

Judges Appointed. ⁴Jehoshaphat dwelt in Jerusalem; but he went out again among the people from Beer-sheba to the highlands of Ephraim and brought them back to the LORD, the God of their ancestors. ⁵He appointed judges in the land, in all the fortified cities of Judah, city by city, ⁶and he said to them: "Take care what you do, for the judgment you give is not human but divine; for when it comes to judgment God will be with you. ⁷And now, let the fear of the LORD be upon you. Act carefully, for with the LORD, our God, there is no injustice, no partiality, no bribe-taking." ⁸In Jerusalem also, Jehoshaphat appointed some Levites and priests and some of the family heads of Israel for the LORD's judgment and the disputes of those who dwell in Jerusalem. ⁹He gave them this command: "Thus you shall act: in the fear of the LORD, with fidelity and with an undivided heart. ¹⁰And in every dispute that comes to you from your kin living in their cities, whether it concerns bloodguilt or questions of law, command, statutes, or ordinances, warn them lest they incur guilt before the LORD and his wrath come upon you and your kin. Do that and you shall not incur guilt. ¹¹See now, Amariah is chief priest over you for everything that pertains to the LORD, and Zebadiah, son of Ishmael, is leader of the house of Judah in all that pertains to the king; and the Levites will be your officials. Take firm action, and the LORD will be with the good."

Chapters 19–20 contain more events not included in Kings. A prophet named Jehu, son of Hanani, rebukes Jehoshaphat for aligning with Ahab, one who hates God (19:1-2). Still, Jehoshaphat dedicates his heart to seek God (19:3), with happy results. He reforms Israel's judicial system by appointing judges dedicated to ancient notions of justice (parallels from Deut 1:16-17; 10:17; and 16:18-20). The most important guide for justice, however, is the divine model: "with the Lord, our God, there is no injustice, no partiality, no bribe-taking" (19:7).

20 **Invasion from Edom.** ¹After this the Moabites, the Ammonites, and with them some Meunites came to fight against Jehoshaphat. ²Jehoshaphat was told: "A great multitude is coming against you from across the sea, from Edom; they are already in Hazazon-tamar" (which is En-gedi). ³Frightened, Jehoshaphat resolved to consult the LORD. He proclaimed a fast throughout all Judah. ⁴Then Judah gathered to seek the LORD's help; from every one of the cities of Judah they came to seek the LORD.

Jehoshaphat's Prayer. ⁵Jehoshaphat stood up in the assembly of Judah and Jerusalem in the house of the LORD before the new court, ⁶and he said: "LORD, God of our ancestors, are you not God in heaven, and do you not rule over all the kingdoms of the nations? In your hand is power and might, and no one can withstand you. ⁷Was it not you, our God, who dispossessed the inhabitants of this land before your people Israel and gave it forever to the descendants of Abraham, your friend? ⁸They have dwelt in it and they built in it a sanctuary for your name. They have said: ⁹'If evil comes upon us, the sword of judgment, or pestilence, or famine, we will stand before this house and before you, for your name is in this house, and we will cry out to you in our affliction, and you will hear and save!' ¹⁰And now, see the Ammonites, Moabites, and those of Mount Seir whom you did not allow Israel to invade when they came from the land of Egypt, but instead they passed them by and did not destroy them: ¹¹See how they are now repaying us by coming to drive us out of the possession you have given us. ¹²O our God, will you not bring judgment on them? We are powerless before this vast multitude that is coming against us. We ourselves do not know what to do, so our eyes are turned toward you."

Victory Prophesied. ¹³All Judah was standing before the LORD, with their little ones, their wives, and their children. ¹⁴And the spirit of the LORD came upon Jahaziel, son of Zechariah, son of Benaiah, son of Jeiel, son of Mattaniah, a Levite of the clan of Asaph, in the midst of the assembly, ¹⁵and he said: "Pay attention, all of Judah, inhabitants of Jerusalem, and King Jehoshaphat!

The Chronicler now relates in chapter 20 a victory in battle over the Ammonites and Moabites, a story not known from Kings. When enemies advance from the East, Jehoshaphat's fear leads him to "consult the Lord" (20:3), the proper religious approach for the Chronicler. This going to God forms part of a larger service of worship, a communal fast and lament service (20:5-12), which leads to God's clear protection of the people. This story shows how postexilic Israel could address God in time of crisis with prayer in the form of communal laments (which address God, complain of their sufferings, petition God to intervene). A similar event is found in a communal fast alluded to in Joel 1–2, when they are facing a natural disaster (probably a plague of locusts).

The LORD says to you: Do not fear or be dismayed at the sight of this vast multitude, for the battle is not yours but God's. ¹⁶Go down against them tomorrow. You will see them coming up by the ascent of Ziz, and you will come upon them at the end of the wadi which opens on the wilderness of Jeruel. ¹⁷You will not have to fight in this encounter. Take your places, stand firm, and see the salvation of the LORD; he will be with you, Judah and Jerusalem. Do not fear or be dismayed. Tomorrow go out to meet them, and the LORD will be with you." ¹⁸Then Jehoshaphat knelt down with his face to the ground, and all Judah and the inhabitants of Jerusalem fell down before the LORD in worship. ¹⁹Levites from among the Kohathites and Korahites stood up to sing the praises of the LORD, the God of Israel, their voices ever louder.

The Invaders Destroyed. ²⁰Early in the morning they went out to the wilderness of Tekoa. As they were going out, Jehoshaphat halted and said: "Listen to me, Judah and inhabitants of Jerusalem!

Let your faith in the LORD, your God, be firm, and you will be firm. Have faith in his prophets and you will succeed." ²¹After taking counsel with the people, he appointed some to sing to the LORD and some to praise the holy Splendor as it went forth at the head of the army. They sang: "Give thanks to the LORD, whose love endures forever." ²²At the moment they began their jubilant praise, the LORD laid an ambush against the Ammonites, Moabites, and those of Mount Seir who were coming against Judah, so that they were defeated. ²³For the Ammonites and Moabites set upon the inhabitants of Mount Seir and exterminated them according to the ban. And when they had finished with the inhabitants of Seir, each helped to destroy the other.

²⁴When Judah came to the watchtower of the wilderness and looked toward the throng, there were only corpses fallen on the ground, with no survivors. ²⁵Jehoshaphat and his people came to gather the spoils, and they found an abundance of cattle and

Then a prophetic figure stands up—the Levite Jahaziel (20:14)—and proclaims God's response to the king's outcry; they should not fear, for God will be with them (20:17). Responding to this promise of victory, the king and people of Jerusalem bow down and worship the Lord (20:17-18). Then Levites arise to praise God with a very loud voice, which they are appointed to do, but here it seems premature, for the victory is still in the future. Jehoshaphat then rises and delivers a speech that sounds like a sermon. Believe God and you will be set firm (20:20); here the Chronicler adapts an old prophetic saying: "Unless your faith is firm / you shall not be firm!" (Isa 7:9). The Chronicler gives a theological commentary on this event: Jehoshaphat faces a test of faith, just as Ahaz faced a test of faith when Isaiah uttered the word to him.

personal property, garments and precious vessels. They took so much that they were unable to carry it all; it took them three days to gather the spoils, there was so much of it. ²⁶On the fourth day they held an assembly in the Valley of Berakah—for there they blessed the LORD; that is why the place is called the Valley of Berakah to this day. ²⁷Then all the men of Judah and Jerusalem, with Jehoshaphat at their head, returned to Jerusalem with joy; for the LORD had given them joy over their enemies. ²⁸They came to Jerusalem, with harps, lyres, and trumpets, to the house of the LORD. ²⁹And the fear of God came upon all the kingdoms of the surrounding lands when they heard how the LORD had fought against the enemies of Israel. ³⁰Thereafter Jehoshaphat's kingdom had peace, for his God gave him rest on every side.

Jehoshaphat's Other Deeds. ³¹Thus Jehoshaphat reigned over Judah. He was thirty-five years old when he became king, and he reigned twenty-five years in Jerusalem. His mother's name was Azubah, daughter of Shilhi. ³²He walked in the way of Asa his father unceasingly, doing what was right in the LORD's sight. ³³Nevertheless, the high places did not disappear and the people had not yet set their hearts on the God of their ancestors.

³⁴The rest of the acts of Jehoshaphat, first and last, are recorded in the chronicle of Jehu, son of Hanani, which was incorporated into the book of the kings of Israel. ³⁵After this, Jehoshaphat king of Judah joined with Ahaziah king of Israel—he acted wickedly. ³⁶He joined with him in building ships to go to Tarshish; the fleet was built at Ezion-geber. ³⁷But Eliezer, son of Dodavahu from Mareshah, prophesied against Jehoshaphat. He said: "Because you have joined with Ahaziah, the LORD will shatter your work." And the ships were wrecked and were unable to sail to Tarshish.

Again the Chronicler views Levites as prophetic speakers. God's spirit came on Jahaziel the Levite in the assembly (20:14) and he publicly utters a salvation oracle in response to the king's lament prayer (20:14-17). This Levite's concern seems more spiritual than tactical; Judah and its leader are to conduct themselves in utter humility and confidence in God, whose deliverance can be expected. The Chronicler seems to address the spiritual yearnings and laments of his own day (Persian-era Judeans). They can realize that God is about to work a new saving action in their day, in the tradition of God's earlier saving acts for Israel.

Jehoshaphat did not always seek God, but he followed the ways of his father Asa, who ended badly (20:35-37). This shift toward unfaithfulness stands as a powerful reminder to the Chronicler's audience: persevere in seeking God. Chapters 21–28 are filled with Judean kings who fail because of disobedience, who do not seek God.

21 ¹Jehoshaphat rested with his ancestors; he was buried with them in the City of David. Jehoram, his son, succeeded him as king. ²He had brothers, Jehoshaphat's sons: Azariah, Jehiel, Zechariah, Azariah, Michael, and Shephatiah; all these were sons of King Jehoshaphat of Judah. ³Their father gave them many gifts of silver, gold, and precious objects, together with fortified cities in Judah, but the kingship he gave to Jehoram because he was the firstborn.

Jehoram's Evil Deeds. ⁴When Jehoram had acceded to his father's kingdom and was firmly in power, he killed all his brothers with the sword, and also some of the princes of Israel. ⁵Jehoram was thirty-two years old when he became king, and he reigned eight years in Jerusalem. ⁶He walked in the way of the kings of Israel as the house of Ahab had done, since the daughter of Ahab was his wife; and he did what was evil in the LORD's sight. ⁷Even so, the LORD was unwilling to destroy the house of David because of the covenant he had made with David and because of his promise to leave him and his sons a holding for all time.

⁸During his time Edom revolted against the rule of Judah and installed its own king. ⁹Thereupon Jehoram with his officers and all his chariots crossed over. He arose by night and broke through the Edomites when they had surrounded him and the commanders of his chariots. ¹⁰To this day Edom has been in revolt against the rule of Judah. Libnah also revolted at that time against his rule because he had abandoned the LORD, the God of his ancestors. ¹¹He also set up high places in the mountains of Judah, prostituting the inhabitants of Jerusalem, leading Judah astray.

Jehoram Punished. ¹²A letter came to him from Elijah the prophet with this message: "Thus says the LORD, the God of David your father: Because you have not walked in the way of your father Jehoshaphat, nor of Asa, king of Judah, ¹³but instead have walked in the way of the kings of Israel, leading Judah and the inhabitants of Jerusalem into prostitution, like the harlotries of the house of

---

21:2–22:1 [cf. 2 Kgs 8:16-24] The reign of Jehoram of Judah

The Chronicler's additions tend to highlight the evils of this reign. The Chronicler lists Jehoram's brothers, who received many gifts from their father Jehoshaphat (21:2-3); Jehoram kills them all as soon as he takes power (21:4). After marrying Athaliah, the daughter of Ahab of Israel, he follows the evil ways of the kings of Israel (21:6; cf. 2 Kgs 8:18). God's anger is provoked, so this king might have been put away except for God's covenant promise not to destroy the royal line of Judah (21:7). His punishment comes in the form of a revolt by Edom and Libnah against Judah (21:10). The Chronicler adds a theological reason for these revolts: Jehoram built high places and led Jerusalem and Judah astray in false worship, thus forsaking God (21:11).

Ahab, and because you have killed your brothers of your father's house, who were better than you, [14]the LORD will strike your people, your children, your wives, and all that is yours with a great plague. [15]You shall have severe pains from a disease in your bowels, which will fall out because of the disease, day after day."

[16]Then the LORD stirred up against Jehoram the animosity of the Philistines and of the Arabians who were neighbors of the Ethiopians. [17]They came up against Judah, breached it, and carried away all the wealth found in the king's house, along with his sons and his wives. He was left with only one son, Jehoahaz, his youngest. [18]After these events, the LORD afflicted him with a disease of the bowels for which there was no cure. [19]Some time later, after a period of two years had elapsed, his bowels fell out because of the disease and he died in great pain. His people did not make a fire for him as they had for his ancestors. [20]He was thirty-two years old when he became king, and he reigned eight years in Jerusalem. He departed unloved; and they buried him in the City of David, though not in the tombs of the kings.

22 **Ahaziah.** [1]Then the inhabitants of Jerusalem made Ahaziah, his youngest son, king to succeed him, since all the older sons had been killed by the band that had come into the camp with the Arabians. Thus Ahaziah, son of Jehoram, reigned as the king of Judah. [2]Ahaziah was twenty-two years old when he became king, and he reigned one year in Jerusalem. His mother's name was Athaliah, daughter of Omri. [3]He, too, walked in the ways of the house of Ahab, because his mother was

The Chronicler adds a letter from the prophet Elijah to Jehoram (21:12-15). His prophecy of doom explains how his evil conduct (especially killing his brothers and infidelity to God) will lead to a plague on his people and a horrible death by sickness of the bowels for himself. Elijah's appearance here is intriguing. First, all the stories about Elijah in 1 Kings are omitted by the Chronicler, so this appearance is unique. Nevertheless, Elijah opposes the house of Ahab in Chronicles as in Kings. Just as he proclaims disaster, so it happens for Judah and for Jehoram. The king dies of some terrible disease of the bowels (21:19), and though he was buried in Jerusalem, it was not in the tombs of the kings. After his death, Jerusalem's inhabitants make his surviving son Ahaziah (Jehoahaz) king in his place (22:1).

22:2-9 [cf. 2 Kgs 8:25-29] The reign of Ahaziah of Judah

The Chronicler adds very little new material and seems to blame his evil on the counsel he followed, much of it from Athaliah and the house of Ahab (22:3-5). So Ahaziah appears as a kind of victim in this text. His ruin came from God because he had sided with Joram, and he was killed in the

his counselor in doing evil. ⁴To his own destruction, he did what was evil in the sight of the LORD, like the house of Ahab, since they were his counselors after the death of his father.

⁵He was also following their counsel when he joined Jehoram, son of Ahab, king of Israel, in battle against Hazael, king of Aram, at Ramoth-gilead, where the Arameans wounded Jehoram. ⁶He returned to Jezreel to be healed of the wounds that had been inflicted on him at Ramah in his battle against Hazael, king of Aram. Then Ahaziah, son of Jehoram, king of Judah, went down to Jezreel to visit Jehoram, son of Ahab, for he was sick. ⁷Now from God came Ahaziah's downfall, that he should join Jehoram; for after his arrival he rode out

with Jehoram to Jehu, son of Nimshi, whom the LORD had anointed to cut down the house of Ahab. ⁸While Jehu was executing judgment on the house of Ahab, he also came upon the princes of Judah and the nephews of Ahaziah who were his attendants, and he killed them. ⁹Then he looked for Ahaziah himself. They caught him hiding in Samaria and brought him to Jehu, who put him to death. They buried him, for they said, "He was the grandson of Jehoshaphat, who sought the LORD with his whole heart." Now the house of Ahaziah did not retain the power of kingship.

Usurpation of Athaliah. ¹⁰When Athaliah, the mother of Ahaziah, saw that her son was dead, she began to kill off the whole royal family of the house

executions of the house of Ahab conducted by Jehu (22:8-9). In deference to his grandfather Jehoshaphat who sought the Lord, they gave him a burial, though the Chronicler does not mention where. So another unfaithful king of Judah has now passed, and the house of David stands at a precarious point, with no obvious successor to the rule (22:9).

22:10–23:21 [cf. 2 Kgs 11:1-20] Athaliah usurps the throne

When Athaliah realizes that her house and that of David are facing extinction and she is the only adult who could claim the throne, she prepares to put to death all of Ahaziah's sons. But Jehosheba, daughter of King Jehoram and sister of Ahaziah, steals away Joash, the only son of Ahaziah still living. She acts to save him from the murderous intentions of Athaliah and to preserve the line of the house of David. The Chronicler emphasizes that Jehoshabeath was married to the priest Jehoiada. This detail fits well with the fact that she and her husband hid the child in the temple for six years, while Athaliah reigned (22:12). The Chronicler says that the child was with "them" in the temple, i.e., husband and wife, rather than with "her" (as in 2 Kgs 11:3). Saving this child involved more than a single person, including cooperation between priests (Jehoiada) and royal family to preserve the Davidic line.

of Judah. [11]But Jehosheba, a daughter of the king, took Joash, Ahaziah's son, and spirited him away from among the king's sons who were about to be slain, and put him and his nurse in a bedroom. In this way Jehosheba, the daughter of King Jehoram, a sister of Ahaziah and wife of Jehoiada the priest, concealed the child from Athaliah, so that she did not put him to death. [12]For six years he remained hidden with them in the house of God, while Athaliah ruled as queen over the land.

23 Athaliah Overthrown. [1]In the seventh year, Jehoiada took courage and brought into covenant with himself the captains: Azariah, son of Jehoram; Ishmael, son of Jehohanan; Azariah, son of Obed; Maaseiah, son of Adaiah; and Elishaphat, son of Zichri. [2]They journeyed about Judah, gathering the Levites from all the cities of Judah and also the heads of the Israelite families, and they came to Jerusalem. [3]The whole assembly made a covenant with the king in the house of God. Jehoiada said to them: "Here is the king's son who must reign, as the LORD promised concerning the sons of David. [4]This is what you must do: a third of your number, both priests and Levites, who come on duty on the sabbath must guard the thresholds, [5]another third must be at the king's house, and the final third at the Foundation Gate, when all the people will be in the courts of the LORD's house. [6]Let no one enter the LORD's house except the priests and those Levites who are ministering. They may enter because they are holy; but all the other people must observe the prescriptions of the LORD. [7]The Levites shall surround the king on all sides, each with drawn weapon. Whoever tries to enter the house is to be killed. Stay with the king wherever he goes."

[8]The Levites and all Judah did just as Jehoiada the priest commanded. Each took his troops, both those going on duty for the week and those going off duty that week, since Jehoiada the priest had not dismissed any of the divisions. [9]Jehoiada the priest gave to the captains the spears, shields, and bucklers of King

---

In 23:1-15 the Chronicler retells the story of the coronation of Joash as king of Judah. The leaders go out to the towns of Judah to enlist support of the Levites and leading families. The Chronicler thus demonstrates widespread support and participation to save the royal line because an unbroken succession in the line of David was so important for all. Levites generally replace the military conspirators of 2 Kings (23:2, 4, 6, 7, 8) and priests are added in two places (23:4, 6). The Chronicler implies that danger to the king is also danger to the temple. In Chronicles these events involve all the people, not just a group of military conspirators. The people of the land sound their trumpets along with singers with their musical instruments and praise songs (23:13). Worship is the overall horizon. Then follows the assassination of Athaliah (23:14-15).

David which were in the house of God. [10]He stationed all the people, each with spear in hand, from the southern to the northern limit of the enclosure, surrounding the altar and the temple on the king's behalf. [11]Then they brought out the king's son and put the crown and the testimony upon him, and proclaimed him king. Jehoiada and his sons anointed him, and they cried, "Long live the king!"

[12]When Athaliah heard the noise of the people running and acclaiming the king, she came before them in the house of the LORD. [13]When she saw the king standing by his column at the entrance, the captains and the trumpeters near the king, and all the people of the land rejoicing and blowing trumpets, while the singers with their musical instruments were leading the acclaim, Athaliah tore her garments, saying, "Treason! treason!" [14]Then Jehoiada the priest brought out the captains in command of the force: "Escort her with a guard detail. If

anyone follows her, let him die by the sword." For the priest had said, "You must not put her to death in the house of the LORD." [15]So they seized her, and when she reached the Horse Gate of the royal palace, they put her to death.

[16]Then Jehoiada made a covenant between himself and all the people and the king, that they should be the LORD's people. [17]Thereupon all the people went to the temple of Baal and demolished it. They shattered its altars and images completely, and killed Mattan, the priest of Baal, before the altars. [18]Then Jehoiada gave the charge of the LORD's house into the hands of the levitical priests, to whom David had assigned turns in the LORD's house for sacrificing the burnt offerings of the LORD, as is written in the law of Moses, with rejoicing and song, as David had provided. [19]Moreover, he stationed guards at the gates of the LORD's house so that no one unclean in any respect might enter. [20]Then he took the captains, the nobles, the rulers

---

Jehoiada the priest acts as a kind of regent for the young king Jehoash after Athaliah's death. He begins with a covenant ceremony between himself, the people, and the king, so they will be a people of the Lord (23:16). Thus they destroy all signs of Baal worship (23:17) and Jehoiada the priest appoints people to rule the temple. The Chronicler specifies that all these officials were responsible to the Levitical priests who had been organized and appointed by David to offer sacrifices with rejoicing and song. The Chronicler mentions gatekeepers for the temple to protect it from entry by people who were unclean; this was clearly a Levitical concern (23:19). Ultimately the Chronicler is more interested in the cultic purity of the temple than in the political plotting. The Chronicler concludes that the whole city was quiet after Athaliah was executed, so the people of the land rejoiced: God has indeed preserved the line of David and his promise to that line (1 Chr 17).

among the people, and all the people of the land, and led the king out of the LORD's house; they came within the upper gate of the king's house, and seated the king upon the royal throne. ²¹All the people of the land rejoiced and the city was quiet, now that Athaliah had been slain with the sword.

24 **The Temple Restored.** ¹Joash was seven years old when he became king, and he reigned forty years in Jerusalem. His mother's name was Zibiah, from Beer-sheba. ²Joash did what was right in the LORD's sight as long as Jehoiada the priest lived. ³Jehoiada provided him with two wives, and he became the father of sons and daughters.

⁴After some time, Joash decided to restore the house of the LORD. ⁵He gathered together the priests and Levites and said to them: "Go out to all the cities of Judah and gather money from all Israel that you may repair the house of your God over the years. You must hurry this project." But the Levites did not. ⁶Then the king summoned Jehoiada, who was in charge, and said to him: "Why have you not required the Levites to bring in from Judah and Jerusalem the tax levied by Moses, the servant of the LORD, and by the assembly of Israel, for the tent of the testimony?" ⁷For the wicked Athaliah and her sons had damaged the house of God and had even turned over to the Baals the holy things of the LORD's house.

⁸At the king's command, therefore, they made a chest, which they put outside the gate of the LORD's house. ⁹They had it proclaimed throughout Judah and Jerusalem that the tax which Moses, the servant of God, had imposed on Israel in the wilderness should be brought to the LORD. ¹⁰All the princes and the people rejoiced; they brought what was asked and cast it into the chest until it was filled. ¹¹Whenever the chest was brought to the royal officials by the

---

24:1-27 [cf. 2 Kgs 12:1-22] The reign of Jehoash

Jehoash, the young survivor of Athaliah's massacre, becomes king at age seven and reigns for forty years (24:1). The Chronicler describes a good and blessed reign, as long as his patron Jehoiada is living, and the king restores the temple. The Chronicler has special emphases. First, Jehoash is rewarded for upright behavior; Jehoiada provides him with two wives and he fathers numerous sons and daughters (24:3). Second, the collection to restore the temple features Levites (in addition to priests) following regulations given by Moses (24:9). Third, the officials and people participate enthusiastically in the collection (24:10). The Chronicler thus portrays the project as a joint venture of priest and king; it probably reflects his vision for cooperation in his own day. In contrast to Kings, where money was not spent for temple vessels, they spend leftover money on temple worship vessels and they actively continue the schedule of burnt offerings in the temple (24:14). Thus far Jehoash seems a model king.

Levites and they noticed that there was a large amount of money, the royal scribe and an overseer for the chief priest would come up, empty the chest, and then take it back and return it to its place. This they did day after day until they had collected a large sum of money. ¹²Then the king and Jehoiada gave it to the workers in charge of the labor on the LORD's house, who hired masons and carpenters to restore the LORD's house, and also iron- and bronze-smiths to repair it. ¹³The workers labored, and the task of restoration progressed under their hands. They restored the house of God according to its original form, and reinforced it. ¹⁴After they had finished, they brought the rest of the money to the king and to Jehoiada, who had it made into utensils for the house of the LORD, utensils for the service and the burnt offerings, and basins and other gold and silver utensils. They sacrificed burnt offerings in the LORD's house continually all the days of Jehoiada. ¹⁵Jehoiada grew old, full of years, and died; he was a hundred and thirty years old. ¹⁶They buried him in the City of David with the kings, because of the good he had done in Israel, especially for God and his house.

Joash's Apostasy. ¹⁷After the death of Jehoiada, the princes of Judah came and paid homage to the king; then the king listened to them. ¹⁸They abandoned the house of the LORD, the God of their ancestors, and began to serve the asherahs and the idols; and because of this crime of theirs, wrath came upon Judah and Jerusalem. ¹⁹Although prophets were sent to them to turn them back to the LORD and to warn them, the people would not listen. ²⁰ Then the spirit of God clothed Zechariah, son of Jehoiada the priest. He took his stand above the people and said to them: "Thus says God, Why are you transgressing the LORD's commands, so that you cannot prosper? Because you have abandoned the LORD, he has abandoned you." ²¹But they conspired against him, and at the king's command they stoned him in the court of the house of the LORD. ²²Thus King Joash was unmindful of the devotion shown him by Jehoiada, Zechariah's father, and killed the son. As he was dying, he said, "May the LORD see and avenge."

After Jehoiada's death, however, things change dramatically in the Chronicler's version—with no parallel in Kings. Judean officials approach Jehoash, who heeds their advice and shifts worship back to the old idols (24:18). Divine anger follows (24:18), but God sends prophets to bring them back. They do not heed the prophets (24:19), so God endows Zechariah, son of the priest Jehoiada, with a prophetic spirit and he issues a stern oracle of judgment. Angered, the king orders his officials to stone the priest/prophet in the temple court, a horrifying sacrilege (24:21). The Chronicler accuses Joash of ingratitude, not remembering Jehoiada's kindness to him, i.e., of breaking the covenant they had made (24:22). The result is a punishment from God in the form of an Aramean invasion (24:23-24). Joash is

Joash Punished. ²³At the turn of the year a force of Arameans came up against Joash. They invaded Judah and Jerusalem, killed all the princes of the people, and sent all their spoil to the king of Damascus. ²⁴Though the Aramean force was small, the LORD handed over a very large force into their power, because Judah had abandoned the LORD, the God of their ancestors. So judgment was meted out to Joash. ²⁵After the Arameans had departed from him, abandoning him to his many injuries, his servants conspired against him because of the murder of the son of Jehoiada the priest. They killed him on his sickbed. He was buried in the City of David, but not in the tombs of the kings.

²⁶Those who conspired against him were Zabad, son of Shimeath from Ammon, and Jehozabad, son of Shimrith from Moab. ²⁷An account of his sons, the great tribute imposed on him, and his rebuilding of the house of God is written in the midrash of the book of the kings. His son Amaziah succeeded him as king.

25 Amaziah's Good Start. ¹Amaziah was twenty-five years old when he became king, and he reigned twenty-nine years in Jerusalem. His mother's name was Jehoaddan, from Jerusalem. ²He did what was right in the LORD's sight, though not wholeheartedly. ³When he had the kingdom firmly in hand, he struck down the officials who had struck down the king, his father. ⁴But their children he did not put to death, for he acted according to what is written in the law, in the Book of Moses, which the LORD commanded: "Parents shall not be put to death for their children, nor shall children be put to death for their parents; they shall each die for their own sin."

⁵Amaziah gathered Judah and placed them, out of all Judah and Benjamin according to their ancestral houses, under leaders of thousands and of hundreds. When he made a count of those twenty years old and over, he found that there were three hundred thousand picked men fit for war, capable of handling lance and shield. ⁶He also hired a hundred thousand valiant warriors from Israel for a hundred talents of silver. ⁷But a man of God came to him and said: "O

---

killed by a conspiracy of his own servants because he spilled the blood of the sons of Jehoiada the priest (24:25). Because of the murder and sacrilege recounted here, the Chronicler claims that he was not buried with the kings of Judah, although his grave was in Jerusalem (24:25). This murder of Zechariah seems to be mentioned in a woe-saying of Jesus against unfaithful people of his own time who shed the blood of prophets (Luke 11:49-51).

25:1-28 [cf. 2 Kgs 14:1-20] The reign of Amaziah

Amaziah reigns for twenty-nine years in Jerusalem. The Chronicler includes most of the material in Kings and concludes that he acted correctly in God's eyes, except "not wholeheartedly" (25:2). His adherence to God's ways is partial. His first move, political and tactical, is to kill those servants

king, let not the army of Israel go with you, for the LORD is not with Israel— with any Ephraimite. [8]Instead, go on your own, strongly prepared for the battle; why should the LORD hinder you in the face of the enemy: for with God is power to help or to hinder." [9]Amaziah answered the man of God, "But what is to be done about the hundred talents that I paid for the troops of Israel?" The man of God replied, "The LORD can give you much more than that." [10]Amaziah then disbanded the troops that had come to him from Ephraim, and sent them home. But they became furiously angry with Judah, and returned home blazing with anger.

[11]Amaziah now assumed command of his army. They proceeded to the Valley of Salt, where they killed ten thousand men of Seir. [12]The Judahites also brought back another ten thousand alive, led them to the summit of Sela, and then threw them down from that rock so that their bodies split open. [13]Meanwhile, the troops Amaziah had dismissed from going into battle with him raided the cities of Judah from Samaria to Beth-horon. They struck down three thousand of the inhabitants and carried off much plunder.

Amaziah's Apostasy. [14]When Amaziah returned from his conquest of the Edomites he brought back with him the gods of the people of Seir. He set these up as his own gods; he bowed down before them and offered sacrifice to them. [15]Then the anger of the LORD blazed out against Amaziah, and he sent a prophet to him who said: "Why have you sought this people's gods that could not deliver their own people from your power?" [16]While he was still speaking, however, the king said to him: "Have you been appointed the king's counselor? Stop! Why should you have to be killed?" Therefore the prophet stopped. But he said, "I know that God's counsel is your destruction, for by doing this you have refused to listen to my counsel."

Amaziah Punished. [17]Having taken counsel, Amaziah, king of Judah, sent

who had killed his father, but he does not kill their children, reasoning from Deuteronomy 24:16 that children should not be put to death because of the sins of their fathers (25:4). The Chronicler adds a story that Amaziah organized his military and hired one hundred thousand northern Israelites. This action invites a prophetic rebuke to rely not on Israel and Ephraim but on God alone (25:7-8). There follow details of acrimonious relations with the North, a successful battle against peoples of Edom and Mt. Seir, and disturbing reports that he then worships the gods of Seir (25:9-14). Another prophet comes to express the Lord's anger that he would trust other gods to deliver him (25:15). Many other disastrous interchanges follow. He is carried back to Jerusalem on horses and is buried there with his ancestors (25:28). The initial evaluation is correct; he acted uprightly, but only partially. Like Jehoash before him, he begins well but does not persevere.

word to Joash, son of Jehoahaz, son of Jehu, the king of Israel, saying, "Come, let us meet face to face." [18]Joash, king of Israel, sent this reply to Amaziah, king of Judah: "A thistle of Lebanon sent word to a cedar of Lebanon, 'Give your daughter to my son in marriage,' but an animal of Lebanon passed by and trampled the thistle underfoot. [19]You are thinking,

'See, I have struck down Edom!'
Your heart is lifted up,
And glories in it. Stay home!
Why bring misfortune and failure
on yourself and on Judah with
you?"

[20]But Amaziah did not listen; for it was God's doing that they be handed over because they sought the gods of Edom.

[21]So Joash, king of Israel, advanced, and he and Amaziah, king of Judah, met face to face at Beth-shemesh of Judah, [22]and Judah was defeated by Israel, and all fled to their tents. [23]But Amaziah, king of Judah, son of Joash, son of Jehoahaz, was captured by Joash, king of Israel, at Beth-shemesh. Joash brought him to Jerusalem and tore down the wall of Jerusalem from the Gate of Ephraim to the Corner Gate, four hundred cubits. [24]He took all the gold and silver and all the vessels found in the house of God with Obed-edom, and in the treasuries of the king's house, and hostages as well. Then he returned to Samaria.

[25]Amaziah, son of Joash, king of Judah, survived Joash, son of Jehoahaz, king of Israel, by fifteen years. [26]The rest of the acts of Amaziah, first and last, are recorded in the book of the kings of Judah and Israel. [27]Now from the time that Amaziah turned away from the Lord, a conspiracy was formed against him in Jerusalem, and he fled to Lachish. But he was pursued to Lachish and killed there. [28]He was brought back on horses and was buried with his ancestors in the City of Judah.

Uzziah's Projects. [1]All the people 26 of Judah took Uzziah, who was only sixteen years old, and made him king to succeed Amaziah his father. [2]It was he who rebuilt Elath and restored it to Judah, after the king rested with his ancestors. [3]Uzziah was sixteen years old when he became king, and he reigned fifty-two years in Jerusalem. His mother's name was Jecoliah, from Jerusalem. [4]He did what was right in the Lord's sight, just as his father Amaziah had done.

[5]He was prepared to seek God as long as Zechariah lived, who taught him to fear God; and as long as he sought the Lord, God made him prosper. [6]He went out and fought the Philistines and razed the walls of Gath, Jabneh, and Ashdod, and built cities in the district of Ashdod and in Philistia. [7]God helped him against the Philistines, against the Arabians who

26:1–23 [cf. 2 Kgs 14:21–15:7] The reign of Uzziah (Azariah)

This king also begins well but ends badly. He becomes king at age sixteen, when his father was killed, and he reigns fifty-two years. The Chronicler gives a much longer account than Kings. At first he seeks God, as

dwelt in Gurbaal, and against the Meunites. [8]The Ammonites paid tribute to Uzziah and his fame spread as far as Egypt, for he grew stronger and stronger. [9]Moreover, Uzziah built towers in Jerusalem at the Corner Gate, at the Valley Gate, and at the Angle, and he fortified them. [10]He built towers in the wilderness and dug numerous cisterns, for he had many cattle. He had plowmen in the Shephelah and the plains, farmers and vinedressers in the highlands and the garden land. He was a lover of the soil.

[11]Uzziah also had a standing army of fit soldiers divided into bands according to the number in which they were mustered by Jeiel the scribe and Maaseiah the recorder, under the command of Hananiah, one of the king's officials. [12]The entire number of family heads over these valiant warriors was two thousand six hundred, [13]and at their disposal was a mighty army of three hundred seven thousand five hundred fighting men of great valor to help the king against his enemies. [14]Uzziah provided for them—for the entire army—bucklers, lances, helmets, breastplates, bows, and slingstones. [15]He also built machines in Jerusalem, devices designed to stand on the towers and at the angles of the walls to shoot arrows and cast large stones. His name spread far and wide; the help he received was wondrous, so strong did he become.

Pride and Fall. [16]But after he had become strong, he became arrogant to his own destruction and acted treacherously with the LORD, his God. He entered the temple of the LORD to make an offering on the altar of incense. [17]But Azariah the priest, and with him eighty other priests of the LORD, courageous men, followed him. [18]They stood up to King Uzziah, saying to him: "It is not for you, Uzziah, to burn incense to the LORD, but for the priests, the sons of Aaron, who have been consecrated for this purpose. Leave the sanctuary, for you have acted treach-

instructed by his advisor Zechariah, so God made him prosperous. The Chronicler describes victory on the battlefield, his construction of cisterns and towers, and his development of farms and vineyards because of his love for the earth. Under him the kingdom is prosperous and secure, and much the same situation prevails in the North. This era, the early eighth century B.C., is a time when superpowers were weakened and Israel and Judah could grow strong. Later he grows proud and personally enters the sanctuary to offer incense (26:16). Usurping the authority of the priests brings the punishment of leprosy for the rest of his days (26:19-20). He lives in seclusion, excluded from the temple, while his son Jotham takes over his judicial duties (26:21). After his death, Uzziah is buried adjacent to a royal burial ground. One of the Chronicler's sources for this story was written by the prophet Isaiah, son of Amoz (26:22). Like his father, Uzziah's richly prosperous reign turns sour at its end as pride guides his actions.

erously and no longer have a part in the glory that comes from the LORD God." ¹⁹Uzziah, who was holding a censer for burning the incense, became angry. But at the very moment he showed his anger to the priests, while they were looking at him in the house of the LORD beside the altar of incense, leprosy broke out on his forehead. ²⁰Azariah the chief priest and all the other priests examined him, and when they saw that his forehead was leprous, they rushed him out. He let himself be expelled, for the LORD had afflicted him. ²¹King Uzziah remained a leper till the day he died. As a leper he lived in a house apart, for he was excluded from the house of the LORD. Therefore his son Jotham was master of the palace and ruled the people of the land.

²²The rest of the acts of Uzziah, first and last, were written by Isaiah the prophet, son of Amoz. ²³Uzziah rested with his ancestors and was buried with them in the field adjoining the royal cemetery, for they said, "He was a leper." His son Jotham succeeded him as king.

27 **Jotham.** ¹Jotham was twenty-five years old when he became king, and he reigned sixteen years in Jeru-

salem. His mother's name was Jerusha, daughter of Zadok. ²He did what was right in the LORD's sight, just as his father Uzziah had done, though he did not enter the temple of the LORD. The people, however, continued to act corruptly.

³It was he who built the Upper Gate of the LORD's house and did much construction on the wall of Ophel. ⁴Moreover, he built cities in the hill country of Judah, and in the wooded areas he set up fortresses and towers. ⁵He fought with the king of the Ammonites and conquered them. That year the Ammonites paid him one hundred talents of silver, together with ten thousand kors of wheat and ten thousand of barley. They brought the same to him also in the second and in the third year. ⁶Thus Jotham continued to grow strong because he made sure to walk before the LORD, his God. ⁷The rest of the acts of Jotham, his wars and his activities, are recorded in the book of the kings of Israel and Judah. ⁸He was twenty-five years old when he became king, and he reigned sixteen years in Jerusalem. ⁹Jotham rested with his ancestors and was buried in the City of David, and his son Ahaz succeeded him as king.

27:1-9 [cf. 2 Kgs 15:32-38] The reign of Jotham

This report is quite positive, a welcome interlude among many negative accounts. He follows the best paths of his father Uzziah, especially in his construction projects in Jerusalem (Ophel hill) and the hill country of Judah, as he established his ways before God (27:6). In one important detail he does not imitate his father: he does not presume to enter the temple (27:2). Ammonites pay him tribute (27:5), and after his death he rests with his ancestors in the city of David (27:9).

28 **Ahaz's Misdeeds.** ¹Ahaz was twenty years old when he became king, and he reigned sixteen years in Jerusalem. He did not do what was right in the sight of the LORD as David his father had done. ²He walked in the ways of the kings of Israel and even made molten idols for the Baals. ³Moreover, he offered sacrifice in the Valley of Ben-hinnom, and immolated his children by fire in accordance with the abominable practices of the nations whom the LORD had dispossessed before the Israelites. ⁴He sacrificed and burned incense on the high places, on hills, and under every green tree.

Ahaz Punished. ⁵Therefore the LORD, his God, delivered him into the power of the king of Aram. The Arameans defeated him and carried away captive a large number of his people, whom they brought to Damascus. He was also delivered into the power of the king of Israel, who defeated him with great slaughter. ⁶For Pekah, son of Remaliah, killed one hundred and twenty thousand of Judah in a single day, all of them valiant men, because they had abandoned the LORD, the God of their ancestors. ⁷Zichri, an Ephraimite warrior, killed Maaseiah, the king's son, and Azrikam, the master of the palace, and also Elkanah, who was second to the king. ⁸The Israelites took away as captives two hundred thousand of their kinfolk's wives, sons, and daughters; they also took from them much plunder, which they brought to Samaria.

Oded's Prophecy. ⁹In Samaria there was a prophet of the LORD by the name of Oded. He went out to meet the army returning to Samaria and said to them: "It was because the LORD, the God of your ancestors, was angry with Judah that he delivered them into your power. You, however, have killed them with a fury that has reached up to heaven. ¹⁰And now you are planning to subjugate the people of Judah and Jerusalem as your slaves and bondwomen. Are not

28:1-27 [cf. 2 Kgs 16:1-20] The reign of Ahaz

This king reverses the positive pattern of his father, Jotham, so the Chronicler narrates nothing positive about his reign. He is responsible for much idolatry. He personally produces metal images of the Baals (28:2), makes incense offerings in the Ben-hinnom valley, and engages in child sacrifices (28:3). Because he has forsaken his ancestral God (28:6), who is thereby enraged (28:9), Ahaz suffers defeats at the hands of the Arameans (28:5), Israelites (28:6-15), Edomites (28:17), and Philistines (28:18), and is oppressed by Assyria (28:16, 20-21).

The Chronicler tells a much more detailed story of battle with northern Israelites. The prophet Oded exhorts the northerners to curb their rage and return Judean captives, arguing that both Judah and Israel have sinned equally (28:9-11). This unusual speech succeeds and many captives are returned. With regard to Damascus and the Arameans, the Chronicler has

you yourselves, therefore, guilty of a crime against the LORD, your God? [11]Now listen to me: send back the captives you have carried off from among your kin, for the burning anger of the LORD is upon you."

[12]At this, some of the Ephraimite leaders, Azariah, son of Johanan, Berechiah, son of Meshillemoth, Jehizkiah, son of Shallum, and Amasa, son of Hadlai, themselves stood up in opposition to those who had returned from the war. [13]They said to them: "Do not bring the captives here, for what you are planning will make us guilty before the LORD and increase our sins and our guilt. Great is our guilt, and there is burning anger upon Israel." [14]Therefore the soldiers left their captives and the plunder before the princes and the whole assembly. [15]Then the men just named proceeded to help the captives. All of them who were naked they clothed from the spoils; they clothed them, put sandals on their feet, gave them food and drink, anointed them, and all who were weak they set on donkeys. They brought them to Jericho, the City of Palms, to their kinfolk. Then they returned to Samaria.

Further Sins of Ahaz. [16]At that time King Ahaz sent an appeal for help to the kings of Assyria. [17]The Edomites had returned, attacked Judah, and carried off captives. [18]The Philistines too had raided the cities of the Shephelah and the Negeb of Judah; they captured Bethshemesh, Aijalon, Gederoth, Soco and its dependencies, Timnah and its dependencies, and Gimzo and its dependencies, and settled there. [19]For the LORD had brought Judah low because of Ahaz, king of Israel, who let Judah go its own way and committed treachery against the LORD. [20]Tiglath-pilneser, king of Assyria, did indeed come to him, but to oppress him rather than to lend strength. [21]Though Ahaz plundered the LORD's house and the houses of the king and the princes to pay off the king of Assyria, it was no help to him.

Ahaz sacrificing to their gods. He collects temple vessels and uses the metal to pay tribute, closes the temple doors (i.e., causes normal worship to cease), and builds altars everywhere. This thoroughly disobedient king was buried in Jerusalem, but not in the royal cemeteries. The Chronicler will move directly to Ahaz's son, Hezekiah, the next king of Judah.

At this point, the Chronicler omits crucial texts: 2 Kings 17 and 18:9-12. The Kings account begins with the reign of King Hoshea of Israel and includes the attack by Shalmaneser, King of Assyria, and his siege of Samaria. Eventually the Assyrians capture the Israelite capital and send its people into exile. The Chronicler does not comment on these events, since he does not specifically narrate the history of the northern kingdom. Some scholars suggest that the condemnations of Israel are not included by the Chronicler so that northerners, the lost tribes of Israel, could be more clearly invited back to union and worship with the southern kingdom of Judah.

Archers of Tiglath-pilneser, king of Assyria, attack a besieged city (2 Chr 28:20).

22While he was already in distress, the same King Ahaz increased his treachery to the LORD. 23He sacrificed to the gods of Damascus who had defeated him, saying, "Since it was the gods of the kings of Aram who helped them, I will sacrifice to them that they may help me also." However, they only furthered his downfall and that of all Israel. 24Ahaz gathered up the utensils of God's house and broke them in pieces. He closed the doors of the LORD's house and made altars for himself in every corner of Jerusalem. 25In every city throughout Judah he set up high places to offer sacrifice to other gods. Thus he provoked the LORD, the God of his ancestors, to anger.

26The rest of his words and his deeds, first and last, are recorded in the book of the kings of Judah and Israel. 27Ahaz rested with his ancestors and was buried in Jerusalem—in the city, for they did not bring him to the tombs of the kings of Israel. His son Hezekiah succeeded him as king.

29 **Hezekiah's Reforms.** 1Hezekiah was twenty-five years old when he became king, and he reigned twenty-nine years in Jerusalem. His mother's name was Abijah, daughter of Zechariah. 2He did what was right in the LORD's sight, just as David his father had done. 3In the first month of the first year of his reign, he opened the doors of the LORD's house and repaired them. 4He summoned the priests and Levites, gathering them in the open space to the east, 5and said to them: "Listen to me, you

---

HEZEKIAH

2 Chronicles 29–32

Hezekiah ranks as one of Judah's three most important kings, after David and Solomon. The Chronicler devotes four chapters to him, most of them without parallels in Kings. The unique material recounts issues of worship at the temple, whereas Kings focuses more on military and political events, especially the invasion of Assyrian King Sennacherib. The Chronicler links Hezekiah's concern for worship with the accomplishments of David and Solomon. The Chronicler transforms the Hezekiah story into a renewal program for the entire people, including northerners who were presumably cut off after 722 B.C. In chapters 29–30 Hezekiah cleanses the temple from the impurity introduced by Ahaz and reestablishes the proper rituals and the joyful celebration of Passover and Unleavened Bread. He delineates duties and roles of Levites and priests, focusing on status and responsibility for the Levites. Thus the Chronicler underscores the importance of worship for Israel's common life. His attention to Sennacherib's invasion and defeat is quite abbreviated when compared with its parallels in 2 Kings 18–19 and Isaiah 36–37. This commentary will emphasize the Chronicler's favorite issues: temple worship, personnel, and the great Passover festival.

Levites! Sanctify yourselves now and sanctify the house of the LORD, the God of your ancestors, and clean out the filth from the sanctuary. 6Our ancestors acted treacherously and did what was evil in the eyes of the LORD, our God. They abandoned him, turned away their faces from the LORD's dwelling, and turned their backs on him. 7They also closed the doors of the vestibule, extinguished the lamps, and failed to burn incense and sacrifice burnt offerings in the sanctuary to the God of Israel. 8Therefore the anger of the LORD has come upon Judah and Jerusalem; he has made them an object of terror, horror, and hissing, as you see with your own eyes. 9For our ancestors fell by the sword, and our sons, our daughters, and our wives have been taken captive because of this. 10Now, I intend to make a covenant with the LORD, the God of Israel, that his burning anger may turn away from us. 11My sons, do not be negligent any longer, for it is you whom the LORD has chosen to stand before him, to minister to him, to be his ministers and to offer incense."

12Then the Levites arose: Mahath, son of Amasai, and Joel, son of Azariah, of the Kohathites; of the descendants of Merari: Kish, son of Abdi, and Azariah, son of Jehallel; of the Gershonites: Joah, son of Zimmah, and Eden, son of Joah; 13of the sons of Elizaphan: Shimri and Jeuel; of the sons of Asaph: Zechariah and Mattaniah; 14of the sons of Heman: Jehuel and Shimei; of the sons of Jeduthun: Shemiah and Uzziel. 15They gathered their kinfolk together and sanctified themselves; then they came as the king had ordered, in keeping with the words of the LORD, to cleanse the LORD's house.

29:1-36 [cf. 2 Kgs 18:1-12] Hezekiah restores temple service

Hezekiah reigns for twenty-nine years and does what God considered right and honest, like David. He restores the temple for worship and for the Passover, after the reign of Ahaz left it with a polytheistic atmosphere. First, he cleanses the temple and rededicates it (29:3-30). Then he assembles the priests and Levites and exhorts them to participate in the cleansing and consecration of the temple (29:5-11). The Levites are prominent in their enthusiastic response. In verses 12-14 the Chronicler lists fourteen Levitical families that participated. The first eight come from the four great Levite families: Kohath, Merari, Gershon, and Elizaphan (29:12-13a), and the next six names derive from three families of singers: Asaph, Heman, and Jeduthun (29:13b-14).

To purify the temple, the priests bring out unclean things, while the Levites receive and dispose of them in Wadi Kidron. The ceremonies take eight days for the outer court and another eight days for the inner house of the Lord; so this entire process takes them to the sixteenth of the first month. Since Passover begins on the fourteenth of the first month, they cannot begin on time since the temple is not yet consecrated. Their only alternative is celebrate Passover in the second month.

121

¹⁶The priests entered the interior of the Lord's house to cleanse it. Whatever they found in the Lord's temple that was unclean they brought out to the court of the Lord's house, where the Levites took it from them and carried it out to the Wadi Kidron. ¹⁷They began the work of consecration on the first day of the first month, and on the eighth day of the month they reached the vestibule of the Lord; they consecrated the Lord's house over an eight-day period, and on the sixteenth day of the first month, they had finished.

¹⁸Then they went inside to King Hezekiah and said: "We have cleansed the entire house of the Lord, the altar for burnt offerings with all its utensils, and the table for the showbread with all its utensils. ¹⁹We have restored and consecrated all the articles which King Ahaz had thrown away during his reign because of his treachery; they are now before the Lord's altar."

The Rite of Expiation. ²⁰Then King Hezekiah hastened to convoke the princes of the city and went up to the Lord's house. ²¹Seven bulls, seven rams, seven lambs, and seven he-goats were presented as a purification offering for the kingdom, for the sanctuary, and for Judah. Hezekiah ordered the sons of Aaron, the priests, to offer them on the altar of the Lord. ²²They slaughtered the bulls, and the priests collected the blood and splashed it on the altar. Then they slaughtered the rams and splashed the blood on the altar; then they slaughtered the lambs and splashed the blood on the altar. ²³Then the he-goats for the purification offering were led before the king and

---

The consecration ceremony (29:20-30) begins with various sacrifices (sin offerings and sprinkling blood against the altar) to make atonement for all Israel. During the public sacrifices Levites are stationed in the temple and begin their music and song, while the priests sound their trumpets. At the same time the assembly bows down in prostration. Hezekiah arranges for burnt offerings accompanied by the Lord's song and the playing of trumpets and other musical instruments of David. Having music, song, and burnt offerings together seems to be a liturgical innovation of Hezekiah. The Levites praise God using the ancient words of David and Asaph.

When the assembly brings thank offerings and burnt offerings (29:31-33), Levites assist the priests to prepare the offerings, until enough priests had consecrated themselves. The Chronicler notes that the Levites "were more careful than the priests to sanctify themselves" (29:34). This was a time of great rejoicing over the revival of worship and the Chronicler offers a message for his own era. Postexilic Israelites should adhere to the great worship traditions, especially Passover and Unleavened Bread, which recall Israel's covenant with their God. Worship should include public sacrifices, music, and song, along with physical prostration; it concludes with personal sacrificial offerings, many of them shared in a liturgical meal with great rejoicing.

the assembly, who laid their hands upon them. ²⁴The priests then slaughtered them and offered their blood on the altar to atone for the sin of all Israel. For the king had said, "The burnt offering and the purification offering are for all Israel."

²⁵He stationed the Levites in the LORD's house with cymbals, harps, and lyres, according to the command of David, of Gad the king's seer, and of Nathan the prophet; for this command was from the LORD through his prophets. ²⁶The Levites were stationed with the instruments of David, and the priests with the trumpets. ²⁷Then Hezekiah ordered the burnt offering to be sacrificed on the altar. At the very moment the burnt offering began, they also began the song of the LORD, to the accompaniment of the trumpets and the instruments of David, king of Israel. ²⁸The entire assembly bowed down, and the song was sung and the trumpets sounded until the burnt offering had been completed. ²⁹Once the burnt offering was completed, the king and all who were with him knelt and worshiped. ³⁰King Hezekiah and the princes then told the Levites to sing the praises of the LORD in the words of David and of Asaph the seer. They sang praises till their joy was full, then fell down and worshiped.

³¹Hezekiah then said: "You have dedicated yourselves to the LORD. Approach, and bring forward the sacrifices and thank offerings for the house of the LORD." Then the assembly brought forward the sacrifices and thank offerings and all their voluntary burnt offerings. ³²The number of burnt offerings that the assembly brought forward was seventy oxen, one hundred rams, and two hundred lambs: all of these as a burnt offering to the LORD. ³³As consecrated gifts there were six hundred oxen and three thousand sheep. ³⁴Since there were too few priests to skin all the victims for the burnt offerings, their fellow Levites assisted them until the task was completed and the priests had sanctified themselves. The Levites, in fact, were more careful than the priests to sanctify themselves. ³⁵The burnt offerings were indeed many, along with the fat of the communion offerings and the libations for the burnt offerings. Thus the service of the house of the LORD was re-established. ³⁶Hezekiah and all the people rejoiced over what God had re-established for the people, and at how suddenly this had been done.

30 Invitation to Passover. ¹Hezekiah sent word to all Israel and Judah, and even wrote letters to Ephraim and Manasseh, saying that they should come

---

30:1-27 The celebration of Passover

This chapter has preparations for the Passover (30:1-12) and the ceremony itself (30:13-27). Invitations to come to Jerusalem for Passover go out also to the northern tribes Ephraim and Manasseh (30:1-2). It seems that the Chronicler aims at some kind of reconciliation with the lost northern tribes. He also invites them for a festival in the second month, as explained in 29:17. The invitation to "return to the Lord" in penitence intends that God might bring back all the exiles to their homeland (30:6). This spirituality

to the house of the LORD in Jerusalem to celebrate the Passover to the LORD, the God of Israel. ²The king, his princes, and the entire assembly in Jerusalem had agreed to celebrate the Passover during the second month. ³They could not celebrate it at the regular time because the priests had not sanctified themselves in sufficient numbers, and the people were not gathered at Jerusalem. ⁴This seemed right to the king and the entire assembly, ⁵and they issued a decree to be proclaimed throughout all Israel from Beersheba to Dan, that everyone should come to celebrate the Passover to the LORD, the God of Israel, in Jerusalem; for not many had kept it in the prescribed manner. ⁶By the king's command, the couriers, with the letters written by the king and his princes, went through all Israel and Judah. They said: "Israelites, return to the LORD, the God of Abraham, Isaac, and Israel, that he may return to you, the remnant left from the hands of the Assyrian kings. ⁷Do not be like your ancestors and your kin who acted treacherously toward the LORD, the God of their ancestors, so that he handed them over to desolation, as you yourselves now see. ⁸Do not be stiff-necked, as your ancestors were; stretch out your hands to the LORD and come to his sanctuary that he has consecrated forever, and serve the LORD, your God, that he may turn his burning anger from you. ⁹If you return to the LORD, your kinfolk

of repentance deepens; when you turn to the Lord you will find mercy before your captors, for your God is merciful and compassionate (30:9).

His invitation to Passover finds two distinct responses. Many northerners ridicule the messengers who bring the invitation, while others humble themselves and go to Jerusalem. For some northerners, answering Hezekiah's invitation carries political ramifications that they could not overcome. Southerners from Judea accept the invitation unanimously (30:12). They celebrate with a huge assembly in Jerusalem for the Unleavened Bread. The Passover sacrifices on the fourteenth of the month (30:14-20) follow prescriptions of the Torah of Moses. There were so many people who needed assistance but had not consecrated themselves that many Levites assisted them in their sacrifices (30:17). The Chronicler mentions large numbers of northerners who had not purified themselves but still ate the Passover meal against regulations. This act poses a challenge for the king. He prays to God for them, especially those who set their heart to seek the Lord (30:18). This shows the importance of a right heart, a spiritual intention in celebrating the festival sacrifice. The Chronicler focuses on inner spirituality in a balance with ritual actions. God listens to the king's prayer and heals the people (30:20). The feast of Unleavened Bread follows for another seven days, and it combines thanksgiving sacrifices and feasting with thanksgiving songs and music; it is another occasion of great joy.

and your children will find mercy with their captors and return to this land. The LORD, your God, is gracious and merciful and he will not turn away his face from you if you return to him."

¹⁰So the couriers passed from city to city in the land of Ephraim and Manasseh and as far as Zebulun, but they were derided and scoffed at. ¹¹Nevertheless, some from Asher, Manasseh, and Zebulun humbled themselves and came to Jerusalem. ¹²In Judah, however, the hand of God brought it about that the people were of one heart to carry out the command of the king and the princes by the word of the LORD. ¹³Thus many people gathered in Jerusalem to celebrate the feast of Unleavened Bread in the second month; it was a very great assembly.

Passover Celebrated. ¹⁴They proceeded to remove the altars that were in Jerusalem as well as all the altars of incense, and cast them into the Wadi Kidron. ¹⁵They slaughtered the Passover on the fourteenth day of the second month. The priests and Levites were shamed into sanctifying themselves and brought burnt offerings into the house of the LORD. ¹⁶They stood in the places prescribed for them according to the law of Moses, the man of God. The priests splashed the blood given them by the Levites; ¹⁷for many in the assembly had not sanctified themselves, and the Levites were in charge of slaughtering the Passover victims for all who were unclean so as to consecrate them to the LORD. ¹⁸The greater part of the people, in fact, chiefly from Ephraim, Manasseh,

---

The entire assembly decides on an additional festival of seven days, a festival not required by Torah and not characterized by burnt offerings or Levitical song and music. However, the notion of joy or rejoicing appears three times in the space of four verses (30:23-26), so typical for the Chronicler. This was an inclusive celebration—with Judeans (community, priests, and Levites), northerners from Israel, and resident aliens (from Judah and Israel). Joy and inclusiveness were sufficient reasons for the Chronicler's enthusiasm: he exclaims that Hezekiah's Passover was like none since the days of David and Solomon (30:26). This celebration shows five important aspects of Israel's public worship. First, it should be an inclusive celebration. Second, it recognizes God's past generosity to Israel, especially the exodus from Egypt. Third, speaking of the Lord as merciful and compassionate highlights the notion of God's everlasting compassion, often related to the exodus tradition. Fourth, a whole heart was crucial for good worship. Fifth, there should be great joy and rejoicing. The Chronicler uses the word for joy six times in these chapters (29:30, 36; 30:21, 23, 25, and 26), suggesting that the rituals of worship, exercised with a full heart, actually lead to great rejoicing and to the experience of unity with each other and their entire tradition (30:26).

Issachar, and Zebulun, had not cleansed themselves. Nevertheless they ate the Passover, contrary to the prescription; because Hezekiah prayed for them, saying, "May the good LORD grant pardon to [19]all who have set their heart to seek God, the LORD, the God of their ancestors, even though they are not clean as holiness requires." [20]The LORD heard Hezekiah and healed the people.

[21]Thus the Israelites who were in Jerusalem celebrated the feast of Unleavened Bread with great rejoicing for seven days, and the Levites and the priests sang the praises of the LORD day after day with all their strength. [22]Hezekiah spoke encouragingly to all the Levites who had shown themselves well skilled in the service of the LORD. And when they had completed the seven days of festival, sacrificing communion offerings and singing praises to the LORD, the God of their ancestors, [23]the whole assembly agreed to celebrate another seven days. So with joy they celebrated seven days more. [24]King Hezekiah of Judah had contributed a thousand bulls and seven thousand sheep to the assembly, and the princes a thousand bulls and ten thousand sheep. The priests sanctified themselves in great numbers, [25]and the whole assembly of Judah rejoiced, together with the priests and Levites and

the rest of the assembly that had come from Israel, as well as the resident aliens from the land of Israel and those that lived in Judah. [26]There was great rejoicing in Jerusalem, for since the days of Solomon, son of David, king of Israel, there had been nothing like it in the city. [27]Then the levitical priests rose and blessed the people; their voice was heard and their prayer reached heaven, God's holy dwelling.

31 Liturgical Reforms. [1]After all this was over, those Israelites who had been present went forth to the cities of Judah and smashed the sacred pillars, cut down the asherahs, and tore down the high places and altars throughout Judah, Benjamin, Ephraim, and Manasseh, until they were all destroyed. Then the Israelites returned to their cities, each to his own possession.

[2]Hezekiah re-established the divisions of the priests and the Levites according to their former divisions, assigning to each priest and Levite his proper service, whether in regard to burnt offerings or communion offerings, thanksgiving or praise, or ministering in the gates of the encampment of the LORD. [3]From his own wealth the king allotted a portion for burnt offerings, those of morning and evening and those on sabbaths, new moons, and festivals,

---

31:1-21 Hezekiah provides for priests and Levites

This chapter adds more information about religious matters during Hezekiah's reign. They continue to remove vestiges of idolatry after the Passover feast. Hezekiah also establishes the work rotations of priests and Levites, similar to the specifications of David in 1 Chronicles 23–27 (31:2). The monarch is responsible for providing animals for sacrifice; royal funding of sacrifices was likely the historical practice in postexilic times. Finan-

as is written in the law of the LORD. [4]He also commanded the people living in Jerusalem to provide for the support of the priests and Levites, that they might firmly adhere to the law of the LORD.

[5]As soon as the order was promulgated, the Israelites brought, in great quantities, the best of their grain, wine, oil, and honey, and all the produce of the fields; they gave a generous tithe of everything. [6]Israelites and Judahites living in other cities of Judah also brought in tithes of oxen, sheep, and votive offerings consecrated to the LORD, their God; these they brought in and heaped up in piles. [7]It was in the third month that they began to establish these heaps, and they completed them in the seventh month. [8]When Hezekiah and the princes had come and seen the piles, they blessed the LORD and his people Israel. [9]Then Hezekiah questioned the priests and the Levites concerning the piles, [10]and the priest Azariah, head of the house of Zadok, answered him, "Since they began to bring the offerings to the house of the LORD, we have eaten, been satisfied, and had much left over, for the LORD has blessed his people. This great supply is what was left over."

[11]Hezekiah then gave orders that chambers be constructed in the house of the LORD. When this had been done, [12]they deposited the offerings, tithes, and votive offerings there for safekeeping. The overseer of these things was Conaniah the Levite, and his brother Shimei was second in command. [13]Jehiel, Azaziah, Nahath, Asahel, Jerimoth, Jozabad, Eliel, Ismachiah, Mahath, and Benaiah were supervisors subject to Conaniah the Levite and his brother Shimei by appointment of King Hezekiah and of Azariah, the prefect of the house of God. [14]Kore, the son of Imnah, a Levite and the keeper of the eastern gate, was in charge of the voluntary offerings made to God; he distributed the offerings made to the LORD and the most holy of the votive offerings. [15]Under him in the priestly cities were Eden, Miniamin, Jeshua, Shemaiah, Amariah, and Shecaniah, who faithfully made the distribution to their brothers, great and small alike, according to their divisions.

[16]There was also a register by ancestral houses of males three years of age and over, for all priests who were eligible to enter the house of the LORD according to the daily schedule to fulfill their service in the order of their divisions. [17]The priests were inscribed in their family records according to their ancestral houses, as were the Levites twenty years of age and over according to their various offices and divisions. [18]A

cial remuneration for priests and Levites is assigned to voluntary offerings of the people, who respond generously (31:4-13). Moreover, one document specifies the organization of Levites and priests for the distribution of tithes to them (31:14-19). The chapter ends with a positive summary of Hezekiah's actions; he has acted with a whole heart, so he prospers. The only other king who prospered, according to the Chronicler, was Solomon (1 Chr 29:23), which means that they both follow God's Torah.

distribution was also made to all who were inscribed in the family records, for their little ones, wives, sons and daughters—thus for the entire assembly, since they were to sanctify themselves by sharing faithfully in the votive offerings. [19]The sons of Aaron, the priests who lived on the lands attached to their cities, had in every city men designated by name to distribute portions to every male of the priests and to every Levite listed in the family records.

[20]Hezekiah did this in all Judah. He did what was good, upright, and faithful before the LORD, his God. [21]Everything that he undertook, for the service of the house of God or for the law and the commandment, was to seek his God. He did this with all his heart, and he prospered.

32 **Sennacherib's Invasion.** [1]But after all this and all Hezekiah's fidelity, there came Sennacherib, king of Assyria. He invaded Judah and besieged the fortified cities, intending to breach and take them. [2]When Hezekiah saw that Sennacherib was coming with the intention of attacking Jerusalem, [3]he took the advice of his princes and warriors to stop the waters of the springs outside the city; they promised their help. [4]A large force was gathered and stopped all the springs and also the stream running nearby. For they said, "Why should the kings of Assyria come and find an abundance of water?" [5]He then looked to his defenses: he rebuilt the wall where it was broken down, raised towers upon it, and built another wall outside. He strengthened the Millo of the City of David and made a great number of spears and shields. [6]Then he appointed army commanders over the people. He gathered them together in his presence in the open space at the gate of the city and encouraged them with these words: [7]"Be strong and steadfast; do not be afraid or dismayed because of the king of Assyria and all the horde coming with him, for there is more with us than with him. [8]He has only an arm of flesh,

32:1-33 [cf. 2 Kgs 18:13–20:21; Isa 36:1–39:8] Invasion of Sennacherib and other events during Hezekiah's reign

The challenges brought on by the Assyrian invasion of Judah take up only one chapter here, but two chapters in Kings (2 Kgs 18:13–20:19) and Isaiah (chs. 36–37). The Chronicler's interest in Hezekiah's political and military affairs focuses more on their religious and theological significance, though his reign was apparently a time of great construction projects in Jerusalem (32:27-30). The discussions and negotiations between Judeans and Assyrians in Kings are shortened by the Chronicler, who then mentions that Hezekiah and the prophet Isaiah pray to God (32:20), who delivers them just as he had delivered Israel during the reigns of Abijah (13:3-20), Asa (14:9-15), and Jehoshaphat (20:1-30). Finally, a very brief version of Hezekiah's illness is mentioned (32:24), distilled from 2 Kings 20:1-11 and Isaiah 38:1-22 (with the famous prayer of Hezekiah).

but we have the LORD, our God, to help us and to fight our battles." And the people took confidence from the words of Hezekiah, king of Judah.

Threat of Sennacherib. ⁹After this, while Sennacherib, king of Assyria, himself remained at Lachish with all his forces, he sent his officials to Jerusalem with this message for Hezekiah, king of Judah, and all the Judahites who were in Jerusalem: ¹⁰"Thus says Sennacherib, king of Assyria: In what are you trusting, now that you are under siege in Jerusalem? ¹¹Is not Hezekiah deceiving you, delivering you over to a death of famine and thirst, by his claim that 'the LORD, our God, will rescue us from the grasp of the king of Assyria'? ¹²Has not this same Hezekiah removed the Lord's own high places and altars and commanded Judah and Jerusalem, 'You shall bow down before one altar only, and on it alone you shall offer incense'? ¹³Do you not know what my fathers and I have done to all the peoples of other lands? Were the gods of the nations in those lands able to rescue their lands from my hand? ¹⁴Who among all the gods of those nations which my fathers put under the ban was able to rescue their people from my hand? Will your god, then, be able to rescue you from my hand? ¹⁵Let not Hezekiah mislead you further and deceive you in any such way. Do not believe him! Since no other god of any other nation or kingdom has been able to rescue his people from my hand or the hands of my fathers, how much the less shall your god rescue you from my hand!"

¹⁶His officials said still more against the LORD God and against his servant Hezekiah, ¹⁷for he had written letters to deride the LORD, the God of Israel, speaking of him in these terms: "As the gods of the nations in other lands have not rescued their people from my hand, neither shall Hezekiah's god rescue his people from my hand." ¹⁸In a loud voice they shouted in the language of Judah to the people of Jerusalem who were on the wall, to frighten and terrify them so that they might capture their city. ¹⁹They spoke of the God of Israel as though he were one of the gods of the other peoples of the earth, a work of human hands. ²⁰But because of this, King Hezekiah and Isaiah the prophet, son of Amoz, prayed and cried out to heaven.

Sennacherib's Defeat. ²¹Then the LORD sent an angel, who destroyed every

---

Still, there are danger signs. Hezekiah is affected by pride (32:25), though he later humbles himself, thus delaying God's anger until after his time (32:26). Sin is followed by repentance, but it seems possible that the exile was occasioned by his pride. Hezekiah's repentance repairs the breach, for he is greatly successful again. Great construction projects date to this era, including diversion of the spring Gihon (32:30), corroborated by Hezekiah's tunnel (visible to this day), with an inscription describing its construction. Also, envoys came to him from Babylon to make inquiries. Finally comes his death notice (32:32-33), with the positive note that he was buried in royal tombs in Jerusalem.

warrior, leader, and commander in the camp of the Assyrian king, so that he had to return shamefaced to his own country. And when he entered the temple of his god, some of his own offspring struck him down there with the sword. ²²Thus the LORD saved Hezekiah and the inhabitants of Jerusalem from the hand of Sennacherib, king of Assyria, as from every other power; he gave them rest on every side. ²³Many brought gifts for the LORD to Jerusalem and costly objects for Hezekiah, king of Judah, who thereafter was exalted in the eyes of all the nations.

Hezekiah's Later Reign. ²⁴In those days Hezekiah became mortally ill. He prayed to the LORD, who answered him by giving him a sign. ²⁵Hezekiah, however, did not respond with like generosity, for he had become arrogant. Therefore wrath descended upon him and upon Judah and Jerusalem. ²⁶But then Hezekiah humbled himself for his pride—both he and the inhabitants of Jerusalem; and therefore the wrath of the LORD did not come upon them during the time of Hezekiah.

²⁷Hezekiah possessed very great wealth and glory. He made treasuries for his silver, gold, precious stones, spices, jewels, and other precious things of all kinds; ²⁸also storehouses for the harvest of grain, for wine and oil, and barns for the various kinds of cattle and flocks. ²⁹He built cities for himself, and he acquired sheep and oxen in great numbers, for God gave him very great riches. ³⁰This same Hezekiah stopped the upper outlet for water from Gihon and redirected it underground westward to the City of David. Hezekiah prospered in all his works. ³¹Nevertheless, in respect to the ambassadors of the Babylonian officials who were sent to him to investigate the sign that had occurred in the land, God abandoned him as a test, to know all that was in his heart.

³²The rest of Hezekiah's acts, including his good deeds, are recorded in the vision of Isaiah the prophet, son of Amoz, and in the book of the kings of Judah and Israel. ³³Hezekiah rested with his ancestors; he was buried at the approach to the tombs of the descendants of David. All Judah and the inhabitants of Jerusalem paid him honor at his death. His son Manasseh succeeded him as king.

33 **Manasseh's Impiety.** ¹Manasseh was twelve years old when he became king, and he reigned fifty-five years in Jerusalem. ²He did what was

---

THE FALL OF JUDAH

2 Chronicles 33–36

33:1-20 [cf. 2 Kgs 21:1-18] The reign of Manasseh

The Chronicler transforms a very negative view of Manasseh in the book of Kings into a vision of hope. Here is a great idolater who becomes a king who is humbled and repents of his sin. His reign of fifty-five years must be seen as a blessing. At first he does evil (as in Kings), rebuilding high places that Hezekiah had torn down, and conducting child sacrifice

The sign showing the water level of Hezekiah's underground tunnel into Jerusalem (2 Chr 32:30).

evil in the LORD's sight, following the abominable practices of the nations whom the LORD dispossessed before the Israelites. [3]He rebuilt the high places which Hezekiah his father had torn down. He set up altars to the Baals, and also made asherahs. He bowed down to the whole host of heaven and served them. [4]He built altars in the house of the LORD, of which the LORD had said: In Jerusalem shall my name be forever; [5]and he built altars to the whole host of heaven in the two courts of the house of the LORD. [6]It was he, too, who immolated his children by fire in the Valley of Ben-hinnom. He practiced soothsaying and divination, and reintroduced the consulting of ghosts and spirits.

He did much evil in the LORD's sight and provoked him to anger. [7]An idol he had made he placed in the house of God, of which God had said to David and to his son Solomon: In this house and in Jerusalem, which I have chosen out of all the tribes of Israel, I shall set my name forever. [8]I will no longer make Israel step out of the land I assigned to your ancestors, provided that they are careful to observe all I commanded them, the entire law, the statutes, and the ordinances given by Moses.

[9]Manasseh misled Judah and the inhabitants of Jerusalem into doing even greater evil than the nations the LORD had destroyed at the coming of the Israelites. [10]The LORD spoke to Manasseh and his people, but they paid no attention.

Manasseh's Conversion. [11]Therefore the LORD brought against them the army commanders of the Assyrian king; they captured Manasseh with hooks, shackled him with chains, and transported him to Babylon. [12]In his distress, he began to appease the LORD, his God. He humbled himself abjectly before the God of his ancestors, [13]and prayed to him. The LORD let himself be won over: he heard his prayer and restored him to his kingdom in Jerusalem. Then Manasseh knew that the LORD is indeed God.

[14]Afterward he built an outer wall for the City of David to the west of Gihon in the valley, extending to the Fish Gate and encircling Ophel; he built it very high. He stationed army officers in all the fortified cities of Judah. [15]He removed the foreign gods and the idol from the LORD's house and all the altars he had built on the mount of the LORD's house and in Jerusalem, and cast them outside the city. [16]He restored the altar

---

in the valley of Ben-hin-nom (i.e., Gehenna, as in the New Testament: Matt 5:22; Mark 9:43; Jas 3:6). The Chronicler's new version in verses 10-17 is surprising. God warns Manasseh and the people to repent (33:10), and then Assyrians capture him and take him to Babylon (33:11). There he prays to his God and humbles himself (33:12; cf. 2 Chr 7:14); his petition is heard and God returns him to Jerusalem, so Manasseh knows that the Lord is God (33:13). Then he pursues ambitious construction projects in the city of David, removing idols and altars, and installing an altar for the Lord. Although his life is changed, the people keep sacrificing on high places,

of the LORD, and sacrificed on it communion offerings and thank offerings, and commanded Judah to serve the LORD, the God of Israel. [17]Though the people continued to sacrifice on the high places, they now did so to the LORD, their God.

[18]The rest of the acts of Manasseh, his prayer to his God, and the words of the seers who spoke to him in the name of the LORD, the God of Israel, are written in the chronicles of the kings of Israel. [19]His prayer and how his supplication was heard, all his sins and his treachery, the sites where he built high places and set up asherahs and carved images before he humbled himself, all this is recorded in the chronicles of his seers. [20]Manasseh rested with his ancestors

and was buried in his own palace. His son Amon succeeded him as king.

Reign of Amon. [21]Amon was twenty-two years old when he became king, and he reigned two years in Jerusalem. [22]He did what was evil in the LORD's sight, as his father Manasseh had done. Amon offered sacrifice to all the idols his father Manasseh had made, and served them. [23]Moreover, he did not humble himself before the LORD as his father Manasseh had humbled himself; on the contrary, Amon only increased his guilt. [24]His officials plotted against him and put him to death in his palace, [25]but the people of the land then slew all who had plotted against King Amon, and the people of the land made his son Josiah king in his stead.

though to the Lord (33:17). In conclusion the Chronicler mentions particularly Manasseh's prayer to God after he had been humbled and that he was buried in his house (33:18-20). These verses replace the condemnation in 2 Kings 21:10-16. The Chronicler omits mentioning that his sin and the evil of Manasseh were the reason for the downfall of Judah in the South.

Unlike other Judean kings, Manasseh's life pattern went from bad to good. The Chronicler seldom invents stories, so this account may be considered historical in some way. Still, his repentance, return, and actions are not portrayed as historical but as acts of God. The Chronicler uses his life as an excellent example of the possibility of repentance, forgiveness, and grace, especially for postexilic Israel. In this tradition is the beautiful Prayer of Manasseh, a prayer of penitence found in the Apocrypha but not in the biblical canon.

33:21-25 [cf. 2 Kgs 21:19-26] The reign of Amon

Manasseh's son, Amon, follows the evil in his father's life rather than humbling himself, as Manasseh had done. Rather, he increases his own guilt (33:23). As in Kings, he was assassinated by conspiratorial servants, who were in turn struck down by the people of the land (33:25). Unlike the Kings account, there is no burial notice or regnal notice for this king.

34 **Josiah's Reforms.** ¹Josiah was eight years old when he became king, and he reigned thirty-one years in Jerusalem. ²He did what was right in the LORD's sight, walking in the way of David his father, not turning right or left. ³In the eighth year of his reign, while he was still a youth, he began to seek after the God of David his father. Then in his twelfth year he began to purify Judah and Jerusalem of the high places, the asherahs, and the carved and molten images. ⁴In his presence, the altars of the Baals were torn down; the incense stands erected above them he broke down; the asherahs and the carved and molten images he smashed and beat into dust, which he scattered over the tombs of those who had sacrificed to them; ⁵and the bones of the priests he burned upon their altars. Thus he purified Judah and Jerusalem. ⁶He did likewise in the cities of Manasseh, Ephraim, Simeon, and in the ruined villages of the surrounding country as far as Naphtali; ⁷he tore down the altars and asherahs, and the carved images he beat into dust, and broke down the incense stands throughout the land of Israel. Then he returned to Jerusalem.

The Temple Restored. ⁸In the eighteenth year of his reign, in order to purify the land and the temple, he sent Shaphan,

34:1-7 [cf. 2 Kgs 22:1-2] The reign of Josiah: early reform movements

After Amon's murder the people of the land make the eight-year-old Josiah their king. Surely other officials administer the kingdom until he reaches his majority at age twenty, the twelfth year of his reign (34:3). Josiah is a notable religious reformer, but the Chronicler's description differs greatly from 2 Kings; there Josiah initiates the reform after his officials find the book of Torah in the temple. For the Chronicler, Josiah's religious concerns come first. At age sixteen he begins to seek the God of David his forebear, removing high places from Judah and Jerusalem. At age twenty, when he begins to rule himself, his religious reforms begin. He removes and destroys idol altars and images in Jerusalem and Judah; then they pulverize all these objects and spread their dust on the graves of their worshipers (34:4). Since corpse pollution is considered a terrible degradation in Israel, these actions would be especially harsh. As elsewhere, the Chronicler extends the reform to northern Israel (34:6). Josiah's religious devotion and concerns come first in his career, which is the Chronicler's preferred order of events (also evidenced in the lives of David and Solomon). The Chronicler also emphasizes that worship and liturgy typify Israel as God's people, more than politics, economics, or warfare.

34:8-18 [cf. 2 Kgs 22:3–11] The Torah book discovered

Josiah's religious concern continues. At age twenty-six he orders his officials to repair the Jerusalem temple, using funds collected by the Levites

son of Azaliah, Maaseiah, the ruler of the city, and Joah, son of Joahaz, the chancellor, to restore the house of the LORD, his God. ⁹They came to Hilkiah the high priest and turned over the money brought to the house of God which the Levites, the guardians of the threshold, had collected from Manasseh, Ephraim, and all the remnant of Israel, as well as from all of Judah, Benjamin, and the inhabitants of Jerusalem. ¹⁰They turned it over to the master workers in the house of the LORD, and these in turn used it to pay the workers in the LORD's house who were restoring and repairing it. ¹¹They also gave it to the carpenters and the masons to buy hewn stone and timber for the tie beams and rafters of the buildings which the kings of Judah had allowed to fall into ruin. ¹²The men worked faithfully at their task; their overseers were Jahath and Obadiah, Levites of the line of Merari, and Zechariah and Meshullam, of the Kohathites, who directed them. All those Levites who were skillful with musical instruments ¹³were in charge of the men who carried the burdens, and they directed all the workers in every kind of labor. Some of the other Levites were scribes, officials, and gatekeepers.

The Finding of the Law. ¹⁴When they brought out the money that had been deposited in the house of the LORD, Hilkiah the priest found the book of the law of the LORD given through Moses. ¹⁵He reported this to Shaphan the scribe, saying, "I have found the book of the law in the house of the LORD." Hilkiah gave the book to Shaphan, ¹⁶who brought it to the king at the same time that he made his report to him. He said, "Your servants are doing everything that has been entrusted to them; ¹⁷they have smelted down the silver deposited in the LORD's house and have turned it over to the overseers and the workers." ¹⁸Then Shaphan the scribe also informed the king, "Hilkiah the priest has given me a book," and then Shaphan read it in the presence of the king.

¹⁹When the king heard the words of the law, he tore his garments. ²⁰The king

from Israel, Judah, and Jerusalem. They give the money to the appointed workers, honest workers supervised by various Levites. In the midst of these operations Hilkiah the priest finds the book of the Torah given through Moses (34:14). He hands it over to Shaphan, an official, who takes it to Josiah to read aloud before the king (34:18). When Josiah hears the words of the Torah he weeps and tears his garments and is moved to repentance by what he has heard. Many scholars today think that this scroll discovered in the temple was a version of the book of Deuteronomy. For the Chronicler, this discovery results from his reforms, whereas in Kings this discovery motivates Josiah to reform.

34:19-33 [cf. 2 Kgs 22:12–23:3] Confirmation by the prophetess Huldah

Eager to learn the status of this document, Josiah sends Hilkiah, Shaphan, and other officials to inquire of the prophetess Huldah. She responds in an

then issued this command to Hilkiah, to Ahikam, son of Shaphan, to Abdon, son of Michah, to Shaphan the scribe, and to Asaiah, the king's servant: ²¹"Go, consult the LORD for me and for those who are left in Israel and Judah, about the words of the book that has been found, for the anger of the LORD burns furiously against us, because our ancestors did not keep the word of the LORD and have not done all that is written in this book." ²²Then Hilkiah and others from the king went to Huldah the prophet, wife of Shallum, son of Tokhath, son of Hasrah, keeper of the wardrobe; she lived in Jerusalem, in the Second Quarter. They spoke to her as they had been instructed, ²³and she said to them: "Thus says the LORD, the God of Israel: Say to the man who sent you to me, ²⁴Thus says the LORD: I am about to bring evil upon this place and upon its inhabitants, all the curses written in the book that was read before the king of Judah. ²⁵Because they have abandoned me and have burned incense to other gods, provoking me by all the works of their hands, my anger burns against this place and it cannot be extinguished.

²⁶"But to the king of Judah who sent you to consult the LORD, give this response: Thus says the LORD, the God of Israel: As for the words you have heard, ²⁷because you were heartsick and have humbled yourself before God when you heard his words concerning this place and its inhabitants; because you humbled yourself before me, tore your garments, and wept before me, I in turn have heard—oracle of the LORD. ²⁸I will gather you to your ancestors and you shall go to your grave in peace, and your eyes shall not see all the evil I am about to bring upon this place and upon its inhabitants."

This they reported to the king.

Covenant Renewal. ²⁹ The king then had all the elders of Judah and of Jerusalem summoned before him. ³⁰The king went up to the house of the LORD with all the people of Judah and the inhabitants of Jerusalem: priests, Levites, and all the people, great and small. He read aloud to them all the words of the book of the covenant that had been found in the house of the LORD. ³¹The king stood by the column and made a covenant in the presence of the LORD to follow the LORD and to observe his commandments, statutes, and decrees with his whole heart and soul, carrying out the

oracle which describes the evil about to overcome Jerusalem and Judah because of their sins (34:23-28). She answers their question only indirectly. She says that God is about to enact all the curses written in the book (presumably those listed in Deut 28:15-68), which implies that Israel deserves the fulfillment of God's word in Deuteronomy. So she implies that this book of Torah is authentic, i.e., it is God's word for Israel. But she also prophesies that Josiah will die in peace rather than in battle, because he repented (34:27-28). She is the prophet who authenticates the Torah document and exhorts the king and people to adhere to it and the covenant with God. She is the one woman prophet of the era of Israel's monarchy.

words of the covenant written in this book. [32]He thereby committed all who were in Jerusalem and Benjamin, and the inhabitants of Jerusalem acted according to the covenant of God, the God of their ancestors. [33]Josiah removed every abomination from all the territories belonging to the Israelites, and he obliged all who were in Israel to serve the LORD, their God. During his lifetime they did not turn away from following the LORD, the God of their ancestors.

35 The Passover. [1]Josiah celebrated in Jerusalem a Passover to honor the LORD; the Passover sacrifice was slaughtered on the fourteenth day of the first month. [2]He reappointed the priests to their duties and confirmed them in the service of the LORD's house. [3]He said to the Levites who were to instruct all Israel, and who were consecrated to the

LORD: "Put the holy ark in the house built by Solomon, son of David, king of Israel. It shall no longer be a burden on your shoulders. Serve now the LORD, your God, and his people Israel. [4]Prepare yourselves by your ancestral houses and your divisions according to the prescriptions of David, king of Israel, and the prescriptions of his son Solomon. [5]Stand in the sanctuary according to the branches of the ancestral houses of your kin, the common people, so that the distribution of the Levites and the families may be the same. [6]Slaughter the Passover sacrifice, sanctify yourselves, and be at the disposition of your kin, that all may be done according to the word of the LORD given through Moses."

[7]Josiah contributed to the common people a flock of lambs and young goats, thirty thousand in number, each

35:1-19 [cf. 2 Kgs 23:21-23] Josiah keeps the Passover

Josiah's religious reform also includes a great Passover celebration at the Jerusalem temple, just as Hezekiah has done. Here again the festival is not family-oriented as in contemporary practice but is an act of public worship. It includes slaughtering Passover lambs, burnt offerings, arrangements for the priests and Levites, singers, and gatekeepers. It is followed by the Feast of Unleavened Bread for seven days. This celebration proceeds according to plan.

One unique aspect of this celebration is the description of roles for the Levites. The Chronicler identifies them as teachers of Israel and changes their responsibilities; no longer do they carry the ark, but they assist in temple liturgy and they help in the flaying of the Passover lambs (35:11). The Chronicler emphasizes that the Levites follow God's word found in the Scriptures: verses 6 and 12 connect their roles with the book of Moses. The Chronicler was very impressed with this festival, noting that nothing comparable had occurred since the days of Samuel the prophet. The Chronicler uses this pattern of an authentic Passover celebration to encourage his community's practice.

137

to serve as a Passover victim for all who were present, and also three thousand oxen; these were from the king's property. [8]His princes also gave a voluntary offering to the people, the priests, and the Levites. Hilkiah, Zechariah, and Jehiel, prefects of the house of God, gave to the priests two thousand six hundred Passover victims along with three hundred oxen. [9]Conaniah and his brothers Shemaiah, Nethanel, Hashabiah, Jehiel, and Jozabad, the rulers of the Levites, contributed to the Levites five thousand Passover victims, together with five hundred oxen.

[10]When the service had been arranged, the priests took their places, as did the Levites in their divisions according to the king's command. [11]The Passover sacrifice was slaughtered, whereupon the priests splashed some of the blood and the Levites proceeded with the skinning. [12]They separated out what was destined for the burnt offering and gave it to various groups of the ancestral houses of the common people to offer to the LORD, as is written in the book of Moses. They did the same with the oxen. [13]They cooked the Passover on the fire as prescribed, and also cooked the sacred portions in pots, caldrons, and pans, then brought them quickly to all the common people. [14]Afterward they prepared the Passover for themselves and for the priests. Indeed the priests, the sons of Aaron, were busy sacrificing burnt offerings and the fatty portions until night; therefore the Levites prepared for themselves and for the priests, the sons of Aaron. [15]The singers, the sons of Asaph, were at their posts as commanded by David and by Asaph, Heman, and Jeduthun, the king's seer. The gatekeepers were at every gate; there was no need for them to leave their stations, for their fellow Levites prepared for them. [16]Thus the entire service of the LORD was arranged that day so that the Passover could be celebrated and the burnt offerings sacrificed on the altar of the LORD, as King Josiah had commanded. [17]The Israelites who were present on that occasion kept the Passover and the feast of the Unleavened Bread for seven days. [18]No such Passover had been observed in Israel since the time of Samuel the prophet; no king of Israel had observed a Passover like that celebrated by Josiah, the priests, and Levites, all of Judah and Israel that were present, and the inhabitants of Jerusalem. [19]It was in the eighteenth year of Josiah's reign that this Passover was observed.

Josiah's End. [20]After Josiah had done all this to restore the temple, Neco, king of Egypt, came up to fight at Carchemish on the Euphrates, and Josiah went out

---

35:20–36:1 [cf. 2 Kgs 23:28-30] The death of Josiah

Despite his religious reforms and despite Huldah's prophecy about Josiah dying peacefully, this king gets caught in the war between Egypt and Assyria. He moves into the path of Pharaoh Neco on his northward battle march through Israel. Chronicles reflects the basic narrative in Kings, but the Chronicler seems troubled by Josiah's untimely, unmerited death.

to meet him. ²¹Neco sent messengers to him, saying: "What quarrel is between us, king of Judah? I have not come against you this day, for my war is with another kingdom, and God has told me to hasten. Do not interfere with God who is with me; let him not destroy you." ²²But Josiah would not withdraw from him, for he was seeking a pretext to fight with him. Therefore he would not listen to the words of Neco that came from the mouth of God, but went out to fight in the plain of Megiddo. ²³Then the archers shot King Josiah, who said to his servants, "Take me away, I am seriously wounded." ²⁴His servants took him from his own chariot, placed him in the one he had in reserve, and brought him to Jerusalem, where he died. He was bur-

ied in the tombs of his ancestors, and all Judah and Jerusalem mourned him. ²⁵Jeremiah also composed a lamentation for Josiah, which is recited to this day by all the male and female singers in their lamentations for Josiah. These have been made an ordinance for Israel, and can be found written in the Lamentations.

²⁶ The rest of the acts of Josiah, his good deeds in accord with what is written in the law of the LORD, ²⁷and his words, first and last, are recorded in the book of the kings of Israel and Judah.

36 **Jehoahaz.** ¹The people of the land took Jehoahaz, son of Josiah, and made him king in Jerusalem to succeed his father. ²Jehoahaz was twenty-three years old when he became king, and he reigned three months in Jerusalem. ³The

Neco, the Egyptian ruler, proclaims to Josiah that he intends to attack the house of Judah but not him, so he should cease his opposition. Josiah does not obey Neco, but the Chronicler explains it in a startling way: "he would not listen to the words of Neco that came from the mouth of God" (35:22). Even an enemy king can mediate God's word to Israel! Perhaps his downfall relates to disbelief in God's word through the Pharaoh, for Josiah is soon shot by archers, mortally wounded, and dies after his servants carry him back to Jerusalem. Judah and Jerusalem all mourn for Josiah (35:24), and Jeremiah utters a lamentation for him, while male and female singers mention him in their lamentations (35:25). These lamentations remind us of the book of Lamentations, usually connected with Jeremiah the prophet. Josiah has a glorious burial, for he has been loyal and faithful to God's Torah (35:26). This death notice is extremely positive for Judah's last independent king.

36:2-4 [cf. 2 Kgs 23:31-35] The reign and dethronement of Jehoahaz

Made king by the people of the land, Jehoahaz reigns only three months before being deposed by the king of Egypt. Neco imposes tribute on the land, replaces Jehoahaz with his brother Eliakim (his name is changed to Jehoiakim), and exiles him to Egypt. The Chronicler's account is so brief—an indignity in itself—that it even omits negative comments about his evils.

king of Egypt deposed him in Jerusalem and fined the land one hundred talents of silver and a talent of gold. ⁴Then the king of Egypt made Eliakim, the brother of Jehoahaz, king over Judah and Jerusalem, changing his name to Jehoiakim. Neco took Jehoahaz his brother away and brought him to Egypt.

Jehoiakim. ⁵Jehoiakim was twenty-five years old when he became king, and he reigned eleven years in Jerusalem. He did what was evil in the sight of the Lord, his God. ⁶Nebuchadnezzar, king of Babylon, attacked and bound him in chains to take him to Babylon. ⁷Nebuchadnezzar also carried away to Babylon some of the vessels of the house of the Lord and put them in his palace in Babylon. ⁸The rest of the acts of Jehoiakim, the abominable things that he did, and what therefore happened to him, are recorded in the book of the kings of Israel and Judah. His son Jehoiachin succeeded him as king.

Jehoiachin. ⁹Jehoiachin was eighteen years old when he became king, and he reigned three months and ten days in Jerusalem. He did what was evil in the Lord's sight. ¹⁰At the turn of the year, King Nebuchadnezzar sent for him and had him brought to Babylon, along with precious vessels from the house of the Lord. He made his brother Zedekiah king over Judah and Jerusalem.

36:5-8 [cf. 2 Kgs 23:36–24:7] The reign of Jehoiakim

The Chronicler greatly abridges Jehoiakim's story in Kings. He removes much of the information in 2 Kings, including hints of the great historical shifts of this time, when Egypt was defeated by Babylon and Judea shifted loyalties from Pharaoh Neco to Nebuchadnezzar of Babylon. He also omits the king's revolt against his Babylonian overlord. For the Chronicler it seems sufficient to mention his reign of eleven years, the evil and abominations of his reign, and his capture and exile to Babylon by Nebuchadnezzar. As usual, the Chronicler's interest focuses on his king's religious posture, so he adds the information that Nebuchadnezzar took vessels from the Jerusalem temple to his temple in Babylon. This deed is noted also in Daniel 1:1-2. The Chronicler's brief account demonstrates his negative evaluation of Jehoiakim based on his religious posture.

36:9-10 [cf. 2 Kgs 24:8-17] The reign of Jehoiachin

This brief reign (three months and ten days) lasts long enough for him to do evil in God's sight, so Nebuchadnezzar takes him to Babylon along with the best vessels from the temple, and in his place installs Zedekiah his brother as king. Overlooking the details of Jehoiachin's surrender to his enemy and the detailed account of exiles to Babylon (2 Kgs 24:14-16), the Chronicler pinpoints religious attitudes and objects as his main interest in this king.

Zedekiah. [11]Zedekiah was twenty-one years old when he became king, and he reigned eleven years in Jerusalem. [12]He did what was evil in the sight of the LORD, his God, and he did not humble himself before Jeremiah the prophet, who spoke for the LORD. [13]He also rebelled against King Nebuchadnezzar, who had made him swear by God. He became stiff-necked and hardened his heart rather than return to the LORD, the God of Israel. [14]Likewise all the princes of Judah, the priests, and the people added treachery to treachery, practicing all the abominations of the nations and defiling the LORD's house which he had consecrated in Jerusalem.

The Fall of Judah. [15]Early and often the LORD, the God of their ancestors, sent his messengers to them, for he had compassion on his people and his dwelling place. [16]But they mocked God's messengers, despised his words, and scoffed at his prophets, until the LORD's anger against his people blazed up beyond remedy. [17]Then he brought up against them the king of the Chaldeans, who killed their young men with the sword in their own sanctuary, with compassion for neither young men nor young women, neither the old nor the infirm;

36:11-17 [cf. 2 Kgs 24:18-20; Jer 52:1-3] The reign of Zedekiah

Appointed by Nebuchadnezzar, this king also does evil in God's sight. The Chronicler summarizes the problem: Zedekiah should have repented and humbled himself before the word of God uttered through Jeremiah (36:12). The prophet Jeremiah contains eight chapters of oracles during Zedekiah's reign, so we cannot identify a specific act of disobedience but rather a general failure to heed God's prophetic word. The Chronicler composes his own version of Judah's end (36:13-17). Zedekiah rebels against Nebuchadnezzar, even though he had sworn by God to serve him: so he offends God and also errs politically (36:13a). More seriously, he hardens his heart against returning to God (36:13b); in biblical language, he refuses to repent, so he is cut off from God. Leaders of the priests and people also act unfaithfully, like the Gentile nations; thus they help to pollute the temple. The Chronicler speaks of the sin and evil in more general terms, but mocking God's prophetic messengers is serious enough to bring divine anger.

Still, the Chronicler claims that God has compassion on his people and temple and keeps sending messengers to call them back (36:15). Even as the Chronicler spells out Israel's sins he carefully juxtaposes God's compassion on the people and temple. God's ultimate action, bringing the enemy to victory over Jerusalem, seems almost an act of divine desperation (36:17). The Chronicler states tersely that God brings against them the Chaldeans, who destroy the temple and its vessels and slaughter the people.

all of them he delivered into his power. [18]All the utensils of the house of God, large and small, the treasures of the LORD's house, and the treasures of the king and his princes, all these he brought to Babylon. [19]They burnt the house of God, tore down the walls of Jerusalem, burnt down all its palaces, and destroyed all its precious objects. [20]Those who escaped the sword he carried captive to Babylon, where they became servants to him and his sons until the Persian kingdom came to power. [21]All ▶ this was to fulfill the word of the LORD spoken by Jeremiah: Until the land has retrieved its lost sabbaths, during all the time it lies waste it shall have rest while seventy years are fulfilled.

Decree of Cyrus. [22]In the first year of Cyrus, king of Persia, in order to realize

36:18-21 [cf. 2 Kgs 25:8-21; Jer 52:12-30] The fall and captivity of Judah

Nebuchadnezzar exiles to Babylon all those who survive the sword in Jerusalem, until the rise of Cyrus the Persian. For the Chronicler, this exile fulfills Jeremiah's prophetic saying about seventy years of exile (Jer 25:11-12; 29:10). In this connection, Leviticus 26:34 mentions times of exile for the people as a time for the land to make up its lost sabbaths with sabbatical years. For the Chronicler this is an opportunity for transformation and change in relationship with God.

The Chronicler follows the story pattern of 2 Kings, but not its details or theology. Missing here is the international political scene, especially struggles between Babylon and Egypt and their impact on Judah. Missing also is the notion that exile to Babylon mostly involved higher echelons of Judeans, with the poorer farmers and peasants left around the destroyed city. Lacking also is the tendency in 2 Kings to blame the Babylonian invasions on the sin of Manasseh (e.g., 2 Kgs 24:3; not repeated in 2 Chr). Manasseh has repented in Chronicles. More significant, the Chronicler tends not to blame present evils on past generations; rather he finds the evil in the kings and Judean social groups of the generations after Josiah's untimely death.

36:22-23 [cf. Ezra 1:1-4]
Cyrus' proclamation about a return to Jerusalem

The Chronicler concludes this history quite differently than Kings, which ends with the image of Jehoiachin, the last king of Judah, under house arrest in Babylon. Here the reader is moved to the next historical period, the

---

▶ This symbol indicates a cross reference number in the *Catechism of the Catholic Church*. See page 147 for number citations.

the word of the LORD spoken by Jeremiah, the LORD roused the spirit of Cyrus, King of Persia, to spread this proclamation throughout his kingdom, both by word of mouth and in writing: [23]"Thus says Cyrus, king of Persia: The LORD, the God of heaven, has given to me all the kingdoms of the earth. He has also charged me to build him a house in Jerusalem, which is in Judah. All among you, therefore, who belong to his people, may their God be with them; let them go up."

Persian Era when Jews return to Jerusalem and Judah. Cyrus the Persian has come to power after defeating the Babylonians, and with him has come a new policy of allowing subject peoples to return to their homelands, under watchful conditions. His proclamation begins the book of Ezra (Ezra 1:1-4) but also concludes 2 Chronicles. It includes a startling image of Cyrus in the service of the Lord God of heaven, i.e., as an instrument of Israel's God. The Chronicler also transforms the doom of exile into a moment of blessing for those who belong to God: May God be with them as they return. Here is a final word of hope, consistent with a theology which envisions the conversion and transformation even of Judea's worst king, Manasseh. In the last sentences the Chronicler looks forward, to a time of renewed hope and blessing, when Israel strengthens its covenant bond with God through committed worship and faithful service.

REVIEW AIDS AND DISCUSSION TOPICS

The Book of First Chronicles

1:1–9:34 Genealogies *(pages 7–28)*

1. Why does the Chronicler pay so much attention to genealogy?

2. Read Matthew 1:1-17, the genealogy of Jesus. What is included from the period covered by 1 Chronicles? How does it compare to this view of history?

3. Discuss the important figures in your family tree. What version of history does your family focus on? Who is included, and who is not? What links to the past has the family wanted to preserve?

9:35–29:30 The History of David *(pages 28–68)*

1. How is King David depicted by the Chronicler?

2. What familiar stories are left out of this account?

3. What is gained by this "whitewashing" of David's history? What is lost? Are there times when it is necessary to tell this kind of story?

4. What are examples of "heroes" of our own time who have benefited from a revised history? Who has lost in the revision of history?

5. What is the effect of learning "the truth" or finding out a more complex story about a person we idolized?

6. What is your take on the position and identity of the United States now? How does our perception of ourselves affect the stories we tell?

7. The Chronicler is very concerned with establishing the liturgical practices for postexilic Israel. Compare the episode in 1 Chronicles 15 where David brings the ark to Jerusalem with the same episode in 2 Samuel 6. What are the significant differences in the story? Do any aspects of present-day liturgy reflect the account in 1 Chronicles 15?

The Book of Second Chronicles

1:1–9:31 Solomon *(pages 69–88)*

1. What are the major differences between this portrayal of Solomon and the account in 1 Kings?

2. In 1 Kings, the extravagance of Solomon's own house was compared to that of the temple. Here, the focus is solely on the temple. What is the significance of the temple? What does the Chronicler want to say about Israel that is different from the portrait during the Exile found in the Deuteronomistic History?

3. What are the elements in the liturgy of the dedication of the temple? How are these elements present in our own liturgies? Do they serve the same purpose?

4. Samuel's long prayer in 2 Chronicles 6:12-42 lists occasions when it is right for Israel to petition God. How is this prayer like the Prayer of the People in the Catholic Mass?

10:1–28:27 The Divided Monarchy *(pages 88–120)*

1. The stories of the prophets Elijah and Elisha are missing in this history. How does this affect the story? If we only had this account, how might that affect our reading of the Transfiguration account in Mark 9:2-14?

2. In chapter 20 the Levite Jahaziel speaks as a prophet. Who are the Levites and what is their traditional role in the Promised Land? How might the gift of prophecy among the Levites help in the unifying project so valued by the Chronicler?

3. Unlike the Deuteronomistic historian, the Chronicler does not go back and forth between the kings of Judah and the kings of Israel but focuses on Judah alone. Why? What is the effect?

4. What is the story of Athaliah?

5. 2 Chronicles 23–24 illustrate the importance of the priest Jehoiada to King Joash's success and faithfulness to God. What do you make of this relationship? Why do you think the history shows God's continued commitment to kings rather than appointing religious leaders (priests or prophets) to rule Israel?

29:1–32:33 Hezekiah *(pages 120–131)*

1. Why is Hezekiah ranked as "one of Judah's three most important kings, after David and Solomon"?

2. Why might the feast of Passover and Unleavened Bread receive such attention in the reconsecration of the people?

3. What is the message in the fact that Passover was held one month late and that many who were not yet consecrated still participated? What role do the Levites play here?

4. Pride brings about Hezekiah's fall and the Babylonian exile of Israel. This parallels Greek tragedy, where a series of kings are brought down for their hubris, an extreme form of pride whereby people think they are equal to or above the gods. How has pride shown itself throughout these histories of Israel? In what way are we susceptible to pride, and what effect does it have on us and our lives?

33:1–36:23 The Fall of Judah *(pages 131–143)*

1. Manasseh is completely transformed in this account from the Deuteronomistic text. Why is this important to the postexilic Israelites?

2. Many believe that deep, mystical prayer or prayerful contemplation of the Bible is always painful because it reveals to us our shortcomings as we draw closer to God. How might this be compared to Josiah's experience with the Torah? Does this reflect our own experience with the Bible? Why or why not?

3. How does the ending of 2 Chronicles differ from the ending of 2 Kings? Why might the Chronicler have made the change?

4. How does the postexilic Chronicler balance joy and hope with the grief and condemnation implied by the fall of Israel? Is the author successful in providing a history and liturgical vision to sustain a people coming out of exile?

5. What lessons of this text might be useful to us in our current historical context?

INDEX OF CITATIONS FROM THE
CATECHISM OF THE CATHOLIC CHURCH

The arabic number(s) following the citation refer(s) to the paragraph number(s) in the *Catechism of the Catholic Church*. The asterisk following a paragraph number indicates that the citation has been paraphrased.

United Monarchy of Israel

- – – – MAXIMUM EXTENT OF THE UNITED MONARCHY
- AREAS OF INFLUENCE
- CONQUERED AREAS
- ■ SITES FORTIFIED BY SOLOMON
- ASHER ISRAELITE TRIBES
- MOAB NON–ISRAELITE GROUPS

0   30 Miles
0   30 Kilometers

Sidon

Damascus

SIDONIANS

Mt. Lebanon

Mt. Hermon

SYRIA (ARAM)

N

Tyre

Abel-beth-maccah

Dan

ASHER

NAPHTALI

Hazor ■

Acco

Chinnereth

Sea of Chinnereth

Ashtaroth

Helam

Cabul

ZEBULUN

▲ Mt. Carmel

Mt. Tabor ▲

MANASSEH

Jokneam

ISSACHAR

Dor

Megiddo ■

Jezreel

Wadi Kishon

Mt. Gilboa ▲

Beth-shean

Rogelim

Ramoth-gilead

Taanach

ISRAEL

The Great Sea

Hepher?

MANASSEH

Abel-menolah

Samaria

Tirzah

Mt. Ebal ▲

Mahanaim

Mt. Gerizim ▲ Shechem

River Jabbok

Zarethan?

River Jordan

Joppa

Shiloh

EPHRAIM

GAD

Beth-horon

Bethel

Rabbah

BENJAMIN

Jericho

AMMON

Baalath?

Gezer

Gibeah

Ashdod

Ekron

Jerusalem

Mt. Pisgah

Beth-shemesh

Bethlehem

▲ Mt. Nebo

Ashkelon

Gath?

Gaza

PHILISTINES

Hebron

Dibon

Gerar

Carmel

Ziklag?

JUDAH

The Salt Sea

Beer-sheba

Arad

MOAB

River Arnon

SIMEON

Kir-hareseth

Brook Besor

The Negeb

Zoar

Brook Zered

Tamar ■

EDOM

LUCIDITY INFORMATION DESIGN, LLC

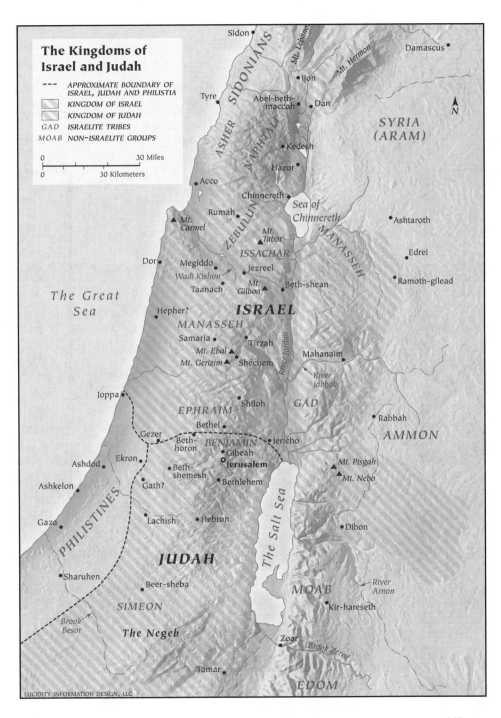

The Kingdoms of Israel and Judah

- - - APPROXIMATE BOUNDARY OF
     ISRAEL, JUDAH AND PHILISTIA

KINGDOM OF ISRAEL

KINGDOM OF JUDAH

GAD ISRAELITE TRIBES

MOAB NON-ISRAELITE GROUPS

0   30 Miles

0   30 Kilometers

N

Sidon

Damascus

Mt. Lebanon

Ijon

Mt. Hermon

ASHER

SIDONIANS

Tyre

Abel-beth-maccah

Dan

SYRIA
(ARAM)

NAPHTALI

Kedesh

Hazor

Acco

Chinnereth

Ashtaroth

Rumah

Sea of
Chinnereth

ZEBULUN

Mt.
Carmel

Mt.
Tabor

MANASSEH

Edrei

ISSACHAR

Ramoth-gilead

Dor

Megiddo

Jezreel

Wadi Kishon

Taanach

Mt.
Gilboa

Beth-shean

The Great
Sea

Hepher?

ISRAEL

MANASSEH

Samaria

Tirzah

Mahanaim

Mt. Ebal

River Jabbok

Mt. Gerizim

Shechem

River Jordan

Joppa

EPHRAIM

Shiloh

GAD

Rabbah

Gezer

Bethel

AMMON

Beth-horon

BENJAMIN

Jericho

Ashdod

Ekron

Gibeah

Jerusalem

Mt. Pisgah

Beth-shemesh

Mt. Nebo

Ashkelon

Gath?

Bethlehem

Gaza

PHILISTINES

Lachish

Hebron

The Salt Sea

Dibon

JUDAH

Sharuhen

Beer-sheba

MOAB

River
Arnon

SIMEON

Kir-hareseth

Brook
Besor

The Negeb

Zoar

Brook Zered

Tamar

EDOM

LUCIDITY INFORMATION DESIGN, LLC

149

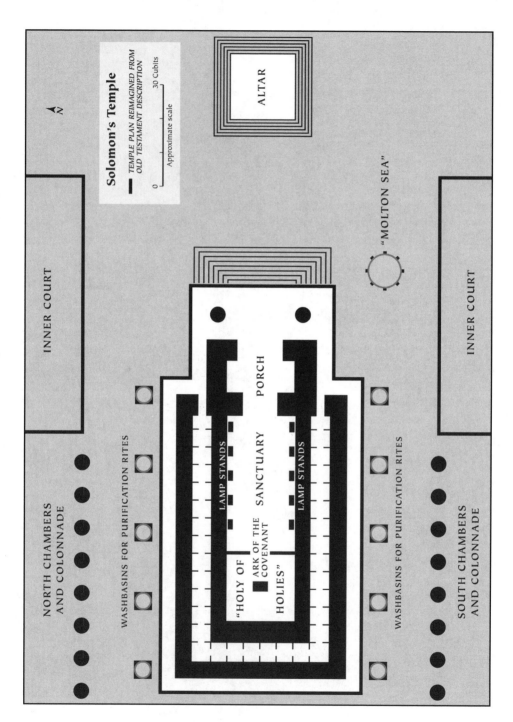

Solomon's Temple

TEMPLE PLAN REIMAGINED FROM OLD TESTAMENT DESCRIPTION

0   30 Cubits
Approximate scale

N

ALTAR

"MOLTON SEA"

INNER COURT

INNER COURT

PORCH

SANCTUARY

LAMP STANDS

LAMP STANDS

ARK OF THE COVENANT

"HOLY OF HOLIES"

NORTH CHAMBERS AND COLONNADE

SOUTH CHAMBERS AND COLONNADE

WASHBASINS FOR PURIFICATION RITES

WASHBASINS FOR PURIFICATION RITES

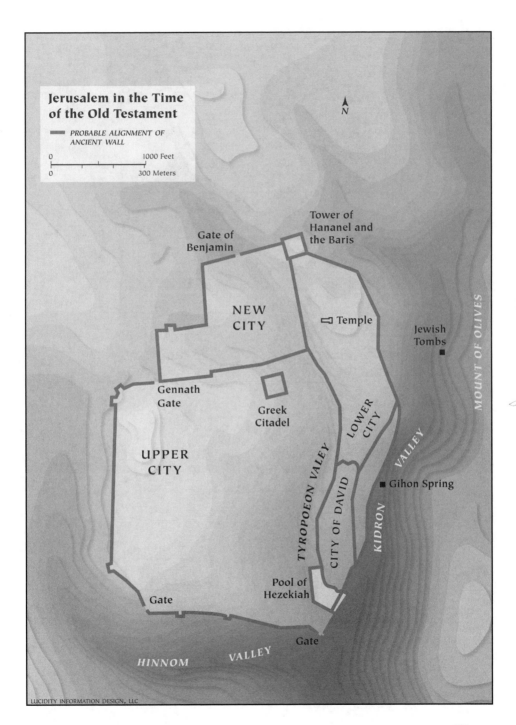

Jerusalem in the Time of the Old Testament

PROBABLE ALIGNMENT OF ANCIENT WALL

0   1000 Feet

0   300 Meters

N

Gate of Benjamin

Tower of Hananel and the Baris

NEW CITY

Temple

Jewish Tombs

MOUNT OF OLIVES

Gennath Gate

Greek Citadel

LOWER CITY

UPPER CITY

TYROPOEON VALEY

CITY OF DAVID

KIDRON VALLEY

Gihon Spring

Pool of Hezekiah

Gate

Gate

HINNOM VALLEY

LUCIDITY INFORMATION DESIGN, LLC

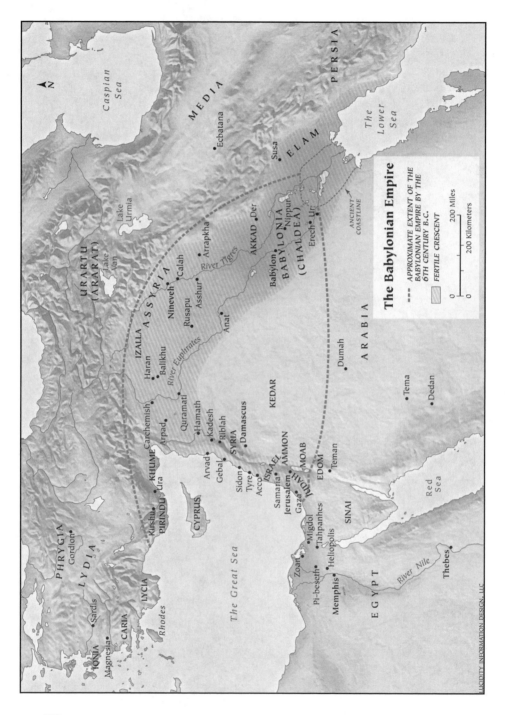

The Babylonian Empire

- - - APPROXIMATE EXTENT OF THE
BABYLONIAN EMPIRE BY THE
6TH CENTURY B.C.

▨ FERTILE CRESCENT

200 Miles

200 Kilometers

PHRYGIA
Gordion

LYDIA
Sardis

CARIA

IONIA
Magnesia

Rhodes

LYCIA

CYPRUS

PIRINDU
Kirshu
Ura

KHUME

Carchemish
Haran
Balikhu
Arpad
Quramati

IZALLA

ASSYRIA

Nineveh
Calah
Asshur
Rusapu

Anat

River Tigres

River Euphrates

Hamath
Kadesh
Arvad
Riblah
Gebal
Damascus
Sidon
Tyre
Acco
Samaria
Jerusalem
Gaza

SYRIA

ISRAEL

JUDAH

KEDAR

AMMON
MOAB
EDOM
Teman

The Great Sea

Migdol
Tahpanhes
Zoar
Pi-beseth
Heliopolis
Memphis

EGYPT

River Nile

Thebes

SINAI

Red
Sea

ARABIA

Dumah

Tema
Dedan

URARTU
(ARARAT)

Lake
Van

Lake
Urmia

Caspian
Sea

MEDIA

Ecbatana

Arrapkha

AKKAD
Der

Babylon
BABYLONIA
(CHALDEA)
Nippur
Erech
Ur

Susa

ELAM

PERSIA

The
Lower
Sea

ANCIENT
COASTLINE

N